WHAT PEOPLE ARE

LESS INCO

This is an important book for those who are curious about the possibility of the existence of other levels of consciousness besides that of the purely physical body. It is based on the research of Waldo Vieira, which includes a very large number of personal experiences, particularly out-of-body experiences, collected throughout his life. Sandie Gustus is excellently placed to describe Vieira's discoveries as she has been practicing and teaching his theories for many years and has considerable personal knowledge of a range of energetic and paranormal phenomena. The book provides practical methods for inducing out-of-body experiences and using them to increase our understanding of the nonphysical components of our conscious experience.

Dr. Peter Fenwick, BA, MB, BChir, DPM, FRCPsych, Consultant Neuropsychiatrist emeritus, Epilepsy Unit, Maudsley Hospital, London, UK; Senior Lecturer, Institute of Psychiatry, London, UK; Co-author (with Elizabeth Fenwick) of *The Art of Dying*

Sandie Gustus has written a provocative and eloquent book focused on those aspects of exceptional human experience that are often overlooked, and even derided and pathologized by mainstream science, medicine, and media. However, these accounts are ignored at society's risk because they can not help but enlarge and enrich the boundaries of the human condition.

Stanley Krippner, PhD., Professor of Psychology, Saybrook University, San Francisco, Calif., USA; Co-editor, *Varieties of Anomalous Experience: Examining the Scientific Evidence*

Any comprehensive understanding of consciousness requires incisive tools for studying the subjective aspects of human experience. The careful and systematic assessment of out-of-body experiences described in this book comprises a valuable scientific resource for approaching this complex and difficult challenge, as well as providing a potentially productive path for self-exploration and personal growth.

Brenda Dunne, Laboratory Manager, Princeton Engineering Anomalies Research (PEAR) laboratory; President, International Consciousness Research Laboratories (ICRL); and co-author (with Robert Jahn) of *Margins of Reality: The Role of Consciousness in the Physical World* and *Consciousness and the Source of Reality: The PEAR Odyssey.*

The information communicated in this book is a true representation of the key themes of the sciences of conscientiology and projectiology as proposed by Brazilian consciousness researcher, Dr. Waldo Vieira, who has been my mentor and a personal friend for 25 years. These sciences have already enabled thousands of individuals around the world to assume control of their personal development in a rational and tangible way that is devoid of any mysticism, allowing them to experience more fulfilling lives. This book, an exciting first attempt to make conscientiology and projectiology accessible to a nonacademic audience, represents, therefore, a contribution of enormous potential.

Wagner Alegretti, President, International Academy of Consciousness (IAC); Author, *Retrocognitions: An Investigation into the Memory of Past Lives and the Period between Lives*

This interesting book about out-of-body experiences and theories exploring the possibility of consciousness existing apart from the body is based on the research and life work of Waldo Vieira, MD. Drawing from personal experiences grounded in the theories presented, Sandie Gustus speaks with the authority of someone who has studied extensively and taught Vieira's work for many years at the International Academy of Consciousness (IAC). The concepts of consciousness being multidimensional and multi-existential are explored in depth and the explanations discussed engender a moral code for living, encouraging readers to consider their own actions with regards to others. The book also offers practical guidance for those curious to experience the phenomena discussed. This is a welcome addition to the literature on the exploration of consciousness.

Dr Penny Sartori, author of *The Near-Death Experiences of Hospitalized Intensive Care Patients: A Five-Year Clinical Study* and Staff Nurse in Intensive Care

This book is pivotal in raising awareness of Waldo Vieira's scientific research among the general population. It thoroughly explains the main principles of his work and provides practical guidelines for understanding consciousness at a very personal level. As we go forward in the twenty-first century and beyond, it is critical to raise awareness of and facilitate regaining contact with the nonphysical realms of existence in order to revolutionize science as we know it and this book makes an important contribution to achieving this.

Dr. Chantal Toporow, Aerospace Engineer; Council Member of the Society for Scientific Exploration

At last, Dr. Vieira's major contribution to both science and spirituality through first-person research of out-of-body experience, subtle energy and psi is made available in "plain English" with accompanying techniques — a must-read for both lay readers and scholars. Sandie Gustus' own experience with these phenomena and their potential to enrich and clarify "regular" life is evident throughout the book, as well.

Nelson Abreu, electrical utility engineer and contributing author of *Filters and Reflections: Perspectives on Reality* (2009) by International Consciousness Research Laboratories.

Less Incomplete

A Guide to Experiencing the Human Condition beyond the Physical Body

Less Incomplete

A Guide to Experiencing the Human Condition beyond the Physical Body

Sandie Gustus

Winchester, UK
Washington, USA

First published by O-Books, 2011
O-Books is an imprint of John Hunt Publishing Ltd., Laurel House, Station Approach, Alresford, Hants, SO24 9JH, UK
office1@o-books.net
www.o-books.com

For distributor details and how to order please visit the 'Ordering' section on our website.

ISBN: 978 1 84694 351 5

A CIP catalogue record for this book is available from the British Library.

Design: Stuart Davies

Cover: Sebastian Kaulitzki and Andy Newbold

Printed in the UK by CPI Antony Rowe
Printed in the USA by Offset Paperback Mfrs, Inc

CONTENTS

Foreword, by Pim van Lommel 1

Acknowledgments 5

Introduction 6

Out-of-Body Experience—A Natural Phenomenon ▪ The Limitations of Conventional Science for the Study of Nonphysical Realities ▪ A New Scientific Approach ▪ The Impact of Discovering I Was More than My Physical Body ▪ A New Direction in Life ▪ What You Can Learn from This Book and How to Apply It to Your Life ▪ How to Handle the Material ▪ Safely Producing Out-of-Body Experiences

PART ONE: Multidimensionality: Insights into a Wider Reality **21**

Part 1 examines one of several fundamental attributes of the consciousness—(soul, spirit)—that it is multidimensional.

Chapter 1. The Bodies of Manifestation of the Consciousness **22**

The Physical Body ▪ The Energy Body ▪ The Extraphysical Body ▪ The Mental Body ▪ What Happens When We Die? ▪ Everyday Experiences of Your Vehicles of Manifestation

Chapter 2. Nonphysical Dimensions **38**

The Extraphysical Sphere of Energy ▪ The Crustal Dimension (Paratroposphere) ▪ The Extraphysical Dimensions ▪ The Mental Dimension

Chapter 3. Nonphysical Consciousnesses; Transdimensional Interactions and Relationships **55**

Helpers ▪ Blind Guides ▪ Intruders

Chapter 4. Bioenergy 78

Bioenergy—A Look Back through History ▪ Bioenergy—Properties and Characteristics ▪ The Subtle Influence and Powerful Effects of Bioenergetic Fields ▪ Energetic Sensitivity, Awareness and Control ▪ Exercises for Improving Energetic Sensitivity, Capacities and Self-Defense ▪ Tips for Mastering Your Bioenergy

PART TWO: Seriality: The Series of Successive Lives 101

Part 2 examines a second fundamental attribute of the consciousness—that it reincarnates.

Chapter 5. Karma and the Multiexistential Cycle 102

The Alternation of Physical and Extraphysical Existences ▪ The Period between Lives ▪ Holokarma

Chapter 6. Clues to Past Lives 117

Phobias ▪ Birthmarks and Birth Defects ▪ Xenoglossy and Glossolalia ▪ Prodigies, Exceptional Talents and Early Achievers ▪ Genius ▪ The Savant Syndrome ▪ Love at First Sight ▪ Aversions ▪ Gender Dysphoria ▪ Ideological Affinities

Chapter 7. The Mechanisms by Which Past-Life Experiences Affect Our Present Lives 136

Holomemory ▪ Paragenetics ▪ Pathologies of the Mental Body ▪ A Case in Point

Chapter 8. Retrocognitions 144

What Defines a True Retrocognition? ▪ The Benefits of Retrocognitions ▪ Factors That Block and Inhibit Retrocognitions ▪ Precautions ▪ Tips for Recalling Past Lives ▪ Techniques for Producing Retrocognitions

PART THREE: The Evolution of the Consciousness 161

Part 3 examines a third fundamental attribute of the consciousness—that it evolves.

Chapter 9. The Evolutionary Process **162**

Recovery of Awareness ▪ Tips for Recovering More Advanced Levels of Awareness (i.e. Awareness of Who You Are beyond the Physical Body) ▪ Existential Self-Mimicry: The Stagnation of Consciential Evolution

Chapter 10. Life Plan **174**

Was My Life Planned? ▪ Mini and Maxi Life Plans ▪ Success and Failure in the Endeavor to Carry Out One's Life Plan ▪ Ten Reasons We Fail to Complete Our Life Plan ▪ The Intermissive Study Course ▪ How Our Life Plan Is Decided ▪ Moratoriums ▪ Melancholy and Euphoria Related to Failure or Success in One's Life Plan

Chapter 11. Identifying Your Purpose in Life **193**

Personal Strong and Weak Traits Formula ▪ Personal Reciprocation Formula ▪ Lucid Out-of-Body Experiences ▪ Retrocognitions ▪ One-Year-More Technique ▪ 50-Times Technique ▪ Books and Courses ▪ Precautions

Chapter 12. Holomaturity **201**

Types of Maturity ▪ Physiological Maturity ▪ Psychological Maturity ▪ Intellectual Maturity ▪ Holomaturity ▪ Examples of Maturities and Immaturities of the Consciousness ▪ Daily Utilization of Time

Chapter 13. Cosmoethics **219**

Ethics Versus Cosmoethics ▪ Self-Incorruptibility ▪ Conscientiality ▪ The Law of the "Lesser Evil" ▪ Fraternity ▪ Thoughts and Intentions ▪ Personal Principles

PART FOUR: The Out-of-Body Experience **231**

Part 4 is dedicated to the out-of-body experience, the tool that enables readers to verify the information contained in the book through their own first-hand experiences.

Chapter 14. Benefits of the Out-of-Body Experience **232**
Therapeutic Benefits ▪ Psychological Benefits ▪ Educational Benefits ▪ Parapsychic Benefits ▪ Specific Practical Uses

Chapter 15. Preparation for the Out-of-Body Experience **235**
External Factors ▪ Physical and Physiological Factors ▪ Psychological Factors ▪ Bioenergetic Factors ▪ Parapsychic Factors ▪ General Comments about Preparation for a Projection

Chapter 16. Lucid Projection Techniques **245**
Tips ▪ Projective Techniques

Chapter 17. Common Sensations of the Take-Off and Return **257**
Signs That a Projection is Imminent ▪ Sensations During Take-Off and Return

Chapter 18. Recall and Analysis **261**
Why Is It Difficult to Remember an Out-of-Body Experience? ▪ The Importance of Extraphysical Lucidity to the Recall of Extraphysical Events ▪ Factors That Favor Recall ▪ Factors Unfavorable to Recall ▪ Types of Recall ▪ Tips for Recalling Projections ▪ Analysis of Extraphysical Events ▪ Diary of Extraphysical Experiences

Conclusion 276
Appendix A 278
Notes 284
Glossary 285
Bibliography 292
About the Author 297
Index 298

for you James

Foreword

Throughout the course of his life, Brazilian consciousness researcher, Waldo Vieira MD, has amassed one of the largest existing libraries on the out-of-body experience (OBE) and is considered one of the most prolific "lucid projectors" alive, reportedly producing intentional OBEs on an almost daily basis. Far from being a guru-type personality, Vieira states that producing lucid OBEs is a natural human ability that everyone can develop. He also insists that you doubt and question everything he says; that you have your own experiences of the OBE and other altered states of consciousness instead to verify his claims. Vieira has written a number of books including the acclaimed diary of personal experiences *Projections of the Consciousness* and a thousand-page tome entitled *Projectiology,* which attracted the attention of a number of science-oriented individuals who were dissatisfied with both materialistic and religious approaches to understanding consciousness.

The current views on the relationship between the brain and consciousness held by most physicians, philosophers and psychologists are too narrow to explain the near-death experience (NDE), which is similar in nature to the OBE and considered by Vieira as a specific type of OBE. Both the OBE and NDE reveal that our consciousness (i.e. our ability to be aware) does not always coincide with brain functions; that we can in fact experience our consciousness independently of the physical body.

It is my pleasure therefore to introduce this book by Sandie Gustus, OBE scholar, instructor and practitioner, who has been volunteering and teaching at the London office of the International Academy of Consciousness (an organization associated with Vieira's work) since 2003. This is the first book to present the fundamental principles of his work to a general, non-academic audience . . . a significant contribution as despite being one of the world's leading authorities on the OBE, Vieira remains unknown to many who are interested in alternative research into consciousness.

Although a fellow physician who similarly questioned conventional theories about consciousness, Vieira's path has been quite different to mine. I was a resident in 1969, working on a cardiac ward, when a heart-attack patient told me that while unconscious he had seen the most beautiful world, with extraordinary music and light. What I still can't forget is the way he described the experience and how deeply impressed he was by what had happened. At the time I wasn't at all interested in consciousness. But I then read *Return from Tomorrow*, a book by George Ritchie, who as a medical student had had a near-death experience. After reading this book I started to ask those of my patients who had survived a cardiac arrest if they had any memory of the period of unconsciousness. And to my enormous surprise, within two years, I had collected 12 personal accounts of an enhanced consciousness during the period of clinical death in 50 survivors of cardiac arrest. Because of this finding I decided to initiate, along with some colleagues, a systematic and prospective trial into this phenomenon of the so-called near-death experience. The results, published in *The Lancet* in 2001, demonstrated that common hypotheses that dismiss the NDE as a real event, such as lack of oxygen to the brain and fear of death, had no correlation to the occurrence of an NDE. Since 2003, I have dedicated myself to researching the NDE phenomenon further, because it challenges our current concepts about the relationship between consciousness and the function of our brain.

As for Vieira, he began experiencing out-of-body experiences at the age of nine. He grew up in Minas Gerais, Brazil and was heavily influenced by a kind of religion known as Spiritism that took the philosophy and psychical study of Frenchmen Allan

Kardec and attempted to merge it with Christianity. Vieira eventually left Spiritism to develop a more scientific approach that was not linked to any particular culture or faith but was instead based on a combination of scientific principles and direct, personal experience. This, of course, flew in the face of conventional scientific rules and expectations! How replicable are these experiences? How can we reach objective conclusions using subjective experience? Vieira suggests that the corroboration of different individual's accounts of remote physical occurrences, and even shared OBEs, indicate an objective dimension to the OBE and its potential as a tool for the reliable exploration of consciousness beyond the physical body, for scientists and lay people alike.

Sandie Gustus provides a fascinating, detailed and highly readable overview of the bases of this scientific and spiritual paradigm conceived by Vieira; now further developed by a number of scholars worldwide who combine personal exploration of nonphysical realms with more conventional third-person, objective research to reach rational, personally verifiable conclusions about the nature of consciousness and the human condition beyond the physical body.

Bearing in mind that there are plausible hypotheses for the OBE that do not necessarily require extraordinary models, as I explain in *Consciousness Beyond Life,* I cannot help but be intrigued by Vieira's experiences and theories. Perhaps Vieira is right but you and I won't have cause to abandon the more conventional, physical explanations unless we have our own, repeated, out-of-body experiences; a consistent theme of this book and one that is supported by numerous techniques for controlling one's energy, developing one's psychic abilities, and producing OBEs and other phenomena at will . . . techniques that Gustus insists can produce results for anyone who has the determination to succeed. One thing rings true, however. While Vieira and I present different approaches to the study of consciousness, it is not so unlikely that the two will be equally important to answer the stubborn questions of consciousness, the brain and beyond.

If, like me, you have not had a lucid out-of-body experience, I invite you to enjoy this compelling book that credibly argues the case for life beyond the physical body with an open mind.

Pim van Lommel, MD

Author, *Consciousness Beyond Life: The Science of the Near-Death Experience*

Acknowledgments

There are many people whose time, effort, energy, sacrifices, encouragement and support inspired me to start this book and allowed me to finish it.

I would like to express my thanks to Nanci Trivellato, Wagner Alegretti, Umberto Correa da Silva, Liliana Alexandre and Jeffrey Lloyd of the International Academy of Consciousness (IAC), whose teaching had such a profound impact on me when I first encountered these ideas back in 2000. A special thank you to Nanci, who helped me make the decision to move to the UK to take up volunteering and teaching with the IAC and for the considerable investment she made in mentoring me and in developing my understanding and knowledge of conscientiology; thanks also to Wagner for the same, as well as for his guidance and support in starting this book.

My sincere gratitude goes to both Wagner and David Lloyd for their thoughtful and thorough revisions of the manuscript and for contributing their extensive experience, knowledge and insights to suggest many valuable improvements.

I thank Robert Bruce for selflessly sharing his experience of publishing and helping guide me through the final phases of preparing for publication; Nelson Abreu for cheerful assistance so willingly given during a last minute dilemma; and my editor, Cynthia Mitchell, for making the work infinitely more readable and for her encouragement.

A special debt of gratitude is owed to my wonderful family and friends, especially my mother, Julie Gustus, and sister, Maryanne Gustus, who provided all manner of support throughout the long and unpredictable experience of getting this book into print.

Introduction

> Science is the tool of the Western mind and with it more doors can be opened than with bare hands. It is part and parcel of our knowledge and obscures our insight only when it holds that the understanding given by it is the only kind there is.
> —*C.G. Jung*.

How many of us have had an experience that suggests that a deeper, unseen reality that extends beyond the purely physical is present in our everyday lives? Most of us have probably had an experience with déjà vu, intuition, synchronicity, premonition or telepathy; felt an instant sense of recognition or familiarity with a complete stranger; or experienced a spontaneous vibrational state . . . or at least know of someone who has. Such indications that our reality is more complex than it appears to be and that there is a kind of 'backstage' to our existence, are commonplace.

Despite this, most people have no direct awareness that we live in a multidimensional environment that extends far beyond the boundaries of our physical world, and that we are, in fact, much more than just our physical bodies.

Fortunately, there is one phenomenon that is natural to all humans that allows us to verify for ourselves, through first-hand experience, that we are capable of acting entirely independently of the physical body in a nonphysical dimension . . . the out-of-body experience (OBE). Anyone who has had a fully lucid OBE, and I count myself among them, will tell you that if you can be lucid outside the body, you will find that all your mental faculties are fully functioning, that you can make decisions, exercise your free will, access your memory, think with a level of clarity that sometimes exceeds your usual capacity, and even capture information from the physical dimension that can later be corroborated . . . and that to experience all this provides you with irrefutable evidence that the physical body is merely a temporary 'house' through which your consciousness (i.e. your soul or spirit) manifests in the physical world.

It is important to make the distinction here between *the consciousness* and *consciousness*. In the context of this book *the consciousness* is used as a synonym of soul, spirit, ego, human essence or intelligent principle. *Consciousness*—on its own—is typically used to imply the state of being aware or lucid. To avoid confusion, some people like to use the word 'self' when referring to *the consciousness*.

Out-of-Body Experience—A Natural Phenomenon

I describe the out-of-body experience (or the projection of the consciousness outside the physical body) as a natural phenomenon, because almost all humans experience some separation between their physical body and a more subtle nonphysical body every night while they're asleep. The reason so few of us are aware of this fact is because most of us experience poor levels of awareness or lucidity whilst out of the body, don't remember what happened or confuse the OBE with a dream. In reality, most people are just sleeping outside the body, as depicted in the illustration below.

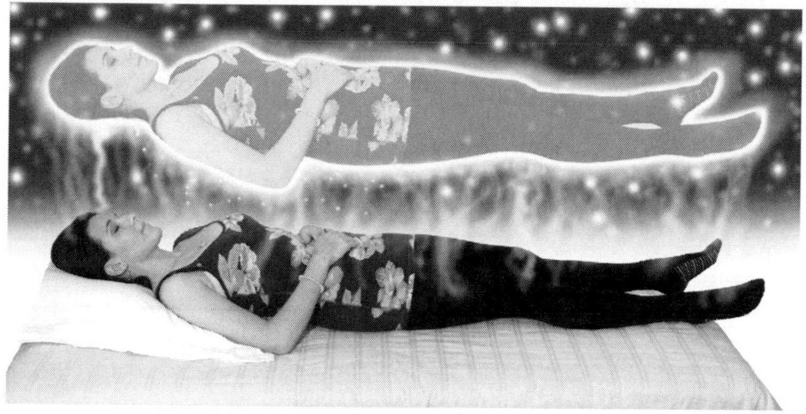

Sleeping outside the body (or unconscious projection)

But it is possible to learn to become more "awake" outside of the body. Anyone who has the will to do this can achieve results. No particular psychic ability is required.

History confirms the prevalence and universality of this unique phenomenon. Human beings have been recording the departure and subsequent return of a subtle body from the physical body with a remarkably high degree of consistency since Ancient Egypt, between 3,000 and 5,000 years ago. A look back through history also reveals that the OBE is common to all people, regardless of their culture, socio-economic status, gender, language, nationality, age, religion or belief system.

Thankfully, in the last few decades, the taboos surrounding the OBE have diminished, making open discussions in public events possible and coverage in the mainstream media more common. Most significantly, the OBE (particularly the near-death experience (NDE), a type of forced OBE) has begun to attract serious attention from the scientific and medical communities.

The Limitations of Conventional Science for the Study of Nonphysical Realities

The perspective of conventional science (i.e. materialist, positivist science, based on the Cartesian-Newtonian model that considers reality to be physical only) is largely inadequate for the study of nonphysical realities, however, because it fails to take into account the possibility that the consciousness can extend beyond the limits of the physical dimension, an aspect considered by the sciences represented in this book, to be fundamental to the consciousness.

To put it another way, current scientific convention does not accept that the consciousness can manifest in a nonphysical body such as it does during an OBE, because the existence of the nonphysical body itself cannot be confirmed, verified or proven by objective observation.

Recognizing that the limitations of such an approach had

serious ramifications for the advancement of human knowledge, a few decades ago one of the world's foremost authorities on the subject of the consciousness (according to *Who's Who in the 21st Century*, 2002), and a lucid projector since the age of nine, Brazilian researcher Waldo Vieira M.D., began to lay the groundwork for a more sophisticated and inclusive scientific approach to studying the consciousness—a hugely complex endeavor.

A New Scientific Approach

As a result of his own extensive personal experimentation and research, and in the face of clear-cut evidence derived from a consensus of experience recorded by ordinary people around the world, Vieira had long been aware that a significant amount of human experience lay beyond the reach of the conventional sciences. So he developed an approach that expanded upon existing scientific precepts to acknowledge the validity and value of *subjective* observation and experience. This book is based almost exclusively on his comprehensive leading-edge theories and the personal experiences I have had to validate them.

In 1986, Vieira formally proposed the science of projectiology to the public and scientific communities with the launch of a highly detailed 1200-page treatise entitled *Projectiology: A Panorama of Experiences Outside the Human Body* (published in the author's native Portuguese), which has a bibliography of 1,957 entries sourced from 28 countries and 18 different languages.

In 1994 he published the bases for the science of conscientiology in a second treatise entitled *700 Experiments of Conscientiology*. The foundation of these new sciences is based on a wider perspective that recognizes the multidimensional nature of existence. Vieira terms this *the consciential paradigm*.

Conscientiology is the science that studies the consciousness (soul, spirit, ego, self, human essence), investigating all of its properties, attributes, capacities, phenomena, bodies of manifestation and lives, based on the consciential paradigm.

Conscientiology is hierarchically structured into a set of subdisciplines—70 in total; projectiology being the subdiscipline dedicated to the study of the projection of the consciousness outside of the physical body (out-of-body experience, OBE). Projectiology is a particularly important subdiscipline as the OBE is the tool that allows the individual (consciousness) to be both the researcher and the object of study; in other words, it allows the consciousness to observe and study itself.

As explained by Vieira in the introduction to *Projectiology*, the massive amount of data he gathered in proposing these sciences was obtained from the following sources:

1. Over 1,100 lucid projections that he independently experienced, analyzed and recorded between 1941 and 1985, (60 of which are described in Projections of the Consciousness: A Diary of Out-of-Body Experiences);
2. Ideas and experiences gathered from fortnightly meetings with a team of lucid projectors from the Center of Continuous Consciousness (CCC), an organization he founded in 1981 in Rio de Janeiro (now disbanded), and from monthly meetings with the general public in the cities of São Paulo, Ribeirão Preto and other cities in Brazil;
3. Personal correspondence received from hundreds of lucid projectors of all levels from all over the world. This material is filed at the International Institute of Projectiology and Conscientiology (IIPC), an organization that was founded by Vieira and a group of researchers from the CCC in 1988, in response to demand in Brazil for a more structured environment in which to study the consciousness. Vieira presided over the IIPC, a nonprofit organization, for more than ten years;
4. Personal interviews conducted with lucid projectors both in

Brazil and all over the world;

5. Direct contact with nonphysical individuals who were, in previous lives, lucid projectors like Vieira. Many of them had studied the subject and had a wealth of knowledge and experience to impart, others were authors in past lives and established a rapport and came into contact with Vieira when he was researching their works;
6. Meetings and field research that took place in Brazil and abroad, particularly in Europe and the US, with directors, editors, researchers and members of institutions, laboratories, studios, bookstores, private and public universities and institutional libraries;
7. Vieira's vast private collection of technical works, dictionaries, anthologies, treatises, manuals, biographies, magazines, newspapers, periodicals, bulletins, reports, expositions, proceedings and dissertations.
(Vieira, Projectiology).

As a result of Vieira's scientific approach to organizing an encyclopedic amount of data gathered from such an extensive variety of sources, a clear consensus as to the true nature of the human consciousness has emerged, making it possible to draw many conclusions about and largely demystify this great enigma of mankind.

Age 78 at the time of writing, and with 50 years of research behind him, Vieira is today based at the campus of the Center for Higher Studies of Conscientiology (CHSC) at Iguassu Falls in Brazil. Supported by a team of more than 100 volunteers, including professional psychologists, engineers, linguists and academics, and drawing on his personal library of some 63,000 items related to the subject of consciousness and associated paranormal phenomena (the largest personal library of its kind in the world), he continues to research and add knowledge to a body of information that is already truly quantum in breadth and scale.

The Impact of Discovering I Was More Than My Physical Body

When I first came across these new sciences in 2001, via the London Educational Center of the International Academy of Consciousness (IAC), an organization associated with Vieira's work, their value struck me immediately. A series of personal experiences that followed soon after and continue to this day, enabled me to verify enough that my understanding of the world around me, my perspective on life, and as a consequence, the way I chose to live it, was irrevocably altered.

Knowing what I now know, there will never be any going back; meaning, I will never be able to "unknow" what I have learned or deny my experiences. So it is now a matter of consistently working towards living my life in a way that is more coherent with what I know and that allows me and others to benefit from the privilege.

Let me explain why conscientiology has had such a profound impact on my life. It quickly became apparent that through the out-of-body experience we have access to a richer, broader, more complex multidimensional existence in which the answers to some of the questions that have puzzled humankind for many centuries were at hand; questions such as:

What happens when we die?
Where will I go when I die?
What is it like there?
Who else will be there?
Where did I come from?
What is the purpose of my life?

These questions are monumental. And they were answered in a rational, logical, nonmystical and nonreligious way, and in a theoretical and practical (personally verifiable) scientific context by the IAC.

And Pandora's Box was opened. For I also came to understand that in transcending my physicality, not only do I survive physical death and spend a period afterwards manifesting in a nonphysical body, but that my broader existence consists of countless such alternations of physical lives with nonphysical periods spent between lives. In other words, my current physical incarnation is just one life of many I have already had, in which I am just one person of many that I have already been.

This realization alone explained so many things for me—strong connections I have with certain people, experiences in which I've felt a sense of familiarity with and affection for a complete stranger, and some oddities of my personality that seem to have no known cause in this lifetime. Just for starters.

I also came to realize that the OBE provides us all with an invaluable opportunity to visit and familiarize ourselves with the dimension in which we will exist after death and to prepare for this certain eventuality. This is so important because without such understanding and knowledge, upon death, people can become confused, traumatized and eventually psychotic as their association of being aware with being alive in the physical dimension is so strong that they're unable to make any sense of their nonphysical state. This is not to say that this condition is irreversible—it's entirely possible that a person is able to get a clearer perspective after a period of time. But for anyone who remains in such a condition, nothing productive comes out of this lengthy period spent between lives. But don't just take my word for it. You can verify this for yourself by projecting to the dimensions that interact and overlap with physical life to see the condition that some nonphysical individuals are in.

By contrast, if we are lucid after death, we can spend this period between lives preparing for our next physical life, planning its purpose and setting goals; goals that relate to advancing our personal development and that of others. It is through processes such as these that we mature, grow, evolve and become more balanced as individuals.

But we don't have to wait until we die to start this work. We can easily choose to begin this process of personal growth now by reprioritizing our lives . . . by prioritizing learning about the broader, multidimensional realities of our existence, and by helping others to do the same.

I decided that this was exactly what I was going to do with my life . . . no matter what.

A New Direction in Life

The "no matter what" part initially consisted of having to exchange paid employment for voluntary work, so I quit my job at the U.N. in Geneva where I was living at the time and moved to London to train to be an instructor with the IAC and to help raise awareness of its work. Eight years have since passed. I have been teaching for seven of them and as each year passes I remain committed to my original goals.

Life is busier, more challenging and more demanding these days, but with the challenges comes the personal growth, the expansion of self-awareness, and the immeasurable satisfaction of helping others to see and live their lives in a broader, more meaningful context. There have been several occasions in which I've been supervising a practical class, for example, the lights are out and I'm sitting there quietly and still in the dark while the students practice a technique I've just taught for leaving the body—and I think to myself, there's nothing else in the world I'd rather be doing with my time.

During these years working for the IAC, it gradually became apparent to me that there was a role to be played as a kind of bridging 'interpreter' between Dr. Vieira and lay readers interested in enriching their knowledge of the human consciousness and the wider realities in which we exist. Vieira's own books are notoriously sophisticated, technical and intellectual in style, but his priority was to further human knowledge by faithfully and accurately recording the details of his research, not to write a bestseller. My endeavor, with this book, is to make his work available to a wider nonacademic audience by presenting it in a language and format that everyone can understand and follow, without compromising the integrity of his ideas in any way. Einstein once said that "it should be possible to explain the laws of physics to a barmaid" so I figure it should be equally possible to explain conscientiology to the general reader. My motivation for making the information more accessible is to provide assistance to those searching for this knowledge.

What You Can Learn from This Book and How to Apply It to Your Life

In part 1, the foundations that are essential to understanding the broader context of your existence are laid down; I describe, for example, the different vehicles or bodies in which you (as a consciousness) can manifest, the various nonphysical dimensions you can visit, the nonphysical beings you can come into contact with in your daily lives (be you inside or outside your body), and bioenergy. Expect to encounter some terminology and concepts that may seem strange at first, but be patient, remain open and accept that this is a normal part of the process of learning something new and original. There is a glossary of terms at the end of the book—if you familiarize yourself with it, you will quickly become accustomed to the terminology. This part of the book is also more theoretical than practical in nature, out of necessity, although it has several practical sections nonetheless. I mention this because I encourage you to persevere through these chapters, because you have to have the knowledge before you can apply it!

Once you have the necessary information under your belt, the book goes on to describe how you can apply the information in a practical way in your own life, to move forward in your personal development.

You will learn, for example:

- how to master your energy and use it as a tool to:
    - experience conscious and controlled OBEs
    - increase your psychic abilities
    - develop energetic sensitivity and perception
    - protect yourself energetically from the influences of both physical and nonphysical individuals
    - heal yourself and others
- how to have more positive helpers (spirit guides) and more positive people around you
- how to facilitate the recollection of past lives, avoid repeating the mistakes of your past, understand the karmic links that connect you to those closest to you and evaluate the quality of those links
- how to know yourself more completely and realize your full potential so you can face and overcome your limitations and shortcomings through frank self-analysis and get the most out of your strong traits
- how to identify your purpose in life and move towards it with discernment, conviction and self-motivation
- how to be more consistently good natured and how to deal better with conflict, misunderstandings and resentments in your relationships
- how to become more mature and more (cosmo)ethical and thus improve your karma
- how to exercise more control over your life
- how to lose your fear of death and prepare yourself for what will happen when you die
- how to take the maximum opportunity of what this life offers to develop and evolve as an individual

In short, how to be a little less incomplete.

How to Handle the Material

I am not suggesting for a minute that to understand how all these things work is the same as putting them into practice. You will need a strong will, determination, a readiness to be frank about your own weak traits and a willingness to practice some new skills until they're mastered. You may find that you have to undo some deep-seated conditionings or beliefs that have been ingrained in you since the day you were born (some may even have their roots in past lives), in order to be able to benefit fully from the ideas presented here. And this may precipitate difficulties or even crises. You will also need to be prepared to go against the norms and trends of society and begin the process of relying increasingly upon your own knowledge, personal experiences and reference points in order to decide how to make your way forward. This too can bring pressure. To give you an example, when I gave up my job in Switzerland to become a volunteer at the IAC, I know some of my friends had trouble accepting that I was prepared to take major decisions about my life based on prioritizing my personal development over the usual concerns, such as status and wealth.

So just be aware that this book is delivering powerful information on topics that are not superficial; please approach it with common sense and maturity.

There are no quick fixes or shortcuts to enlightenment in this book. It has taken us 350,000 years (i.e. some thousands of lives) to evolve from caveman to modern day man. We will probably need thousands more lives to reach the point of being so evolved that there is nothing left to learn from being a physical human being and we can discard the body for the last time and commence a period of existence in which we live exclusively in a more subtle body.

I hope you're still reading! What I can tell you is, if you apply the ideas described in this book to your own life, to the very best of your ability, you will have ongoing opportunities to reevaluate and reprioritize your life and to lead a more fulfilling and purposeful life. You will notice immediate changes and improvements in your life that will have positive consequences now and for the remainder of your current physical life—and for the entirety of your existence. This is the journey you're headed on if you think this book is for you.

A final word on how to handle the material in this book; history shows us that truth is not absolute, but is relative; that is, it is a reflection of the best knowledge available to man at any given time. Neither Dr. Vieira nor the many thousands of people who are teaching, studying or working on furthering his original ideas are saying that "we have the final knowledge." No. So I urge you to use your own mental capacities, your intellect, logic, rationality and discernment when thinking about the ideas presented here. I cannot encourage you enough to *not* just accept everything that is written in these pages but to use the OBE and to have your own experiences and *know your own truth* for yourself.

Safely Producing Out-of-Body Experiences

The final part of the book, part 4, is entirely dedicated to helping you have lucid, controlled, out-of-body experiences and to remember them when you return to the normal, physical waking state. A number of techniques are described in detail. Although learning to produce OBEs at will is by no means the sole objective of this book, the OBE is the tool that allows us to discover the aspects of our existence that lie outside of our direct awareness. To this end, its value is immeasurable and to master it is of key importance.

It is important to point out that if you correctly follow the instructions of the practical exercises in this book that relate to producing lucid OBEs, mastering your bioenergies, recalling past lives or any other subject, there is no need for a personal teacher or guide. It is quite safe for you to work on your own—

there is nothing to fear. Many myths and misconceptions about paranormal phenomena are totally unfounded and cause a lot of unnecessary apprehension.

My experiences with conscientiology will not necessarily be yours so I don't focus on my experiences throughout this book. I acknowledge that we are all individuals with our own histories, with our own unique ways of responding to different information, with the right to exercise our free will and to choose what we want and need from life. But it is with untold pleasure that I share here with you what I have learned, so that you can have the opportunities I have had, should you be looking for them.

PART ONE

Multidimensionality—Insights into a Wider Reality

Reality is merely an illusion, albeit a very persistent one.
—*Albert Einstein*

Chapter One

The Bodies of Manifestation of the Consciousness

> Just as the dweller in his body passes through childhood, youth, and old age, so at death he merely passes into another body. The wise are not deceived by that.
> —*Sri Krishna*

One of the most fundamental principles of conscientiology is that the consciousness, being composed of neither energy nor matter, is not limited by form, space or time and is therefore able to present itself (or manifest) not only in the physical world but in more subtle dimensions that lie beyond what we can perceive with our physical senses.

In total, the consciousness uses one of four different bodies (or vehicles) recognized by conscientiology to manifest; namely:

- the physical body in the physical dimension
- the energy body (which, although unable to house the consciousness as such, enables us to affect or alter our manifestation)
- the astral body in nonphysical dimensions
- the mental body in the mental dimension

Although the word "astral" is a popular term that most people can easily relate to, I'm going to use the word "extraphysical" instead of astral, as a synonym of nonphysical, in order to avoid suggesting any mystical or religious connotations.

Each body or vehicle of the consciousness adapts to and corresponds to the specific properties of the dimension in which it manifests and each one presents particular attributes of the consciousness.

Understanding that the consciousness is multidimensional is crucial to enabling a complete picture of the reality of human existence to emerge. So let's consider in more detail what being multidimensional means and how this really works.

The Physical Body

In order for the consciousness to exist in and interact with the energetically dense physical environment, it uses a body made of energy and matter . . . the physical body. The physical body is perfectly adapted to the physical dimension in that it can process the resources it requires for survival such as food, water and air, and has numerous automatic psycho-physiological responses that further enhance its chances of survival. But while our physical existence preoccupies us a great deal, if we stop for a moment to examine ourselves more closely, we see that there are clues liberally scattered throughout our ordinary, everyday lives to the idea that we are consciousnesses, not just physical bodies. For example, the way we sometimes think and feel can be driven by experiences such as emotions, mental insights and energetic connections, none of which are physical, none of which we can see, touch, map, measure or quantify.

The Energy Body

The consciousness also has an energy body that is roughly the same shape as the physical body only slightly larger. The part of the energy body that visibly extends beyond the physical body is known as the human aura.

The energy body is not a vehicle of the consciousness per se, but an interface between the physical body and the extraphysical body.

When the physical and extraphysical bodies are in a state of

The part of the energy body that visibly extends beyond the physical body is known as the human aura

nonalignment such as occurs during a projection, part of the energy body forms what is commonly known as the silver cord. The silver cord connects and secures the consciousness to the physical body when it is projected into other dimensions.

Although the energy body is not officially recognized by conventional medicine, it has long been acknowledged by traditional Chinese medicine and is a vital component of several complementary therapies such as acupuncture, acupressure, homeopathy, Reiki and shiatsu massage. Interestingly, the British Medical Association, who used to call complementary treatments "alternative," as they were considered to represent an alternative to conventional medicine, changed the term to "complementary" in recent years as, increasingly, medical doctors and complementary therapists began working together using treatments that they both recognized to be of value. (Lewith, 2002). This suggests that the allopathic medical community has taken a small but significant step towards acknowledging the energy body and the important role it plays in healing.

Characteristics of the Energy Body

Known in conscientiology as the holochakra, and also known as the aura or etheric double, the energy body is not static but constantly absorbs, metabolizes and externalizes energies in a process of exchange with other living beings and with the natural energies produced by the environment—the air, water, earth, plants, food and the universe.

This process of energetic exchange sustains the energy body. It is also responsible for the energetic replenishment and balance of the physical body and, as such, the sustenance of human life. Mostly it takes place while we are asleep and slightly projected out of the body, which also explains why we feel refreshed after a good night's rest.

This exchange of energy mainly takes place via numerous

energetic vortexes within the energy body, known as chakras. Conscientiology recognizes ten main chakras (the sole chakras, the root or sex chakra, the spleen chakra, the umbilico-chakra, the palm chakras, the heart chakra, the throat chakra, the frontal chakra [third eye], the nucal chakra [back of the neck] and the crown chakra), most of which correspond to physical organs. The millions of microchakras, links and channels that actually circulate the energies and connect the chakras to their counterparts in the extraphysical body are known as nadis, or in acupuncture, meridians.

The Extraphysical Body

The extraphysical body (known in conscientiology as the psychosoma, but also as the astral body, emotional body, astral double, human double, spiritual body and subtle body, among many other terms) is the vehicle used by the consciousness to manifest in the multilayered extraphysical dimension. The extraphysical dimension is where most people find themselves during an out-of-body experience. This is also where we go when we die. Many people have reported encountering loved ones who have already passed away during a projection in the extraphysical dimension. This is more commonly experienced during a near-death experience (NDE, a kind of forced OBE). Such experiences can be very powerful, as they allow personal verification of our immortality.

According to Vieira's extensive personal experimentation and research, which is corroborated by the results of numerous other researches (such as the online OBE Survey conducted by IAC researchers Nanci Trivellato and Wagner Alegretti, to which over 10,000 participants have responded), due to the subtlety of the energies of extraphysical dimensions, the consciousness is significantly less limited in the extraphysical body than it is in the physical body and because of this, presents characteristics that are remarkably different.

Characteristics of the Extraphysical Body

As there is no air in most extraphysical dimensions, the extraphysical body isn't burdened by the incessant need to breathe. This can be a little frightening for those who suddenly find themselves lucid outside the body for the first time and realize they are not breathing. (Note: if there is any interruption in the breathing of the *physical* body during a projection however, the projection automatically terminates). But not needing to breathe outside the body can trigger an unrivalled, euphoric sense of freedom.

One of the people interviewed by Raymond Moody in *Life After Life* described the intensity of the euphoria he experienced during an NDE as follows:

"Life is like imprisonment. In this state, we just can't understand what prisons these bodies are. Death is such a release—like an escape from prison. That's the best thing I can think of to compare it to." (from *Life After Life* by Raymond Moody, published by Rider. Reprinted by permission of the Random House Group Ltd.)

Similarly, when manifesting in the most subtle extraphysical dimensions where there is no gravity, the extraphysical body is not bound to the earth's crust, so can think about a place and instantly transport itself there in an amount of time equivalent to some seconds.

Other characteristics of the extraphysical body include indestructibility; weightlessness; 360-degree vision and the capacity to pass through material objects, emit light, communicate more efficiently using telepathy and change its appearance or be invisible. However, these skills are not inherent and may have to be learned when projected. Usually the extraphysical body takes on the same appearance as the current or most recent physical body because most people have a strong attachment to the present or most recent human form.

You may also have to learn how to defend yourself in the

extraphysical dimension or how to help consciousnesses in need through the transmission of your energies. Don't just assume that you are able to do all these things when projected. But if you can't, take heart. These skills can be acquired if you have the will to learn.

Assuming you are lucid as to your condition outside of the body, your capacity to associate ideas; process information; remember things; apply your will and use your rationality, decision-making abilities and critical analysis is often heightened because you're not restricted by the limitations of the physical brain. But lucid individuals who are adept at controlling the extraphysical body, navigating the extraphysical dimension and carrying out preplanned extraphysical tasks and objectives represent only a small minority of the human population. These skills have to be learned.

As I mentioned in the introduction, although every human being experiences some separation between their physical and extraphysical bodies several times a night while asleep, the vast majority do so with either low levels of lucidity or no lucidity at all. Statistics arising from international opinion polls and surveys suggest that approximately 10 percent of the population has semi-conscious OBEs that are usually mixed with dreams, while approximately 80 million people, representing 1.2 percent of the population, have lucid, fully conscious OBEs.

In addition, there is an intrinsic difference in the way we experience emotions in the physical and extraphysical bodies. Emotions are more pronounced and we feel them more keenly in the extraphysical body because there is no physical shield to protect us from the impact of the intentions, ideas, thoughts and feelings of others. In the physical dimension by contrast, people often mask their true thoughts and intentions behind their words and expressions for the very purpose of avoiding conflict and emotional repercussions.

A friend of mine once had a projection that demonstrates very well the difference in how we can experience our emotions in the extraphysical dimension. He was projected with a reasonable level of lucidity when suddenly he perceived some pressure from behind. He turned around and noticed, in the far distance, an extraphysical individual looking at him intently. The impact of the stranger's attention completely unbalanced him and he tore off, fearful and anxious, before being snapped back into the body. What is interesting to note here is the contrast between this behavior and a likely reaction to a similar event in the physical body. As he said himself, if he'd been walking down the street in the physical dimension, sensed someone staring at him from behind, and turned around to see someone looking at him from the other end of the street, it would have been entirely inconsequential.

An out-of-body experience is not, however, an inherently destabilizing process. And of course the level of emotional stability we experience outside of the body is also in part a function of our personal level of maturity, openness and wisdom.

The Mental Body

In terms of density, the mental body (or mentalsoma), which hosts the consciousness during an OBE in the purely mental dimension, is the most subtle body of manifestation. During a mental projection, the consciousness acts in an isolated manner without the human body, the extraphysical body or the silver cord but is secured to the extraphysical body via a formless connection called the golden cord.

Probably the most important thing to understand about the mental body is that the consciousness resides here. Because of this, the mental body is the seat of our awareness and the core of who we are. Let me explain more precisely what I mean by this.

When we are in the physical dimension, we are restrained by

certain limitations. For example, we are subject to gravity, we have to sleep, eat, drink and breathe in order to survive. Our memory is incomplete. We don't remember all the details of our dreams, we remember little of our experiences outside of the body and most of us remember nothing about our past lives.

As we have already seen, when we manifest in the extraphysical body, either projected or between lives, we are much freer and more advanced than we are in the physical dimension in the way we capture and process information, communicate with others, move about, interact with our environment, see and remember things.

If we can do all of those things with the extraphysical body, can you imagine how much more we can do with the mental body when everything we've ever learned, everything we know and the memory and wisdom gained from everything we've ever experienced in previous lives is accumulated there?

In this state of absolute freedom from the restrictions imposed by the more energetically dense dimensions, the mental body is much more refined and complex, is able to realize many more of the consciousness's potentialities and is therefore in a condition that is significantly closer to the core of who it really is. For this reason, it is understood that the mental body is the seat of one's awareness.

Characteristics of the Mental Body

The characteristics and attributes of the mental body lie well beyond the model for existence widely accepted by conventional science. A unique attribute of the mental body, for example, is the complete memory of the existence of the consciousness, as mentioned above. So when manifesting in the mental body, the consciousness is able to access all the details and information pertaining to its past lives and periods spent between lives, including all the skills and knowledge about different subjects that it acquired, all the relationships it had, the countries in which it resided, languages it spoke, decisions it took, mistakes it made and so on. Those who have experienced a projection to the mental dimension will tell you that this information doesn't even have to be recalled or accessed as such. It is just there, imprinted in the complete memory of the consciousness.

In terms of characteristics, the energies of the mental dimension are so subtle that no shapes can be formed there, so when projected in the mental body the consciousness is completely formless and cannot be detected by the human sensory organs or by regular extrasensory perceptions. The mental body has no gender or sexual impulse. It expresses refined sentiments such as serenity, universality and fraternity instead of the courser emotions typical of the extraphysical body. And it is known to transcend the human notions of time and space, so long periods spent in the mental body can strangely occur in the equivalent of mere minutes passed in the physical dimension.

The mental body is also the source of all the positive attributes that will help us to become aware of our broader multidimensional reality and to understand how, why and where we fit into it. These attributes include self-awareness, many different forms of intelligence, concentration and attention, memory, wisdom, logic, rationality, discernment, lucidity, self-organization, self-control, objective criticism, ethics and will, among many others. In truth though, only a minute percentage of the human population is using these attributes for the purpose of developing and evolving themselves. Most modern societies are motivated instead by financial gain, prestige, status, comfort and gratification and have very little awareness of or interest in realities that lie beyond the material world.

Pathologies of the Mental Body

If we can have attributes of the mental body, it stands to reason that we can also have pathologies of the mental body, a pathology being any deviation from a normal healthy condition.

Robotization, a condition in which we allow ourselves to be controlled by mental routines and fixed ideas all the time is one example of this. Some people are robotized to the point that they barely use their mental body at all, such as those who blithely watch hours of TV every day, absorbing and accepting everything they see with no discernment.

Any limitation we have that blocks our progress, growth and evolution as a consciousness can be considered to be a pathology

The vehicles of manifestation

of the mental body. We can overcome such limitations, however, through "personal renovation." We each have established patterns of behavior and responses to given circumstances based on, in some instances, lives of repetitive experience. Self-renovation requires recognition of improved ways of viewing the world around us and of engaging with it, and the formation of new responses that will gradually supersede existing, more harmful ones. So the mental body is like software. If we are going to evolve we have to constantly update it, assimilate new ideas, confront and eliminate our weaknesses, and develop techniques that will help us to change. Experiences such as lucid OBEs that enable us to verify for ourselves that our reality is multidimensional and that there is life after death, often bring significant change and reprioritization to people's lives.

When a person is alive in the physical sense, his or her vehicles of manifestation are arranged as shown in this image. But what happens when we die?

What Happens When We Die?

At the moment of physical death (the first death), the silver cord, which is responsible for maintaining the connection between the physical body and the extraphysical body, ruptures. Part of the energy body remains with the extraphysical body until such time as the individual becomes aware that he is no longer alive in the physical sense . . . in other words, that he has died.

When this realization occurs, the energy body is discarded (second death) and the individual returns to the original, natural condition of an extraphysical consciousness. It can take hundreds of lives to develop this level of multidimensional awareness however. The reality is that the majority of people who are unprepared for life after death do not completely discard the energy body.

Once a person has passed through the second death, only the

extraphysical and mental bodies remain. These two bodies continue the cycle of new physical lives and periods spent between lives, joining with a new physical body and passing through physical death hundreds of times over many thousands of years.

But the more knowledge and awareness we have of the multidimensional nature of our existence, the more we experience things that most people think are just fiction, such as producing lucid OBEs at will, perceiving and communicating with extraphysical individuals and controlling some psychic and energetic phenomena. As we accomplish these things, we advance our mental body. We expand its capacity, lucidity and level of understanding. At the same time we become less emotional because the logic, rationality and more refined sentiments of the mental body start to dominate the emotional tendencies of our extraphysical body. As our emotionality decreases, the extraphysical body becomes more and more subtle until we reach a point where it no longer serves a purpose and we discard it (the third death). At this point the consciousness will exist only in the mental body and won't return to the cycle of physical life.

Everyday Experiences of Your Vehicles of Manifestation

In the introduction I spoke about the importance in conscientiology of having your own experiences. So here are some examples of experiences you may have already had that confirm the existence of your extraphysical and mental bodies.

Have you ever dreamt that you were falling from a great height and then jerked awake, heart pounding? Sometimes, of course, this really is a dream. As already mentioned though, most people experience some level of separation between the physical and extraphysical bodies at night while they're asleep. If the extraphysical body is not just floating above the physical body but is some distance away and for any one of many possible reasons the silver cord pulls it back suddenly, usually you will return at a great speed. When the extraphysical body reenters the physical body very suddenly, the "impact" of the landing can cause us to jerk awake. I think most people have had this experience.

Another example that you may have experienced is a phenomenon known as sleep paralysis (or more technically, projective catalepsy). As explained in an article written by my colleague Nanci Trivellato and myself, this is the phenomenon that occurs either at the onset of sleep or as you are starting to wake up, where you become aware at a moment in which your physical and extraphysical bodies are not fully aligned. You feel yourself to be inside the body, but due to the nonalignment of the two bodies of manifestation the physical brain doesn't respond to your commands. In such instances the paralysis experienced is the sensation of being unable to move, not an actual incapacity to do so, so there is nothing to fear.

To fully realign the extraphysical body with the physical body, just relax and focus on making a small movement, such as taking in a deeper breath and expanding your lungs or moving a toe or a finger, and the sensation of paralysis will disappear.

As we mention in the article, "the ideal means by which to control projective catalepsy and a range of psychic phenomena associated with dreaming and the OBE is to be able to master your own subtle energies, also known as bioenergy, *chi* or *prana*." (Trivellato and Gustus, 2003) Bioenergy and techniques for controlling it are discussed in depth in chapter 4.

History has recorded many incidences of man manifesting in his mental body during a mental projection of the consciousness. Other terms used to describe the projection of the mental body include cosmic consciousness, *nirvana* (Buddhism), *satori* (Zen), *samadhi* (yoga), ecstasy (mystics) and exaltation (mediumship).

As a concept, the projection of the mental body is incomprehensible to those who have never had the experience and it can only be properly understood by those who have. Even so, many who have enjoyed the experience find words quite inadequate to describe this state of being, as it's so far removed from our understanding of reality.

Waldo Vieira provides the following insights into his personal experience of the phenomenon in *Projections of the Consciousness*:

> There, in that nonexistent place, nothing existed, but everything was existing. I experienced 'touchable' ideas, unshakable certainties, indescribably serenity and undreamed of well-being.
>
> Even with my experience of automatic writing, channeling, clairvoyance, precognition, physical effects and many hundreds and various types of projections, I have experienced nothing in this life that compares to the wonders of the "sightless vision" and "emotion of structural peace" that was "seen" and "felt" in this fully conscious projection using the mentalsoma. (Vieira, 1997)

Those who are able to achieve a full, lucid projection with their mental body may also experience cosmoconsciousness, an intangible, somewhat indescribable state of expanded awareness, of all-knowingness, that allows a global view in which the entirety of all things is perceived, understood and appreciated as a single whole. The experience, in which the consciousness transcends space, time and form, is commonly reported as promoting a profound sense of peace and harmony with everyone and everything.

William Bulhman, author of several books on the OBE, quotes a participant of his international survey in *The Secret of the Soul*, who gave the following account of just such an experience:

> My awareness was stretched across the universe. Words

> cannot describe any of this, for I was far beyond form and substance. I was suddenly in an incredible ocean of pure living light. Everything was there—all knowledge, all awareness, and all answers. I was part of it all. I didn't ever want to leave. (Robert J., York Beach, Maine. *The Secret of the Soul,* William Bulhman, 2001, HarperCollins Publishers)

Cosmoconsciousness has been studied by many of the world's traditional and nontraditional religions and is the benchmark of enlightenment against which all other spiritual experiences are measured. It is worth pointing out here that although the experience eclipses even the most elevated state of awareness available to the consciousness manifesting in the human form, it is not a mystical event. I define a mystical event as one that literally cannot be explained. But I appreciate that many people use the word "mystical" to describe any experience that occurs beyond normal physical reality.

The reference points that shape our understanding of existence are generally based upon cultural influences; education; beliefs systems; the dogmas of most religions and the subjectivity, conditionings, assumptions, limitations, fears and misunderstandings inherent to all of these factors. As these influences mold us from the day we are born, in order to learn more about the true nature of what we really are, we first have to undo some deep-seated beliefs in preparation for discovering what we are not.

We are not just the physical body.

Chapter Two

Nonphysical Dimensions

> It is the commonest of mistakes to consider that the limit of our power of perception is also the limit of all there is to perceive.
> —*C.W. Leadbeater*

Of all the fascinating facts and tidbits of information peppered throughout Vieira's classic work *Projectiology,* one of the most telling describes humankind's overwhelming acknowledgment of the multidimensional structure of existence. Vieira cites the studies of Chinese researcher Professor Solon Wang, who classified the world's fourteen most important schools of knowledge as follows:

Western religions—Christianity, Islam and Judaism
Western philosophies—European Spiritualism, Greek and Materialism
Eastern religions—Buddhism, Hinduism and Zoroastrianism
Eastern philosophies—Confucianism, Taoism and Yoga
Sciences—natural (ancient) and new (psychic)

Only two of the fourteen (Materialism and ancient science) mandate physicality as a condition of reality. The other twelve acknowledge that the physical dimension is but one of several dimensions of which the true conformation of existence is composed. (Vieira, 2002)

In the face of such evidence, it is a paradox that many followers of these schools of knowledge accept nonphysical dimensions as reality within the context of their belief systems and faiths, yet not within the context of their ordinary, everyday lives. For example, many people fully subscribe to the concept of an afterlife, yet in complete contradiction to that belief, are totally skeptical of the possibility of being able to function with awareness independently of the physical body.

Extraphysical dimensions and layers are often characterized according to their levels of frequency, vibration or subtlety. To expand this understanding, extraphysical districts can be described as different levels of reality determined by the density of energies, and the level of lucidity and the quality of thoughts, ideas and emotions of the consciousnesses residing or transiting there. This makes sense when you take into account the most essential principle of nonphysical geography, which is that extraphysical environments are not places with geographical locations but states of consciousness.

This is not such an easy concept to grasp at first, but if you are interested in understanding the various realities of the extraphysical world, a serious dose of neophilia (openness to new ideas) is required, because the extraphysical dimensions are not governed by the laws of our material existence.

We can, nonetheless, draw some parallels to facilitate our understanding of nonphysical realities.

For example, when thinking about where the extraphysical dimensions are, we can say that many of them coexist and share space with the physical dimension. They are all around us. They are right here, right now. This fact is much easier to understand when we remember that we are also sharing space with innumerable invisible artificial electromagnetic waves, such as those used to broadcast television and radio and to transmit data across mobile phone networks and between aircraft and military installations. Radio alone broadcasts over hundreds of different frequencies and bands. Strictly speaking, there are an infinite number of frequencies across the electromagnetic spectrum.

When you choose one station and stay there, that is your experience and your reality for a short while. But that doesn't mean the other stations don't exist. In exactly the same way as there are an infinite number of frequencies across the electromagnetic spectrum, there are an infinite number of dimensions or extraphysical layers that make up our existence. Broadly speaking however, it is correct to say that our existence is composed of the physical dimension, the extraphysical dimension and the mental dimension, with the extraphysical dimension being separated into multiple layers, many of which are further divided into districts or zones.

Let's take a closer look at the similarities, differences and peculiarities of the extraphysical layers, starting with the denser layers more closely connected to and associated with the physical dimension.

The Extraphysical Sphere of Energy

If a projector is able to experience the detachment and take-off of the extraphysical body from the physical body with full awareness, the first place he is likely to find himself is in the extraphysical sphere of energy. This extraphysical force field surrounds the human body, extending four meters in every direction (having the physical head at its center). Since this force field overlaps with the physical dimension, its energies are relatively dense in comparison to other extraphysical layers. As such, the extraphysical sphere of energy acts as an interface between the physical and extraphysical dimensions.

When the extraphysical body is floating within the extraphysical sphere of energy, in close proximity to the physical body, one's energy body undergoes a transformation as part of it begins to take the shape of the silver cord. Before this transformation has been fully completed, the silver cord can easily retract to reform the energy body, vigorously pulling the extraphysical body with it. So for those wanting to spend extended periods outside the body, the aim would be to move away from the human body as quickly as possible. The influence of terrestrial gravity in the extraphysical sphere of energy is also notable and has the effect of making the extraphysical body feel heavier than when it is outside of the sphere.

Various phenomena also occur with greater intensity here due to the density of the energetic field, for example:

- instability of the extraphysical body—characterized as a rocking or oscillation.
- extraphysical double awareness—a sensation that can accompany the transition of the consciousness from the brain of the physical body to the (para)brain of the extraphysical body in which the projector experiences his lucidity in the physical and extraphysical bodies at the same time. Note however that the consciousness does not divide itself but can only be present in its entirety in one body of manifestation at any given moment.
- extraphysical double vision—when part of a person's vision is in the human body and part is in the extraphysical body; in other words, when one's normal physical vision and clairvoyance operate simultaneously.
- slow-motion extraphysical movement—often described as the feeling of wading through mud or water.

As the extraphysical sphere of energy is a new environment for most of us and exhibits many unique characteristics with which the majority of us are unfamiliar, it can take a little time to adapt to the sensations and phenomena that are commonly experienced there.

The Crustal Dimension (Paratroposphere)

Slightly less dense energetically than the extraphysical sphere of energy is the earth's crustal dimension (or paratroposphere), which lies within the earth's atmosphere. As the environments of the paratroposphere are closely connected to earth, they duplicate terrestrial environments and life there coexists and overlaps with human life. This extraphysical zone has been given many names throughout history and is commonly known as the crustal plane, the astral plane, the after-death world, and the spiritual world . . . the place in which spirits or lost souls remain earth-bound.

Because of man's indoctrination to his material, physical existence and general lack of openness to and preparedness for the actual nonphysical realities of life after death, when most people die their lucidity dramatically diminishes. Simply put, they don't understand what's going on. Their natural tendency then is to gravitate towards the familiarity of the paratropospheric communities that coincide with the earth's area of influence. The paratroposphere is, as such, densely populated in the same way that our planet is densely populated.

Inhabitants of the Paratroposphere

While a lower level of lucidity characterizes most inhabitants of the earth's paratroposphere, many of its inhabitants are *completely* unaware of their extraphysical state . . . they have no idea that they are dead. One cause of this condition is an excessive attachment to physical life. Many people believe that physical life is everything; it's all there is, and that when they die they will cease to exist. Their attitude doesn't change just because they die, so as long as they experience their awareness, they think they're still alive in the physical sense. This explains why individuals in this condition typically remain earth-bound. Many stay close to former family and friends, attempting to participate in their former lives. Usually, they eventually degenerate into an unbalanced state of despair and confusion as their physical loved ones are unable to perceive or interact with them, they are unable to make any sense of their experiences, and also because they are affected by the confusion and distress of others in their proximity. Many also become disturbed by a literally insatiable hunger for the emotions they derived from physical activities such as giving and receiving affection, eating, drinking, taking drugs and having sex; activities that they can no longer partake in because they don't have the means (i.e. a human body) to do so.

This common condition, often characterized by an intense stare, is known as post-mortem parapsychosis (from the Latin *post-mortem* meaning after death, *para* meaning beyond the physical, and psychosis meaning any severe form of mental disorder). Although the crustal layers are crowded with consciousnesses in this condition, we more commonly hear about the very few who are able to use the dense energy known as ectoplasm to perform direct actions in the physical dimension . . . the poltergeists or hauntings. Poltergeists can move physical objects or cause them to fly, produce noises, smells, air currents and apparitions etc.

I mentioned earlier that extraphysical environments are states of consciousness, as opposed to geographical locations that fall within our current understanding of space. The mechanics of how a state of mind is the underlying cause that gives rise to the creation of a particular environment is demonstrated very well by the paratropospheric extraphysical communities.

It is understood in conscientiology that a consciousness's thoughts, emotions and energy are inextricably linked; in other words, that the quality of an individual's energy is influenced by the quality of his thoughts, intentions, ideas and feelings. So when large groups of kindred extraphysical consciousnesses reflect and dwell on the same subject, consistently producing fixed ideas that persist over hundreds of years, eventually the energies of the group generate powerful, permanent thought-forms, nonphysical energetic expressions of ideas that behave like and appear to be actual structures. The thought-forms are not permanent in the strictest sense, but they no longer require direct, conscious management by anyone to be sustained. They have become part of a nonphysical environment because they are accepted and simply by being acknowledged, energy is added to them.

Let's consider, for example, the fact that many thousands of extraphysical individuals whose most recent life was spent living in London are suffering from post-mortem parapsychosis. The heavy influence of the environment in which they now exist (and to which they contribute due to their diminished lucidity) coerces them into maintaining the fantasy that they are leading a 'normal' physical existence. In other words, they contribute with their energies to the maintenance of existing thought-forms that have been built up by others in the same condition over many centuries. Over time, these thought-forms have molded an extraphysical replica of the city of London that approximates its streets, buildings and landmarks. This process is even more intense when large groups of people pass through the first death and go together to the extraphysical environment at (or around) the same time, as happened during the London Blitz in World War II.

In these sorts of environments individuals create the way in which they interact with their reality for themselves. There is no external influence that imposes change (as often happens in the physical environment where people are forced to change when they lose a job or are promoted, lose or gain a partner, contract a life-threatening disease, etc.), so until they decide to do something different, nothing changes. Because of this, some people, lacking the lucidity to understand their own predicament, become stuck and may spend hundreds of years in a condition of very low awareness. Often, in order to be rehabilitated, enlightened as to their state and moved to a more suitable environment (some projectors refer to this activity as a rescue or retrieval), they still require human resources such as dense energy, and this is something that conscious projectors can provide as the extraphysical body departs the physical body carrying some proportion of the energy body with it.

Most large human cities have an extraphysical equivalent. Can you imagine what might be going on in the extraphysical duplicate of Jerusalem, the sacred place of three major religions with its long and complicated history? Yes. There is war in the crustal dimension. Most human problems we experience in the physical dimension are echoed in the extraphysical world. Human nature is human nature everywhere we go.

When extraphysical layers overlap with physical life in this way, often the extraphysical buildings mirror both the exterior appearance and interior decoration of actual physical homes and may even be temporarily inhabited by a deceased person who resided there during his last physical incarnation. This characteristic of the crustal layers causes much confusion among conscious projectors who sometimes find themselves in environments that are intimately familiar yet not exactly the same as those they know, as slight modifications or variations are common in the extraphysical duplicate.

For example, Wagner Alegretti, the President of the IAC, recounts how during one of his first projections as a teenager he passed out through the roof of his house and was peering down at the empty field next door. But instead of seeing the usual grass and the one tree he knew to be there, he could see a construction that appeared to be an office block of some kind. All this was very confusing until he realized that when you are outside the body you can still distinguish some elements of the terrestrial dimension as you start to see parts of the extraphysical dimension. This is how the dimensions overlap.

Robert Monroe recounted several visits to the crustal dimension in his three books, reporting the following in the second, *Far Journeys:*

> But I knew the next ring[1] inward. It wasn't nice. Beyond that was physical life. The two were tightly interwoven, the thick ring just slightly out of phase with physical matter. It was the interface between one reality system and another. Even from this perspective, it was difficult for a novice to distinguish instantly the differences between the two. But I could.
>
> That was the problem. The inhabitants of this ring couldn't. They didn't or couldn't or wouldn't realize they were no longer physical. They were physically dead. No more physical body. Thus they kept trying to be physical, to do and be what they had been, to continue to be physical one way or another. Bewildered, some spent all of their activity in attempting to communicate with friends and loved ones still in bodies or with anyone else who might come along, all to no avail. Others were held attracted to physical sites in which they had instilled great meaning or importance during their previous human lifetime. (Far Journeys, Robert Monroe, Doubleday and Eleanor Friede Books)

Author Bruce Moen, in *Voyage Beyond Doubt*, the second volume in the Exploring the Afterlife series, offered similar insights when describing his work helping such individuals to become aware of the fact they were dead during his out-of-body travels.

> During past experience doing retrievals, I'd discovered people sometimes get 'stuck' after they die. Often the circumstances of their death or their beliefs about an afterlife are responsible for their being "stuck". (Moen, 1998)

Moen makes two points that are very interesting to note. First, that in addition to erroneous beliefs about the afterlife, sometimes people are completely unaware they have died due to the circumstances of their death. This might include people who died unexpectedly in their sleep, such as victims of sudden natural disasters like landslides and earthquakes, or victims of unforeseen traffic accidents. Second Moen also notes that people's beliefs about the afterlife can cause them to be "stuck." For example, if a person has been indoctrinated to a belief system that maintains that a life well-lived (a highly relative notion) will be rewarded with an eternity floating in the lush environs of paradise and then the reality doesn't match up, the ensuing downward spiral into post-mortem parapsychosis can be extremely difficult to reverse.

The fact that you are open to reading the information in this book and to considering various afterlife realities will help you to be more prepared for what awaits you after death. The ideal, however, would be to take advantage of the opportunities offered by the out-of-body experience, by using it as a tool to visit the earth's paratroposphere while you are alive, to witness and experience for yourself the condition of those who reside there. This will help you to fulfill any expectation you may have of spending your next period between lives in a state of awareness of your extraphysical condition and of passing your time there doing something other than mimicking your current existence.

Paratropospheric Communities

The crustal layers are composed of an extraordinarily diverse range of communities, as is our physical world. The majority of consciousnesses gravitate towards colonies that reflect the mentality of groups with which they associated in former physical lives. There are, for example, communities formed by individuals with a predominantly masculine or feminine mentality while others have predominantly homosexual tendencies. Some communities are defined by the former profession of its inhabitants. There are colonies of former politicians, musicians, writers, scientists, military personnel, criminals, mafia and those employed in the sex trade who continue to lead promiscuous existences between physical lives.

Some zones in the crustal dimension echo the misery, squalor and moral degeneration of human slums where homelessness, violence, drug-trafficking, extortion, gangs and delinquency are the order of the day. Others, inhabited by consciousnesses suffering from schizophrenia and other mental illnesses, are chaotic places devoid of any semblance of organization, where past traumas are relived over and over. Certain places are considerably worse than anything found on earth. Scenes from films such as *What Dreams May Come* and more recently, *Constantine*, that depict seething masses of lost, panicked people crawling all over one another, are not inaccurate reflections of some truly sorrowful extraphysical realities.

It is important to emphasize that the communities dwelling in the earth's paratroposphere reflect human nature, so we find the good as well as the bad and the ugly there. What is common to all these communities is their attachment to the physical dimension, (in terms of affinities not proximity). So the quality of any particular extraphysical area, ethically-speaking, may be influenced by the quality of the terrestrial environment or community to which it is linked. There are paratropospheric communities associated with the offices and work of humanitarian aid organizations in various countries around the world, for example. Equally, however, it can be argued that it is the quality of a particular extraphysical area that influences the quality of the terrestrial environment to which it is linked. As always, we have the chicken and egg scenario. Which came first—the physical community or the extraphysical community? In fact, both scenarios are possible.

The less evolved paratropospheric districts have been visited by numerous conscious projectors over the centuries and their characteristics have been well-documented. Readers of Robert Monroe's books would know these areas as Locale II while others may know them by one of several other names given to them by projectors throughout history such as Hades, Inferno, Kamaloka, Purgatory or Umbral. (Vieira, 2002)

The Extraphysical Dimensions

Moving away from the paratropospheric regions that lie within the earth's atmosphere, the energies of the extraphysical layers become more subtle. These layers are inaccessible to individuals residing permanently in the crustal layers who have not passed through the second death and so are still laden with the dense energies of the energy body. For them, trying to access more subtle dimensions is akin to mixing oil with water.

Throughout the extraphysical dimension, we see an extraordinary diversity and complexity of existences, including everything that lies within accepted parameters of what is real and a whole lot that doesn't.

In the crustal layers, as we've just seen, the majority of consciousnesses are not creating anything new but are just copying physical life. Other extraphysical dimensions are inhabited by communities that are locked in unevolved levels of existence reminiscent of our Middle Ages and even the primitive ages. There are zones that coincide with our underground and with the deepest abysses of the ocean, and others that are nothing but a void. No thought-forms have been created there.

By contrast, in some layers you can interact with the environment on many different levels. You can touch, feel, see, smell and sense in much the same way as you can in the physical plane. Things feel solid. You can lift them. Some extraphysical objects can't be broken or even scratched because their internal cohesion is so strong. Other objects can't be moved. This means that the individuals who created these thought-forms did so with large quantities of energy, or the thought-forms were created and reenforced over a very long period of time.

Some nonphysical areas don't have a ground as we know it.

They are adapted to the needs of residents who fly, so rather than having floors, roads and motorways, the communities are vertical and the buildings resemble bell towers, open on all sides to facilitate the coming and going of the consciousnesses living there.

There are places in which space is not transparent as it is here. You can still see a good distance, but everything is cloaked in a type of fine mist or fog. Some environments don't have stars, planets or a sun, and the only light is the self-illumination of your extraphysical body or of the surrounding extraphysical matter.

Projectors have reported visiting zones that have meteorological-like conditions and others that have periods of calm interspersed with extraphysical storms that rain a type of fire instead of water, sending all the residents scurrying for shelter. You see extraphysical nature in some places . . . flora and fauna that are often very different to what we know. Waldo Vieira once came across a kind of miniature giraffe while he was out of the body. He was able to communicate with it telepathically and found it to be quite intelligent. In terms of flora, there are some equivalents of plants. The leaves, not always green, can be luminous or transparent.

Advanced Nonphysical Communities

Elsewhere in the vast extraphysical dimension that is as limitless as the physical are futuristic communities that are significantly more advanced than ours, where the consciousnesses are using tools and updated technologies superior to anything we know. Some of these areas have absolutely no commonality with the physical dimension at all and could be described as the nonphysical equivalent of extraterrestrial environments inhabited by extraterrestrial life-forms. (Alegretti, 2005)

Residing in the most subtle, rarefied energetic layers of the extraphysical dimension, closer to the mental dimension, are communities of more lucid, evolved nonphysical beings.

In general, people exhibit the same capacities in their physical and extraphysical existences. So by no means are all extraphysical consciousnesses operating at full capacity. For example, some can't fly or pass through solid, physical objects because they don't believe they can and are restricted by their own limitations. More lucid consciousnesses by contrast, understand the mechanism of materializing thought-forms as objects and, limited only by their imagination, create tools, technologies, houses and other buildings to fabricate existences that rival our best science-fiction movies.

The more organized, advanced nonphysical communities are usually involved in one of two tasks, either preparing individuals for the next physical life or welcoming and rehabilitating those who have recently died.

Those consciousnesses who are lucid and are preparing to be reborn commonly undergo a kind of training for their next physical life. This subject is discussed in more detail in chapter 10.

Many more of the advanced extraphysical communities, however, are dedicated to the ongoing and problematic work of assisting those who have recently died and have arrived in the extraphysical dimension from physical life, often in a state of trauma, shock or bewilderment. Individuals from these more-evolved layers work in extraphysical clinics and hospitals working with people who are in need of help and healing. The ambience of these places of convalescence is bleak, in stark contrast to those involved in preparing candidates for human life, which are typified by positive feelings of hope, opportunity and the anticipation of achieving planned goals.

Some advanced communities not involved in the various functions already described might be inhabited by geniuses, while residents of other evolved layers might be examples of serenity and ethics. If you project to places like this, you find beauty and order beyond your imagination. Projected human beings have brought back many inspirations from these extraphysical communities for various forms of art such as painting and sculpture, and music and literature. By the same process, however, some people have reconstructed accurate representations of actual extraphysical environments to create the horror-movies of our worst nightmares. In a similar fashion, some of the music that plays over the radio in the physical dimension echoes the music of some unevolved paratropospheric colonies.

So what is more real—the physical dimension or the extraphysical dimensions? Which is copying which? Just as so many people do not believe in extraphysical realities, many extraphysical consciousnesses do not believe in and are totally skeptical of our physical reality. When we insist that the framework of our material existence provides fixed reference points within which everything else must fit, we severely limit the way in which we experience our existence.

The Mental Dimension

Beyond the extraphysical dimension lies the mental dimension, which is native to the mental body and is the native environment of the consciousness *per se*.

We can say the mental dimension is right here right now, as is the extraphysical dimension. We don't perceive it totally, but there is an interaction in the same way there is with the extraphysical dimension. But as we saw in chapter 1, the reality of the mental dimension is so subtle and different from our reality here that we need a different type of sensitivity and a significant amount of maturity, balance and openness to perceive it.

The best way to study the mental dimension is to have a mental projection. When we are between lives, existing in the extraphysical dimension, we have projections in the mental dimension. So we will already have some memory of these episodes in the integral memory of our mental body.

Characteristics of the Mental Dimension

But what is the mental dimension like? The energies of the level of existence there are so subtle that nothing has form. In the extraphysical dimension there is a reality that we can see, but in the mental dimension there's not enough energy attached to your thoughts to shape anything. You think, but no forms are created. Everything remains in the realm of ideas. So in the mental dimension there is nothing to see.

Nor is there space in the way there is here, so there is no separation between one person and another there even though everyone maintains his individuality. If we were to meet there I wouldn't be able to say you are on my left, I am on your right. There is no above, beyond, floor or ceiling.

Similarly, there's no time. There is no before and after. Sometimes when we are projected in the extraphysical body with no restriction from the physical brain, we can access memories of our past lives or have some precognitions of the future. With the mental body, however, as we're dealing purely with ideas with no concept of time, then something that happened in a past life is just there, imprinted on our mental body. This information is easily accessed in this dimension.

Even though there is no form in the mental dimension, we can immediately perceive and recognize one another on a purely parapsychic level with our memories, thoughts, emotions and energies. We have our whole existence to identify us there. Our core is on display, not like in physical life where we can easily hide or mask our true thoughts, opinions and ideas behind our facial expressions and words.

But how do we communicate there? Because we can't even quantify the distance between us, there is no distance between you, your idea and me. So the moment you have an idea, I know. The moment I react to your idea, you know. Ideas are communicated en bloc via a sophisticated form of nonphysical telepathy that has no articulated words or symbols. Whole blocks of thoughts and ideas just suddenly enter the consciousness. For example, if we were together in the mental dimension and I was to communicate the contents of this book to you, I could convey the information to you en bloc, instead of word by word as we are doing here.

The consciousness manifesting in the mental dimension can also acquire new information that presents itself in a sudden insight. Profound knowledge, intellectual structures or visions may be acquired in this way. These are insights of a complexity whose magnitude far exceeds the most enlightened view of the most capacious human being restricted by his physical brain, insights that clearly never occurred to the same person while in the ordinary, physical waking state. Some outputs of the acquisition of such original ideas include poetry, prose, solutions to all manner of problems, inventiveness and scientific discoveries.

So to experience the mental dimension is to experience an expansion of the consciousness, and a level of freedom, richness and sophistication of ideas, memories and information not available in other dimensions. Sadly, the unlimited nature of the experience is not so easy to remember because of the restriction imposed by the physical form of the brain.

It is interesting to note the parallels between conscientiology and some of the world's greatest religions in terms of the different "places" that exist in the afterlife. Certainly, according to anecdotal evidence provided by hundreds of lucid projectors throughout history, there are areas in the extraphysical dimensions that could be described as paradise or heaven-like and others as hell-like, while we have already discussed the crustal dimension in which many consciousnesses are stuck in a kind of limbo where nothing changes. To compartmentalize the nonphysical dimensions into three afterlife destinations, however, is to over-simplify the diversity and complexity of the extraphysical realities that may be experienced after death.

Chapter Three

Nonphysical Beings: Transdimensional Interactions and Relationships

> Men do not attract that which they want, but that which they are.
>
> —James Allen

We don't change when we die. The deactivation of the physical body simply means that the nature of our *manifestation* has changed so that we can no longer manifest in the physical dimension and the focus of our attention shifts back to the extraphysical dimension. Think of it as a change of address!

Nor does the process of physical death have any bearing on one's actual level of evolution—for better or worse. When we discard our biological body, our weak traits, strong traits, intelligences, pathologies, fears, beliefs, attitudes and ideas accompany us. Because of this, the behavior we see expressed in the extraphysical dimensions related to earth is nothing more than human nature . . . the same human nature that we deal with every single day in our physical world.

It has been interesting to witness over time how the portrayal of this reality in the mainstream entertainment media has become increasingly accurate. Whereas once, extraphysical consciousnesses were typecast as terrifying poltergeists, now we are more regularly being treated to productions that are both technically correct and sympathetic in their portrayal of how extraphysical beings cope with life after death. Some good examples of films of this genre are *Truly, Madly, Deeply; Ghost; The Sixth Sense; The Others; Field of Dreams; Made in Heaven* and *What Dreams May Come.*

But the extraphysical realms are not only inhabited by consciousnesses that were recently human. Some haven't had a physical existence as a human being for many centuries while others have never been human but have led physical existences on other planets in other parts of the universe.

This may sound incredulous, but consider this: The reincarnation of the consciousness is a fundamental principle not only of conscientiology but of many philosophies and religions. But if reincarnation is confined to the rebirth of a consciousness who has already lived a human existence then how can we account for the phenomenal growth in the earth's population from an estimated 300 million 2,000 years ago to 6.5 billion today? As stated by Peter and Elizabeth Fenwick in *Past Lives: An Investigation into Reincarnation Memories* the planet's ever-increasing population "makes a nonsense of the argument that every one of us has lived another human life before." (*Peter and Elizabeth Fenwick*, 1999)

To date, conventional science has had little success in detecting the presence of intelligent life on other planets, but numerous conscious projectors, including Waldo Vieira, Wagner Alegretti and Robert Monroe, among others, have visited planets outside our solar system where they have interacted with a variety of intelligent physical life forms and have met countless extraphysical consciousnesses out of the body who had physical incarnations on other planets in previous lives. When we consider these facts along with what we already know about human nature, the sheer scale of the diversity of extraphysical consciousnesses quickly becomes apparent.

In recognition of the complexity of the various areas of research, the science of conscientiology regularly uses basic categorizations to facilitate understanding of subjects under investigation. In this instance, conscientiology begins the process of classifying extraphysical consciousnesses by dividing them into three groups, termed helpers, blind guides and intruders.

Helpers

Helper is a nonmystical, nonreligious term used to describe an extraphysical consciousness who acts as a benefactor to one or more physical individuals.

A helper is sufficiently mature and personally versed in the reality of physical life and the process of individual growth so that he has an overview of the life of and opportunities available to the people he is supporting.

A helper's task is not to assist a person to have an easier, more comfortable life, but to support and assist him to take maximum advantage of the opportunities offered by the current physical life to become more aware of multidimensional realities, to grow and evolve throughout the entirety of his physical and extraphysical existences and to eventually undertake to help others to do the same.

More popularly known as angels, guardian angels, spirit guides or mentors, helpers are not mystical beings as is commonly thought. They are like us, only in a better condition, more advanced or evolved. They have had physical lives and will have again. Some people currently living among us were helpers in previous nonphysical periods spent between lives.

Characteristics and Behaviors of Helpers

Notable characteristics and behaviors of helpers include the following:

- They are fully aware that they have discarded the physical body (i.e. passed through the first death) and because of this, have discarded their energy body (i.e. passed through the second death).
- Their raison d'être, as their name suggests, is to assist others. Assistance is their specialty. They have the intention to assist in all circumstances and conditions and can fulfill their intentions in many cases.

- While they genuinely care for us, they are not dependent on us nor do they create situations in which we become dependent upon them. One of the ways they do this is by not helping us every time they can. They have the capability to solve most of our problems, but if they were to do this, we would become reliant on them. They understand that it is only in making our own decisions and dealing with the consequences of our choices that we grow. So they provide assistance when appropriate and necessary but otherwise they step back and just monitor us.
- They work in discreet ways. They won't, for example, show themselves to us. If we could see them so easily we would be calling on them for help all the time and not learning how to help ourselves.
- They are not demanding of us. They don't demand that we improve or develop ourselves. It is our always our choice.
- They respect our free will, never applying pressure, forcing or imposing anything on us.
- They analyze us but don't judge us.
- They manifest a heightened level of awareness—meaning they have deliberately been using their mental body more over many physical and extraphysical lives to seek and have new experiences from which they have learned and grown as consciousnesses.
- Being in contact with helpers generates an increase in our lucidity and rationality. For example, you may be about to make a critical decision and many ideas and suggestions come to you. Imagine you are working with an aid organization in a third-world country and you find that you don't have enough medicine and food to keep everyone alive, so you have to decide who receives the assistance and who doesn't. The helpers will help you to think with rationality and to consider all the consequences of the

possible decisions or may give you an intuition about other alternative solutions to the problem.

- They have specific skills. For example, if you want to help homeless people, a helper who has experience with this will come to assist you. If you want to do medical research to find a cure for a disease, a helper who has expertise in this field will come to work with you.
- Their behavior is always cosmoethical—meaning, their behavior is aligned with more evolved moral principles that are not subjective in nature or specific to one particular culture or religion, but are applicable and appropriate in all circumstances, cultures, countries, continents and dimensions. (The subject of cosmoethics is explored in depth in chapter 11).
- They never assist us to do something that is not cosmoethical.
- They don't help us at the cost of someone else.
- They know what our specific purpose in life is. They give us tips about our life task and provide us with opportunities to increase our awareness of this important aspect of our lives until we know what we have to do.
- We almost always have karmic connections with our helpers.

Not everyone has helpers. This reality conflicts with the mystical notion that everyone has his own personal guardian angel watching over him. But serial killers, dictators who commit genocide, terrorists, pedophiles and drug traffickers, for example, don't have helpers. But if a moment arrives in the lives of people like this when they begin to reflect, turn inwards and start working on self-improvement with some commitment and perseverance, they would attract the attention of the helpers.

Helpers are not with us around the clock but are with us when we're in need and when we're doing things that are related to our development and growth. They're always giving assistance, so when we're just taking time out to relax or when we're engaged in activities that are not cosmoethical, they're off making best use of their time helping someone else.

We don't always have the same helper with us throughout our life. There are several reasons for this. Some helpers specialize, for example, in protecting children. Others specialize in fields such as projectiology (assisting interested, cosmoethical individuals to leave the body with lucidity), evolution, research, or the dissemination of ideas. As we develop and evolve, we may need more advanced helpers or simply helpers with different areas of expertise. Sometimes helpers leave us to be reborn.

It is possible to learn to perceive the presence of the helpers if you're not able to do so already. Tips and techniques for developing your parapsychic capacities to the point where you can accurately discern who is around you extraphysically are discussed at length in the next chapter.

How Can I Have More Helpers Around Me?

But what if you perceive that you don't have many helpers close to you? If this is your case and you would like to enhance and increase the frequency of your interactions with helpers, you will attract them to you by being more like them. Remember, who we have around us both physically and extraphysically is a function of affinities—like attracts like. So if we spend more time trying to improve and develop ourselves, and assisting others by happily giving of our time, attention, love, energy, wisdom, money (when appropriate) and any of the many other resources we have at our disposal, we will attract helpers to us. When we help others we create an atmosphere around us with our positive thoughts and intentions that allows the helpers to be close to us. If, on the other hand, we surround ourselves with physical and extraphysical consciousnesses whose attitudes, intentions and behaviors are negative, the helpers can't get close to us.

One important thing to remember about the helpers is that as they are specialists in assistance, they know their job much better than we do. So we can ask our helpers to help someone else but if we ask them to help us, we are, in effect, telling them that they don't know how to do their job. This shows a lack of appreciation. Nor should we constantly make demands of them. They are not our servants and they merit more respect than that.

Mechanisms by Which Helpers Communicate with Us

The helpers use a variety of mechanisms to intervene in our lives and to communicate with us. Here are some examples.

Synchronicity

Reports of an unseen force assisting people at a critical point in their lives are not uncommon. My good friend Sam, for example, was vacationing with his family on Phuket in Thailand when the tsunami struck on Boxing Day, 2004, and through a long sequence of unlikely synchronicities, they all escaped with their lives. First, as they had decided to spend Christmas in Thailand at the last minute, all the beachfront hotels were fully booked so they stayed at Club Med, which was set back from the beach and raised on the incline of a hill. Second, having enjoyed spending all of Christmas Day playing on the beach, they decided to spend the following day there as well. As they were passing the pool on the way to the beach Sam's daughter jumped in, laughing. So he got in with her. It was only minutes later that the first wave struck. Third, the hotel pool wasn't on ground level but was on the first floor. Sam's girlfriend, having just finished a yoga class on the ground floor, was making her way up the stairs to the pool when the wave struck, and was out of harm's way. Fourth, and to their immense credit, Club Med had full emergency evacuation procedures in place and rather than abandoning their guests, the staff put them into practice. The surviving guests were guided to the safety of a monastery on top of the hill as soon as the first wave subsided, a collection of passports from the hotel rooms was organized during the night, and four Air France aircraft were flown especially from Paris to Bangkok and then onto Phuket as soon as the airport reopened. The Club Med guests were on the first planes out of the country the next day.

Was it the helpers hard at work in the days leading up to and then during the disaster that kept my friends safe? Unfortunately, with an event of such magnitude it would be impossible for the helpers to protect everybody.

While some people have some level of awareness of the direct intervention of a helper in a moment of need or crisis, most people interpret synchronicities that bring about positive outcomes in their lives as good luck.

Helpers may also use synchronicities as a means of providing us with some inspirations and ideas.

Secondary Messenger

Perhaps you have had an experience in which a person acted as a "secondary messenger" of the helpers and passed you a message that didn't make any sense to them but made perfect sense and was very helpful to you.

I had this happen several years ago when I was out to dinner one night with a man who later became my partner. At that time we were not involved but were having a lovely dinner and a great chat. Towards the end of the night, the group of people at the table next to us, with whom we'd talked a little throughout the evening, stood up to leave. One of the men leaned very close over our table, between us, and said, "You two have a fantastic connection." He looked each of us square in the eyes and said, "If only you'd realize it." All three of us were quite stunned by what he said, considering he was a complete stranger who had no way of knowing what the nature of our relationship was or wasn't. But along with all the other pieces in the complicated jigsaw of relationships, it helped bring us together.

Intuition

Have you ever been struck by an intuition so strong that you felt compelled to act upon it? Sometimes the helpers use this mechanism of communication to do things like prevent accidents, large or small, and even to save lives. Wagner Alegretti was on the receiving end of just such an intervention when he was a small baby. He was lying asleep in a bassinet under a massive set of kitchen cabinets when all of a sudden his mother, who was ironing on the other side of the room, was struck by a powerful instinct to rush over and snatch him from the bassinet, which she did. Seconds later, the entire shelving unit laden with crockery, pots and pans, and other heavy kitchen equipment collapsed and fell from the wall, crushing the bassinet beneath it.

The film *Touching the Void* also portrays an excellent example of how a helper might intervene through the mechanism of intuition. The film recounts the true story of two climbers and their treacherous assault on the Siula Grande in the Peruvian Andes in 1985. Disturbingly, Englishman Simon Yates had to sacrifice the life of friend Joe Simpson in order to save his own when a storm struck soon after their descent from the summit. As this occurred during a whiteout and at night, Simon wasn't to know that Joe actually survived after being released from a rope, falling over a cliff and into a ravine.

When Simon eventually reached the base camp, which was nothing more than a backpacker they'd met on their travels waiting with a tent and some food, he felt strangely compelled to linger, which he and backpacker Richard Hawking did for four days. This seemed incongruous in light of the ordeal he had just suffered and was against Richard's wishes. On the fourth night however, the two men woke to hear Joe, who had maneuvered his way out of a deep ravine despite hideous injuries to one leg, descended thousands of feet down the mountain and then crawled several kilometers over rocks in excruciating pain and with severe dehydration, hunger, frostbite and then delirium, to reach the camp, despite fully expecting that no one would be there.

What was it that compelled Simon to stay? What was it that drove Joe to overcome the utter hopelessness of his circumstances and inch his way down the mountain? In Joe's case, as he later admitted that he hates to be defeated and is incredibly strong-willed, it seems to me that the helpers took advantage of these strong traits by amplifying them with suggestions to keep moving forward, one painful step at a time.

In a chapter of *Projections of the Consciousness* entitled "Ideal Assistance," Waldo Vieira describes a projection to a neighborhood in Rio de Janeiro in which he met an extraphysical man, a helper, who appeared to be a doctor. Through the process of telepathy, the helper explained that his regular work involved assisting consciousnesses in need and spoke of his plans to expand the team he currently coordinated to regularly incorporate projected individuals whose dense energies would greatly facilitate the work. (As the helpers have passed through the second death and discarded the energy body, they need and use the dense energies of projectors in order to carry out certain types of assistance.)

The helper told Waldo that his team, which is more active at night when human suffering tends to be most acute, from 6:00 p.m. onwards, works with the problems that arise from the loosely structured relationships typical of big cities, such as loneliness and sadness, depression and despair, doubts, longings and resentments.

Before leaving Waldo, the helper conveyed to him this message related to ideal assistance. Waldo recounted it in *Projections of the Consciousness* and I think it's pertinent to quote it here:

Every act of social assistance, no matter how small, signifies fraternity, is productive and deserves praise. Any kind of human assistance is better than none. Nevertheless, the ideal social assistance has its own unmistakable universalistic characteristics.

It is not official since it is spontaneous.
It is not a tax deductible donation.
It does not have a professional title.
It has no secondary or political intentions.
It does not back a personal image or cultivate myths.
It does not encourage segregation of any kind.
It is not restricted by prejudice.
It does not expect gratitude nor require public understanding.
It does not disseminate the act of assistance, regardless of circumstances.

It is the donation of one's self—simple, pure and direct—without mediation, demands or conditions. And everyone can practice it in silence. (Vieira, 2007)

Blind Guides

Blind guides are nonphysical consciousnesses who know us from previous lives. They may have been our spouses, partners, lovers, siblings, children, parents, friends, neighbors or colleagues. Perhaps we were even followers of theirs once, or vice versa. Our blind guides cannot be objective in the way they relate to us because of the strong connections, associations and links between us that stem from the history, affinities, emotions and karma that we share. Blind guides are people just like us, with more or less the same level of evolution as us.

Characteristics and Behaviors of Blind Guides

Notable characteristics and behaviors of blind guides include the following:

- Some have only passed through the first death, meaning they are unaware that they are no longer alive in the physical sense and, consequently, have not discarded their dense energy body. Others have passed through the second death, and are aware of their nonphysical condition.
- Their intentions are neither intrinsically positive nor negative. Although in their own minds their intentions are good, they show no discernment.
- They like us but often disregard our free will.
- Their behavior is not always cosmoethical.
- They do not know what our specific purpose in life is.
- They have about the same level of evolution as us.

So blind guides can be best described as extraphysical beings with poor lucidity and objectivity who are not very advanced or mature. They are blind in terms of evolution.

Typically, blind guides want what's best for us but due to the personal nature of their relationship with us they aren't capable of analyzing objectively what that is. They use whatever resources they have at their disposal to produce outcomes in our lives based on their own subjective opinion of what helping means, and this may not always be what's best for us or what we want.

For example, sometimes former family members (both of this life or previous lives) don't approve of our choice of partner so try to create events that appear to be coincidences or synchronicities in order to block the relationship.

To draw another analogy with physical life, imagine a person has good intentions and wants to help a sick friend by performing surgery on her, but he has no medical training. He will surely end up harming his friend. Blind guides are like that.

Knowing that our blind guides are "on our side" so to speak and supportive of us, we should always be careful of what we wish for others, because our blind guides may try to carry out our wishes. People who were leaders in previous lives are particularly likely to notice some "coincidences" in which their unspoken resentments towards others are fulfilled, because they probably have blind guides around them who were their followers in previous lives and are accustomed to carrying out their orders.

Blind guides can also assist others, but unlike the helpers, are unable to be detached from the circumstances in which they find themselves and usually indulge their personal preferences. So the assistance they lend is more like an indoctrination whereas real assistance respects the individuality and free will of the person being helped.

Intruders

I begin this section by acknowledging the additional, significant research and development of Vieira's work on the subject of intrusion, carried out by Wagner Alegretti and Nanci Trivellato. Alegretti and Trivellato offer a 40-hour course on becoming permanently, totally free of intrusion, and many of the ideas they have contributed are explored in this chapter.

I have given more emphasis to this category of extraphysical consciousnesses so you will find this section longer than the others. If we can develop a solid understanding of the process of intrusion, how it can destabilize our lives, and even the role that we play in allowing it, we are presented with many unique and invaluable opportunities to exercise more control over our daily experience of life. All this will become clear as you read on.

The term "intruder," which applies equally to physical consciousnesses as to extraphysical consciousnesses, is used to describe someone who, intentionally or otherwise, negatively influences another through the transference of a combination of his thoughts, emotions and energy. This transference occurs when two consciousnesses are drawn together through common underlying feelings and couple aurically through the fusion of their energetic fields, a concept that will be described in the next chapter on bioenergy.

Intrusion can occur in the following combinations:

- An intrusion of one physical consciousness on another physical consciousness
- An intrusion of an extraphysical consciousness on a physical consciousness, and vice versa
- An intrusion that occurs between two extraphysical consciousnesses

As this chapter is about nonphysical beings, it is the extraphysical intruders and the ways in which they relate to human beings that are of particular interest to us here. But it is interesting to note the other combinations of intrusion as they help us to see that intrusion occurs naturally within and across dimensions and is also very much a part of the human condition.

To give just a few examples, as humans we intrude on others when we compete for power, force others to put up with our shortcomings and limitations; are manipulative, greedy, picky, insistent, interfering and selfish; when we gossip, impose our ideas on others, try to change others, prioritize our own gratification and rob others of their energy. In the case of extraphysical intruders, we may not see or even perceive them but they are just as able to exert a negative influence over us and steal our energies as humans.

Intrusion, physical and extraphysical, is all about human nature—a reality we deal with every day. For this reason, without trivializing the seriousness of it, intrusion shouldn't

overly frighten or worry us. In the same way that helpers are just like us only more evolved, intruders are also just like us, only more pathological.

Characteristics and Behaviors of Intruders

Notable characteristics of extraphysical intruders include the following:

- Only a small minority are lucid as to their nonphysical condition and have passed through the second death (discarded the energy body).
- As the majority of them still have their energy body, they are "energivorous," meaning, they lack and are in need of dense energy from the physical environment. They get the energy they need from living beings.
- Because of this, most of them dwell in the crustal dimension that overlaps with earth.
- Most of them are not evil, just needy.
- Because they can only connect with us when we share affinities with them, they are particularly competent at amplifying emotions and thoughts that we already have.

Why Do Intruders Intrude on Us?

So why do extraphysical consciousnesses intrude on us? In the vast majority of cases, the intruders are unaware that they're no longer alive in the physical sense, they are still carrying their dense energy body, and they are living within the earth's paratroposphere. Although the energies there are relatively dense as far as extraphysical environments go, they are very subtle compared to the physical dimension. These intruders are not able to absorb the thin energy of the paratroposphere and so intrude on humans to take from us the energy that they need, energy that we have pre-processed and make readily available as most of us have no notion of these realities and therefore no knowledge of how to prevent our energy from being stolen. Although this sort of intrusion is not intentional, when intruders steal our energy, they harm us to a greater or lesser extent.

I realize that this may sound alarming for some of you. Please remember that many extraphysical intruders were once alive, walking among us and that there are also physical intruders around us in our normal, everyday lives. Fearing coming into contact with extraphysical intruders is therefore the same as fearing coming into contact with humans. To give an example, do you have any "friends" who call you when they are down or in difficulty and alleviate the stress they're feeling by "unloading" their problems on you? The exchange is not mutual. There is no reciprocity. It is them demanding your time and attention, support, sympathy and energy. So they are stealing your energy. But do you fear it? No. Likewise, there is nothing to fear from the same process occurring across the dimensions. Nonetheless, as I stated before, when intruders steal our energy, they take something from us that we shouldn't knowingly give, so there is much to be gained from learning how to prevent it. There are several effective techniques for dealing with intrusion that will be discussed later in this chapter, but first let's look at some other forms of intrusion.

In some cases, the intruders are aware of their condition and know exactly what they are doing. They intrude on humans in order to satisfy hungers and craving for specific sensations, thoughts and emotions. For example, if an extraphysical intruder was addicted to sex in previous physical lives and didn't manage to overcome the addiction, he will still be in a condition in which he can think of nothing but sex. So he intrudes on humans who share these appetites in order to feed his insatiable psychological need for sexual energy and the sensations that accompany sexual activity. Prostitutes and others who are promiscuous would be likely targets for intrusion of this variety.

In this context, anything we are addicted to is a problem, be it love, money, a house, a person, alcohol or drugs, because we attract intruders to us who share our addiction.

For example, pathological love is a fairly common cause of intrusion. Sometimes when a person dies, he craves the energies and affection of a former lover to whom he was pathologically attached or addicted. The separation causes him to be in such a state of despair that he intrudes on his former partner, stealing his or her energy and the emotional and mental information it carries.

Possessiveness is another relatively common cause of intrusion. Post-mortem parapsychotics who don't know that they're dead and are very attached to the places where they previously lived can become extremely agitated and resentful when newcomers move into their former homes. If they can access and process enough dense energy to produce outcomes in the physical environment (psychokinesis or PK) intended to scare off the human "interlopers" they become what are known as poltergeists. The film *The Others* demonstrates the motivations behind this particular poltergeist phenomenon very well.

In other instances, our intruders might try to pressure us to do different things that we greatly enjoyed doing together in a previous life such as getting very drunk, controlling or manipulating the opposite sex, or being obnoxious and arrogant. More lucid intruders can also pressure us to produce intense emotions and thoughts as the energy we generate when we experience certain emotions can be extremely powerful and attractive to them in their pathological condition.

Some intruders have a dark sense of humor and play with humans for no better reason than to amuse themselves, in much the same way that bullies tease young children, are cruel to animals, or vandalize the property of others.

Common Symptoms of Intrusion

There are many different symptoms or effects that may suggest we are under intrusion, but I can't emphasize enough here that these very same symptoms may have other causes that are in no way related to intrusion. Not every human problem, mistake or accident is caused by intrusion.

Common symptoms of intrusion include:

- Feeling weak or energetically drained
- Unexplained tiredness or exhaustion (which can manifest as sleeping at any time in any place)
- Insomnia
- Sensing a heavy weight on the shoulders
- An abrupt and/or extreme change of mood
- Unexpected temperamental outbursts
- Fixed ideas or memories that play over and over
- Anxiety
- Confusion
- Unjustified irritability
- Some headaches
- Accident-proneness
- Anger, rage and bad temper
- Laughing or crying without cause
- Persistently bothering others
- Provoking pointless arguments
- Some nightmares
- Fear
- Laziness
- Extreme lack of motivation
- Feeling that something is wrong when it's not
- Talking to oneself
- A sensation of apprehension or imminent catastrophe
- Bad humor and sarcasm
- Pessimism

- Loss of perspective
- Violence
- Sudden crazy thoughts (Trivellato and Alegretti, 2003–2004)

We have to learn to distinguish when these symptoms are totally unrelated to intrusion and have perfectly rational explanations and when they are the result of intrusion. For example, if we are feeling irritable maybe it's because a minor incident occurred at our workplace that annoyed us initially. An intruder then couples with us energetically, contaminates us with his thoughts and magnifies the irritation until it is way out of proportion with the event that caused it. He then takes the energy charged with the irritation that we produce, if this is what he likes. Or maybe we are irritated because we are hungry, tired, cold or suffering from menstrual pains. So while we have to be aware that intrusion is a reality, we have to be balanced, discerning and aware that not everything is intrusion.

How to Detect Intrusion

Vieira has been very interested over the years to try to establish some figures that more or less accurately represent the proportion of extraphysical consciousnesses to physical people. After discussions with high-level helpers on exactly this topic over several decades and according to his own extensive experience out of the body, he estimates that for every physical person on this planet there are nine extraphysical beings. I repeat—these figures are didactical approximations. No one has yet found a way to perform a census of the extraphysical population. It is the best we know for the time being.

But if for now we consider that the extraphysical population is significantly greater than the human population, and that we always have some extraphysical beings around us, some more or less at our level (blind guides), some more advanced (helpers) and some pathological (intruders), then we need to learn how to distinguish who is with us at any given moment in time, in order to be able to recognize when we are being intruded—the first important step towards stopping it from happening.

Whether we are conscious of it or not, we are never alone.

One way of becoming more perceptive of who is around us is to pay attention to the sensations we experience and the thoughts and emotions we're having at the moment, then five minutes later and again twenty minutes later. Ask yourself how you feel. If you have a helper close to you, some of the sensations you might experience are a sense of calmness, serenity and well-being; you feel more relaxed and that everything's OK. Similarly, your thoughts and emotions are balanced and positive. When you're feeling down or negative, and experiencing any of the symptoms of intrusion listed in the previous section, intruders or blind guides may be there with you.

The Mechanism behind Intrusion

To help us understand the mechanism of intrusion, just as we attract helpers to us when we behave like them, intruders intrude on us when we behave, think or feel like them. In other words, intruders can't produce a certain response or reaction from us from nothing. What they can do is amplify or pressure us to exaggerate the thoughts and feelings that we already have.

If we consider the fact that consciousnesses from both dimensions resonate with each other as they exchange, knowingly or unknowingly, thoughts, feelings, intentions, ideas, beliefs, attitudes and energy, etc., then these are the points of connection that link us to and determine our extraphysical company. As Vieira explains in *Projections of the Consciousness*, "An empty brain cannot be directly influenced." (*Vieira*, 1997) So we can say therefore, that every intrusion starts with a self-intrusion. That's the first problem. We have a predisposition for a certain type of energy. We have been open to it. The second problem is that an intruder with a similar affinity has attached himself to us energetically. So we are never completely, 100 percent a victim. We are a part of the equation based on the mental, emotional and energetic affinities we have with our extraphysical company.

An example of how this might unfold on a practical level—you might be having a normal, average day when suddenly you have a passing thought that makes you feel a bit down. An intruder who has a tendency for depression couples with you energetically, exaggerates your feelings and in no time you are feeling irritable, melancholic and depressed . . . but you don't know why.

Tips and Techniques for Preventing Intrusion

The good news is that there are techniques—energetic exercises—that we can apply to perceive and identify our extraphysical company and defend ourselves against intrusion, such as sending out (exteriorizing) our energies and the vibrational state. Detailed instructions for applying these techniques and the numerous additional benefits of these powerful tools for energetic self-defense are discussed in the next chapter.

Other effective means of dealing with intrusion include

- Identifying our shortcomings, i.e. the points of connection that allow the intruders to get close to us in the first place, and then developing a long-term strategy to overcome them—to change. The strategy in the short-term is the vibrational state. An example of how an intrusion may start with our own shortcomings is when people allow themselves to be intruded within intimate relationships because they prefer to put up with the intrusion (in the form of manipulation, domination, physical or verbal abuse, etc.) than to be alone. The long-term strategy for dealing with this intrusion would be to overcome the weakness that permits it in the first place.
- Applying what is known as "mental hygiene," which means to be conscious of your thoughts. When you get stuck on a negative vein of thinking that arouses your anger, frustration or sense of being unfairly treated, for example, quite literally force yourself to think of something else. Do whatever is necessary. Go and see a movie, play an absorbing computer game or go to your favorite restaurant with some good friends. In changing your thoughts, you sever the link that keeps the intruders connected to you and frees you from their influence.
- Standing up and taking action against the physical intruders in our lives. The more we're able to defend ourselves against intrusion physically the more we'll eventually be able to do so extraphysically. For example, most of us know someone who constantly bends our ear, someone who talks and talks at us with no awareness or

concern for whether or not we have the time or inclination to listen to their trivia. People like this are also stealing our energy. Why would we knowingly accept this? Some of us worry about not being nice or that others won't like us, but we can just say firmly and politely, "Excuse me, I'm busy." If we can't stop someone from bending our ear at the water cooler in the office what hope do we have of getting rid of an extraphysical intruder who was our lover in a previous life?

- Don't justify the personality traits that link you to intrusion. If you know a particular impulse is not correct, don't rationalize it to yourself by saying, "This is just the way I am. This is my personality." Be sincere with yourself.
- The flip side of this coin is to consciously develop traits and habits that link us to helpers. For example, try to cultivate an optimistic, positive attitude; evaluate the quality of your thoughts—e.g. do you see the best in people first and then see their weaker points, or do you only see their failings? Practice allowing your rationality to dominate your emotionality, be sincere with yourself and others and persevere with your efforts. (*Trivellato and Alegretti*, 2003–2004)

We need to get used to the idea that we are the masters of our own reality and that we have all the power we need to change many things about our lives that we're not satisfied with. In essence, what this means is that if we suffer intrusion it's because we allow it and putting an end to it is largely a question of will.

Above all, to become free of intrusion is to know and apply the highest level of cosmoethics in every thought, emotion and action.

Chapter Four

Bioenergy

No man is free who is not master of himself.
—*Epictetus*

In the previous chapter, we started to look how our thoughts and feelings modulate the quality and orientation of our energies, and how the quality of our energies in turn, determines who we have around us both physically and extraphysically. In other words, we only connect with energies that have an element of similarity to ours. So we can see that energy plays a key role in the transdimensional interactions and relationships we have with both physical and nonphysical beings.

In this chapter we're going to take a closer look at the properties and characteristics of energy, further examine the fundamental role it plays in our multidimensional existence, and learn how we can improve our energetic sensitivity, capacities and self-defense.

Bioenergy—A Look Back through History

In conscientiology, the term *bioenergy* is used to describe the basis of the individual energetic field that emanates from and encompasses every living being.

Although bioenergy can't be detected using the physical senses, its existence has been recognized by almost every spiritual tradition. Authors John White (who with astronaut Edgar Mitchell founded The Institute of Noetic Science) and Stanley Krippner claimed in *Future Science: Life Energies and the Physics of Paranormal Phenomena* that references are made to the human energy fields or the aura of the body in 97 different cultures. (White and Krippner, 1977)

Synonyms commonly used to describe this type of energy include *qi/chi* (China), *prana* (India), subtle energy, vital energy, vital fluid (Spiritism), universal life energy (Rei-Ki), astral energy and cosmic energy. There are many others. (Vieira, 2002)

As far back as 5,000 years ago, bioenergy was acknowledged by the spiritual tradition of India as the universal source of all life. They called it *prana*. It was the yogis who proposed the system of chakras and nadis as points throughout the energy body (etheric double) through which energy is exchanged between the extraphysical body and the physical body. These are also the channels through which we absorb energy from and send energy out (exteriorize) to the environment. Both of these processes are necessary for the maintenance of our energy levels and the sustenance of vitality, health, longevity and indeed, life itself.

Practitioners of Qigong discovered numerous related benefits of reaching a certain level of proficiency or mastery of their *chi*, including improved psychic abilities such as telepathy and clairvoyance and a generally heightened (psychic) awareness of what was going on around them extraphysically on a moment to moment basis. These consequences were found, in turn, to promote overall spiritual healing and maturation.

According to *The Oxford Dictionary of World Religions*, all religions have a more or less holistic view of healing, placing it within the broader context of life and acknowledging the close relationship that it has with the "psychosomatic unit of the human entity," (*Bowker*, 1997) which includes the energy body.

Many scientists have attempted to invent equipment for detecting and recording bioenergy. Kirlian photography, discovered by accident by Russian Semyon Kirlian in 1939, applies a high-voltage electric field to an object placed on a photographic plate, producing an image of the signals emitted which is said to represent the object's bioenergetic field.

(Trivellato and Gustus, 2003) A more recent development is the PIP (Polycontrast Interference Photography) scanner devised by British scientist Harry Oldfield. This system uses a digital video camera and a computer program to analyze the way in which a person's bioenergetic field interacts with light and to generate a moving image of the person's aura.

Among other experiments performed by scientists in this field, many noteworthy investigations, such as the research into the Human Energy Field (HEF) conducted by Dr. Victor Inyushin at Kazakh University in Russia (Alvino, 1996) have confirmed a relationship between the balance of one's energy field and good health. Research into parapsychic phenomena has also demonstrated that bioenergy is an intrinsic component of numerous phenomena such as the bending of metal at will, moving an object without touching it, dematerializations and rematerializations, ectoplasmy (when bioenergy condenses in order to manifest in a compound condition in the substance called ectoplasm) (Vieira, 2002), homeopathy, poltergeist activities, teleportation, telepathy and psychic surgery. (Trivellato and Gustus, 2003)

Despite such consistent acknowledgment throughout history by different cultures, religions and fields of science, bioenergy is, in the main, an inconspicuous element of the modern-day materialistic western world, an element of which very few people have any direct, consciousness awareness, making the following quote by Winston Churchill seem particularly apt: "Man will occasionally stumble over the truth, but usually manages to pick himself up, walk over or around it, and carry on."

Whether we are aware of it or not, bioenergy plays a pivotal role in the daily lives of all ordinary folk as well as the more energetically sensitive. Here is how it works.

Bioenergy—Properties and Characteristics

Much of the content of this section is drawn from an article I co-authored with Nanci Trivellato entitled "Bioenergy: A Vital Component of Human Existence," first published in *Paradigm Shift* magazine in 2003.

Your bioenergetic field is a part of you that is in a constant state of flux; adapting, reacting, changing, responding and exchanging energies, via the chakras and nadis, with other living beings and with the environment.

In and of itself, bioenergy is neutral. In the case of human beings however, it never exists in isolation but is inextricably linked to a person's thoughts (be they conscious, subconscious or unconscious) and emotions. So if someone's personal bioenergetic field is positive, this is because the factors that drive his thoughts and feelings, such as his ideas, intentions, ethics, interests and objectives, are positive. All of this information about him is carried in his energies. Equally, of course, negative thoughts and feelings produce negative energies. Simply put, the quality of a person's energies is determined by the quality of his thoughts and emotions.

As it is true to say that very few people are in a condition of complete self-awareness, very few of us totally control the quality of our energetic field. As stated in the article mentioned earlier, "As our energetic field is open, flexible and 'porous' then unless we have good awareness and control of our energies, we are subject to the influence of the energies of the people and environments around us. Conversely, regardless of our level of awareness, we also affect, to varying degrees, the energetic fields of the people and places we encounter in our everyday lives." (Trivellato and Gustus, 2003) An example that illustrates these processes with which many of us will be familiar is when our physical, psychological or mental disposition shifts as a result of coming into contact with another person. (ibid, 2003) Does the mere fact of being in the same room as a particular person make your scalp burn, your motivation soar or your rationality diminish, for example?

This also explains why we can instinctively feel a sense of rapport or familiarity with people who share our outlook on life but may feel uneasy, irritable or even unwell around people with whom we have nothing in common. Another example of an unconscious reaction to the bioenergies of others occurs when we couple energetically with someone we are spending time with so strongly that we assimilate their emotions or physical ailments and begin to experience whatever they are feeling, e.g. calmness, euphoria, grief, depression, or even a physical pain such as a headache. (ibid, 2003) Energetic coupling occurs when the bioenergetic fields of two people overlap and interfuse, as is shown in this image.

We can assimilate the disposition of those around us via the process of energetic coupling.

In the same way that the quality of people's energies varies, the way in which people exchange energy with others and with the environment also varies. When we feel well within ourselves, relaxed, confident and inclined towards others, our energies are usually more open and flow more intensely and readily. On the other hand, when we repress our emotions or stew over things such as when we have a broken heart, feel that someone has done us wrong or can't forgive ourselves a mistake, our energies can become blocked. Many complementary medicines not only acknowledge the effect that energetic blockages can have on our physical well-being but also the relationship between the location of the blockage and the specific nature of the illness. For example, failing to "speak up" and voice your true thoughts for fear of what people will think of you might cause a blockage in the laryngo-chakra (throat chakra) after some time, which may eventually lead to a thyroid problem; failing to deal with the cause of a stress that makes your stomach knot might eventually lead to a blockage in the umbilico-chakra which can cause digestive disorders such as hypochloridia (low stomach acid), leaky stomach, stomach ulcers or stomach cancer.

The Subtle Influence and Powerful Effects of Bioenergetic Fields

We have seen how a person's presence and energetic field can affect or influence another on a personal level. But the same process can also take place on a much larger scale. When you have a group of people whose thoughts, emotions and energies are aligned, the force of the group's influence can be sufficient to change the way others think, feel or behave. This can happen in ways that are obvious or in ways that are so subtle we may not be completely aware of what's happening. Sometimes when people say, "I got carried away," or ,"I got caught up in the moment," they are referring to this process.

Author and healer William Bloom provides a compelling example that illustrates just how powerful the effects of mass energies can be in his book *Feeling Safe*. He writes:

> Throughout the world, you can see individuals and groups of people suddenly caught up in a mass movement and behaving in ways that they never thought possible. Perhaps you remember the photographs of the Rwandan women with machetes and knives—including mothers, professionals and highly educated women—on a rampage to kill and maim members of another ethnic group. There is, of course, a mass field of energy that contains violence and aggression. In this case, these normally benevolent women were overwhelmed by the energies of the herd instinct and carried along into psychopathic behavior. (Bloom, 2002)

Violent hooliganism at football games provides another example of this process. The bigotry common to hooliganism usually begins with a few pockets of radical individuals. Their fanatical thoughts, based around separating the crowd of supporters into those who are "with" them and those who are not, are combined with emotions fueled by hostility and antagonism. In the same way that a chant or a "wave" can be picked up and imitated by tens of thousands of people at a football game, energies carrying the thoughts, emotions and intentions of hooligans can also pass across a crowd in a type of bioenergetic contagion, touching those who have some affinity with the ideas and gaining in intensity as they join in. The tension of this type of energetic field builds like a pressure cooker until it takes just one punch to ignite a dangerous riot.

A bioenergetic field doesn't only relate to individuals or groups of people. It can also define the characteristics of a specific place. Consider some of the upscale department stores along Oxford Street in London for example. Almost every day of the year, every year, hundreds of women pile in and shop frenetically for the latest clothes. The music is upbeat, the shop assistants are all looking cool in their branded gear, the shoppers' thoughts are focused on their appearance and thousands of dollars of transactions are taking place every hour. Reinforced on a daily basis, the energies in these stores are loaded with a heady mix of fun, flirtation, excitement, sexuality, anxiety, one-upmanship, euphoria and the addictive sense of bountiful abundance that some people get from "retail therapy" when fulfillment is lacking in other areas of their lives. Try spending half an hour in such a store and coming out without being at least tempted to buy something and you may be able to observe a subtle influence at play.

The bioenergetic field of a specific place can just as easily cast influence on a much larger scale. The undeniable power of the collective energies of an entire country was very well portrayed in Michael Moore's film *Bowling for Columbine.* The film, which won the 2003 Oscar for best documentary, explores America's obsession with guns and shows how, over many decades, American politicians and the media have bred a culture of fear and paranoia of violent crime among Americans. The objects of the fear and paranoia are mostly African Americans and Arabs and for the most part, Americans genuinely believe themselves to be at risk. To defend themselves against the apparent ever-present threat they support laws that facilitate the procurement of guns and ammunition, ironically giving rise to much of the violence and crime they fear. The following staggering statistics demonstrate just how influential a bioenergetic field can be when people allow themselves to be caught up in it on a mass scale:

- Approximately 30,000 Americans die from gun violence every year. Of these, around 1,250 result from unintentional shootings. (Coalition to Stop Gun Violence)
- The rate of firearm deaths among children under the age of 15 is almost 12 times higher in the United States than in 25 other industrialized countries combined. (Centers for Disease Control and Prevention)

- American children are 16 times more likely to be murdered with a gun, 11 times more likely to commit suicide with a gun, and nine times more likely to die from a firearm accident than children in 25 other industrialized countries combined. (Centers for Disease Control and Prevention)

Without knowing, Michael Moore actually refers to bioenergetic fields when he compares the vastly different incidences of gun deaths despite comparable levels of gun ownership in US/Canadian border towns separated only by a river. Likewise, he questions if the shooting at Columbine High School in Denver, Colorado, could have been influenced or predisposed in any way by the fact that the biggest weapons facility in the US is located at the nearby town of Littleton.

Can a bioenergetic field extend even beyond the borders of a country? Yes. Think of the energies in the regions in Asia affected by the Boxing Day tsunamis of 2004. A series of horrors involving hundreds of thousands of people all occurred in the same region at the same time; tidal waves, floods, shipwrecks, train pile-ups, landslides, cave-ins, building collapses and fires. The energies of these areas are likely to be laden with the emotional terror of those who died; the fear, confusion, loss and grief of those who survived and the immense suffering caused by the hunger, thirst, lack of shelter, disease and crime that followed the disaster.

Such natural catastrophes, as well as man-made acts of terror, have a profound impact on the human environments affected. The trauma becomes integrated into the living memory of the disaster zones, affecting those who live or pass through there in a variety of both obvious and subtle ways.

Continuing on up the scale, the quality (or lack thereof) of certain bioenergetic fields can even characterize an entire continent. Anyone who has lived in Africa, for example, will know that the overriding thoughts and intentions of the inhabitants of many of the African nations have been shaped by their long history of fighting for survival in the face of drought, famine, deadly diseases, civil war and genocide. History has produced a continental bioenergetic field charged with a dog-eat-dog mentality that seemingly feeds off itself—one in which corruption, violence and crime have become the very fabric of everyday life.

So these are different examples of how a bioenergetic field produced by a particular group of people or inherent to a specific place can influence or affect us in some way. In conscientiology, a new term was created to describe such a bioenergetic field . . . *holothosene* . . . *holos* from the Greek meaning whole and *thosene* from combining the *tho* from thought, the *sen* from sentiment (or emotion) and the *e* from energy.

Dr. Rupert Sheldrake, revolutionary biologist and director of the Perrott-Warrick project for research on unexplained human abilities funded by Trinity College, Cambridge, presents a similar vision of what he calls a "a living, developing universe with its own inherent memory" via his theory of Morphic Fields and Morphic Resonance.

Energetic Sensitivity, Awareness and Control

It is important for us to ascertain if we have enough mastery of our own energies and thoughts not to be carried along by the collective energies present in certain groups of people or places. Are we independent in our thinking? Do we question, analyze, apply our critical judgment and discernment to what we see on TV, read in the press and hear on the radio? Do we allow our thinking to be influenced by the predominant group mentality?

People who are sensitive to energies will perceive certain bioenergetic fields in different ways. They may experience the emotions with which the environment is impregnated. For example, they may enter a funeral home and feel a sense of loss, an abattoir and experience terror, a prison and feel a sense of degradation. Alternatively, they may feel nauseated, light-headed or have stomach cramps depending on the intensity of the bioenergetic field and their level of sensitivity to it. (Trivellato and Gustus, 2003)

The bioenergetic field of specific places can also affect us positively. We may, for example, feel more compelled to study or research and find we can do so with greater ease and concentration in a library than at home. People often expect that the renewed enthusiasm for intellectual pursuits that they get when visiting an inspiring place such as a library will last, but are nonetheless unable to maintain the motivation when they return to the well-established bioenergetic fields generated by the routines and distractions of their daily lives.

If people are able to perceive the effects of bioenergetic fields and have some control over their own energies however, they can actively maintain their energetic equilibrium and be untainted by pervading influences, all the while remaining aware of the quality and nature of the energies of the environments around them.

Most people though, do not have enough sensitivity or awareness to be able to "read" the bioenergies specific to a crowd or a particular place so are either unaffected or unaware of how they are affected. They may just suddenly feel inspired, moody, joyous, irritable or drained for example (depending on the quality of the field), but have no idea why.

As stated in the article, sometimes "subtle maladies that have no apparent cause are the result of exactly these types of intrusions of energies that are not compatible with ours, into our own energy field via one of our chakras." (ibid 2003)

Exercises for Improving Energetic Sensitivity, Capacities and Self-Defense

The good news is that it is within the capacity of all of us to learn to become aware of and to assess the quality of our energies, to control them, and to perform self-diagnosis and therapy when necessary.

With practice, it is also within our capacity to attain a level of mastery of our bioenergies that will enable us to increase our extrasensory perceptions to the point where we can read the positive or negative energies of a particular environment and perceive, interact and communicate with our nonphysical companions, be they helpers, blind guides or intruders. The importance of developing such a level of perception cannot be underestimated. This is the first, vital step that will enable us to identify the strong traits and fissures in our personality that allow the helpers and intruders to connect to us. Then we need to strengthen the connections we have with the helpers and take action against the countless varieties of intrusions that we regularly experience. In so doing, we assume a much greater level of responsibility for and control over our lives.

Vieira devised and recommends three energetic exercises that, with regular practice and training, can help us to develop and/or improve our control of and sensitivity to bioenergy.

Before describing these, I would like to emphasize that bioenergy is a powerful resource, that *really* exists, and that moving energies is a very real endeavour. No amount of visualization or imagination will ever be sufficient to perform any of these exercises, so I'm not going to instruct you to employ these methods. The key to success in working with energies is to remain physically relaxed, to block any interference from the external environment and to actively focus on moving bioenergy through the application of your ironclad will. Most people unfamiliar with working with energies have little or no perception of the movement of energy at first. But the mere attempt usually produces some small results, even if you are unaware of them, so don't give up, persist. Regular practice will bring improved, tangible results in almost all cases.

Absorption of Energies

Definition: The act of absorbing or interiorizing energies

Comments:

Perform this exercise in a place where you know the energies to be positive. The ideal would be to do it in a natural environment as the energies of nature do not carry any information (in terms of thoughts or emotions), so go to a place like a park or garden, forest, mountain, ocean or river if you can.

How do I do it?

Relax in any way you would normally, breathe normally, and using your will and concentration, try to become aware of the energies of the environment around you. Try to tune into them, to sense them, to perceive how positive they are and how good they make you feel. Now turn your attention to absorbing this positive energy through your chakras. It might take some practice before you start to become aware of the sensations that accompany this action and will confirm that you are actually moving energy, so don't be discouraged if this is your case. Persevere.

Often the temptation in the beginning is to absorb energy as you inhale. Try in time to establish a rhythm that is independent of the rate of respiration. The reason for this is because you don't want to become dependent upon being able to breathe at a certain rate, or on anything else for that matter, in order to be able to absorb energy.

How does it feel?

Common sensations include a change in temperature (e.g. feeling warmer or colder), energetic "shivers" that sweep through part of or your whole body or a tingling sensation. Some people may experience clairvoyance (i.e. perceptions of the extraphysical dimension).

What are the benefits?

The main reason to absorb energy is to replenish your reserves of energy and invigorate your bioenergetic field if you are feeling energetically depleted or drained. Symptoms of this with which we're all familiar are tiredness, lethargy, lack of motivation and heaviness.

Conscious Donation (Exteriorization) of Energies

Definition: the transmission of energy

Comments:

Before exteriorizing energies, check your thoughts and emotions. If you are preoccupied or not in a good condition, wait until your thoughts are balanced and your emotions are positive so as you add only positive energy to your surrounds or the environment.

How do I do it?

Relax and focus your attention on what you are about to do. Perhaps, at first, until you become accustomed to moving your energy, you could focus on accumulating energy in your hands. As our hands are very sense oriented and we are used to "doing" things with our hands, it's often easier to perceive energy moving through them. So think of accumulating energy in your hands and then use your will to do it. When you can sense your energy there, concentrate on flowing it out through your palm chakras. Experience has shown it's easier to move a larger volume of energy by exteriorizing in regular pulses or waves rather than in a continuous flow, so try to do this also. Once you have mastered this, practice exteriorizing energy through your whole body, through all of your chakras simultaneously.

How does it feel?

The sensations are the same as when we absorb energy—feeling warmer or colder, energetic "shivers," tingling, the possibility of clairvoyance, etc.

What are the benefits?

When we exteriorize energy that is infused with positive thoughts and emotions we perform a kind of energetic cleansing that improves the energetic quality of the environment around us.

Bioenergy is also a powerful resource for assisting others in both the physical and extraphysical dimensions, including animals and plants. Assistance can either be offered through the direct transferal of energy to the person/animal/plant in need, or it can be donated to the helpers who then use it to help others (with their consent of course).

Direct energy transferal could be used, for example, to calm someone who is emotionally distraught or has suffered a trauma, to alleviate or prevent some physical ailments, to inject life into a dying plant or to settle a pet before the dreaded visit to the vet. In the extraphysical dimension, bioenergy can be used by projectors to calm and capture the attention of disorientated, recently deceased individuals, or to treat extraphysical consciousnesses who can manifest every variety of illness and pathology that we see here in the physical dimension, and more besides.

I had an interesting experience a few years back in which I donated bioenergy to the helpers who then used it to help my cat who had gone missing. She had come to live with us as an adult cat only two months previously and had obviously decided it was time to go off exploring beyond her new territory and had got herself lost. I went to bed during her second night away concerned, as it was a typical winter's night in London—raining hard, biting wind and bitterly cold—so I explained to the helpers that little Scragglepuss has good perceptions of the extraphysical dimension (something I knew from previous experiences with her), so if they had the time, could they please try to get her attention and guide her home, and that they were welcome to avail themselves of as much of my energy as they needed for the task. I lay quietly in bed and consciously donated energy for well over an hour, checking regularly that it was still flowing and that I felt well and balanced. Eventually I had an intuition to stop so I got up, it was 2:00 a.m. I switched the lights on in the conservatory and the back garden, sat down to write an email, and five minutes later the little fur ball appeared through the cat flap, unhurt but famished and clearly well-pleased to be home. Happy days. Thanks to the helpers.

Another benefit of exteriorizing energy is to use it as a means of "fixing" your day. It is good practice, at the end of every day, to analyze what happened during the day and ask yourself "Who did I disturb? Who did I neglect to help? Who did I not want to help?"And then send the best energies you have to those people as a way of balancing your relationships and your day.

Exteriorizing energy also acts as a safe-guard against intrusion. You can safe-guard your bedroom, your home or your office, for example, by exteriorizing energy to perform an energetic cleansing for five to ten minutes on a daily basis. In time, this will create an energetic field that acts like a protective shield. It makes sense doesn't it—if you exteriorize energy when you are well and positive every day, eventually you will establish a strong energetic environment in your home that the intruders have no affinity with. This will prevent them from entering into your home. Do not however, exteriorize energies at the same time every day while you are working to establish the energetic shield. Remember in the last chapter I described how most intruders are not able to absorb the thin energy of the paratroposphere and so intrude on humans to take from us the energy that they need? If we exteriorize energy in the same place at the same time every day we attract their attention, so vary the time as much as you can. Once the field is established, you can exteriorize energy less frequently as you will only be working to maintain the field. The ideal would be to start in the bedroom and create the energetic shield around it first—as this is the room in which you sleep and project from. Then gradually do the other rooms in your house until your whole home is an energetic haven.

Being proficient at exteriorizing energies is also a great tool for self-defense when you are out of the body. As you still have access to your dense energies via the silver cord (in addition to the energies of the extraphysical body itself), if any extraphysical consciousnesses bother you while you're projected, exteriorize energy to them with your best wishes but also with the very clear signal that you want nothing to do with them and that they should leave you be. In the vast majority of cases, one single pulse of energy sent in their direction is enough to send most intruders on their way.

Vibrational State

Definition: "The condition of maximal and simultaneous dynamisation of the chakras, promoted by the conscious mobilization of one's energies up and down the body." (Trivellato and Gustus, 2003) May also occur spontaneously.

Comments:

Unlike the absorption and exteriorization exercises, there are no restrictions as to where or when you should install a vibrational state as it is the most powerful tool we have at our disposal for energetic self-defense.

How do I do it?

Be relaxed, sit, or lie down if you prefer, and focus on accumulating and sensing your energies in your head. Then slowly, will yourself to move the energy down through the internal core of your body (as opposed to feeling the sensations on your skin or on the outside of your body), towards your feet. Pay attention to where you can and can't perceive the energy. If you can't feel the energy in a particular area of the body it may be because there is an energetic blockage there. Keep the energy moving, back up towards the head, and then down again to the feet, and so on. Remember that most people unfamiliar with such exercises have little or no perception of the movement of energy at first. But the mere attempt usually produces some small results, even if you are unaware of them, so don't give up. Persist. Gradually, increase both the intensity and the speed of the flow of energy, moving it faster and faster up and down the body, until such time as you "lose" the flow of the energy and you reach the vibrational state.

How does it feel?

The following authors offer these descriptions:

> The vibrational state is characterized by the movement of internal pulsating waves similar to electrical vibrations whose occurrence, frequency and intensity can be controlled at will to be fast or slow, strong or weak. These waves sweep the immobilized soma (body) from head to hands and feet, returning to the brain in a steady cycle of a few seconds. The occurrence at times seems like a burning torch, surging and ebbing, or a ball of tolerable electricity guided at will. Not uncommonly, the vibrations produce a sensation of inflation common in psychophony (vocal channeling) with the apparent expansion and swelling of the hands, feet, lips, cheeks, chin and solar plexus area. (Waldo Vieira, *Projections of the Consciousness*)

> In spite of being very exotic and intense, the sensation of vibration is quite pleasant, and sometimes through its intensification a sort of *energetic climax* is reached. (Wagner Alegretti, *Retrocognitions: An Investigation into the Memory of*

> *Past Lives and the Period between Lives*)

> It is as if a surging, hissing, rhythmically pulsating wave of fiery sparks comes roaring into your head. From there it seems to sweep throughout your body, making it rigid and immobile. (Robert Monroe, *Journeys Out of the Body*)

According to my own experience, I can best describe the vibrational state as a condition in which you are acutely aware that every single cell in your body, including the cells of your skin, in your blood and internal organs, your bones, your brain, etc., is furiously vibrating against the cell next to it. The experience promotes a deep sense of well-being.

What are the benefits?

As explained in the article written with Trivellato, the correct use of the vibrational state has significant benefits. When we install the vibrational state, we establish an energetic shield around us that prevents anyone from aurically coupling (energetically interfusing) with us. So the vibrational state "enables us to neutralize unwanted influences and intrusions that we have either knowingly or unknowingly come into contact with, and to play therefore a more active, decisive role in our lives. This in turn stimulates personal maturation and evolutionary growth." (Trivellato and Gustus, 2003)

The vibrational state should be used in advance and in anticipation of intrusion, in other words, before any situation in which you can predict that someone will try to force his energies on you or steal your energies. Next time you find yourself about to enter a challenging situation in which you might, for example, have to deal with an aggressive customer, make your point in a hostile meeting, confront someone over the telephone or handle any other situation in which you anticipate being imposed upon energetically, try to install the vibrational state beforehand and see what results.

Similarly, install the vibrational state before entering any area or environment where you suspect or perceive extraphysical intruders to be. If you do become aware of being intruded, don't just accept it. Do the vibrational state and get rid of it otherwise a superficial intrusion can become a profound one.

As the installation of the vibrational state promotes flexibility and looseness of the energy body, it also greatly facilitates the disconnection of the extraphysical body from the physical body and therefore, the promotion of lucid out-of-body experiences. Some people frequently enjoy spontaneous vibrational states as precursors to conscious projections.

The vibrational state and the conscious exteriorization of energy are also techniques for clearing energetic blockages, and can be very useful as a means of preventing mini-illnesses in that regard. If I ever feel myself coming down with a cold or the flu, for example, I do the vibrational state as much as I can and exteriorize energy through my throat chakra several times a day. Often, the symptoms quickly disappear. I have had very few colds or flus take hold since I began consciously working with energies in this way nine years ago.

Tips for Mastering Your Bioenergy

It is important to emphasize here that everyone has the capacity to work consciously with bioenergies in all the ways I have described. It is not necessary to have any particular aptitude or to be especially sensitive. The reason that relatively few people are consciously working with bioenergy in their everyday lives is simply because most of us were never taught how to do it. If, from a young age, your parents had showed you to how to do these energetic exercises and activities in the same way that they had taught you how to ride a bike, you would have mastered your bioenergies before you reached your teens.

The most important factor in attaining mastery of one's bioenergies is willpower. Improving our energetic performance via any of the three techniques mentioned may appear simple enough on paper, but the amount of personal discipline and effort required to produce worthwhile results is not to be trivialized. (ibid, 2003)

The ideal is to aim to be able to work with energies in any conditions and circumstances (internal or external), and not to be dependent upon being alone, being able to lie down and relax or on performing any other unnecessary ritual, as neither physical nor extraphysical intruders will wait until the conditions are ideal for you to be able to defend yourself before imposing themselves. While most determined individuals are able to achieve good results in terms of absorbing and exteriorizing energy within some months of practice, being able to install an effective vibrational state, anywhere, anytime—no matter what—is an endeavor that may take some years of effort to accomplish.

Having said that, many thousands of people all around the world are already deriving enormous benefit from controlling their bioenergies. Many have developed their paraperceptions to the point of knowing what is going on around them nonphysically—precisely who is there and exactly where they are—and are able to maintain their balance regardless. As a result, they experience greater self-confidence and serenity, safe in the knowledge that the control over their lives is very much in their hands, and they enjoy the many unique benefits of being in direct contact with the advanced, extraphysical helpers. Mastering bioenergies also enables practitioners to: sense and clear energetic blockages, which leads to greater general equilibrium and well-being, and improved health; promote flexibility of the energy body, which in turn triggers the nonalignment of one's vehicles of manifestation—and leads to conscious projection; and increase their overall level of lucidity regarding their multidimensional reality.

So while the level of commitment and discipline required to achieve mastery of your bioenergies may seem high, the rewards and benefits for you in terms of your personal development in the short, medium and long term (i.e. in your future lives) will be immeasurably greater.

PART TWO

Seriality: The Series of Successive Lives

Reincarnation is not exclusively a Buddhist or Hindu concept, but is part of the history of human origin.
—Dalai Lama

Chapter Five

Karma and the Multiexistential Cycle

Destiny is no matter of chance. It is a matter of choice. It is not a thing to be waited for, it is a thing to be achieved.
—*William Jennings Bryan*

The Alternation of Physical and Extraphysical Existences

Another fundamental principle of conscientiology is that the consciousness undergoes a series of successive lives in which it alternates physical lives with extraphysical periods spent between lives. This process is more popularly known as reincarnation. In conscientiology, the interval between lives is referred to as the intermissive period or intermission. The alternation of physical and extraphysical existences is known as the multiexistential cycle.

The natural, basic state of the consciousness is extraphysical, with the periods spent inside the dense energy-matter vehicle of the human body being temporary phases that provide, as we will see in part 3, unique opportunities to mature and evolve. Support for this claim is evident in the fact that during the nightly sleep of most of the advanced life forms (i.e. humans and animals), the consciousness returns several times, usually unconsciously, to the extraphysical dimension to rest and restore itself in its more natural state. (Alegretti, 2004)

When the consciousness is about to begin a new physical life, the extraphysical body approaches the physical dimension and absorbs the denser energies that will form the energy body (if it passed through the second death and discarded the previous energy body). The consciousness begins to establish an energetic connection with its new parents, particularly the mother—a connection that is fortified by the natural energies of the environment—and at the moment at which the mother's egg is fertilized, the first connections of the silver cord connecting the consciousness to the developing fetus are established. (Alegretti, 2004)

An important point to understand about this process is that because the extraphysical and mental bodies of the consciousness accompany it throughout its long series of lives (as explained in chapter 1) the consciousness is able to perpetuate much of its personality from one life to the next, including some of the behaviors, skills, knowledge of subjects, capacities and attributes it has learned in previous lives. Just how much of its "innateness" a consciousness recovers as it matures through the new physical life depends on many factors, but mostly on the amount of awareness regarding its wider multiexistential reality it manages to retrieve, assuming of course that it had any to begin with.

In conscientiology, we study and research only the multiexistential cycle of the consciousness, which represents but a dot in the broader evolution of the consciousness. Although we don't know what happened prior to the very first physical manifestation of the consciousness, we do know that the series of successive physical lives will end at the point at which we pass through the third death (see chapter 1).

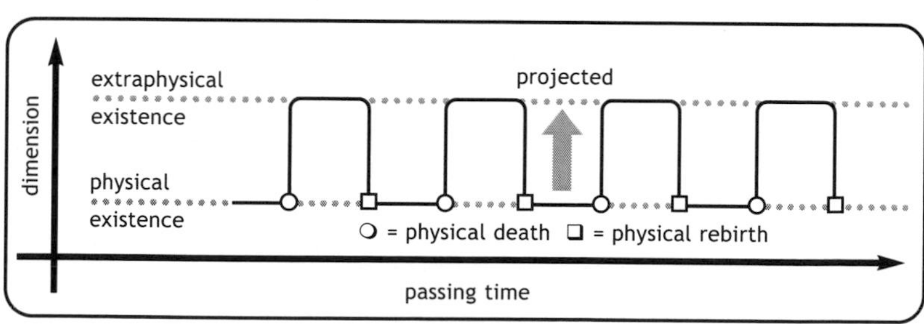

The multiexistential cycle

This diagram shows the three states in which we exist during the multiexistential cycle: the physical state, the extraphysical state and the projected state (as occurs during an OBE). The more lucid OBEs we have and recall, and the more we learn about our wider reality from these experiences, the more prepared we will be for both our intermissive periods and the time when we will permanently be without a physical body. These learning experiences therefore play an important role in bridging the gap between the different dimensions and in bringing us closer to the point of concluding the multiexistential cycle.

So, answer these questions for yourself:

What is my current level of awareness of my existential seriality?

What value do I ascribe to my existential seriality?

These questions truly merit some serious reflection, because when you have understanding and awareness of your existential seriality, you comprehend that you are much more than your current physical incarnation, which is just one life of many you have had and are yet to have, in which you are just one person of many that you have already been and are yet to be. This realization is the first critical step towards understanding that your current physical life is not an arbitrary, random existence but one of value, purpose and countless opportunities to evolve and to influence the nature and quality of the remainder of your multiexistential cycle.

Of course, this realization would be greatly facilitated if we could remember anything at all of our past lives. The main reasons that most of us don't, along with tips and techniques for being able to, are discussed in chapter 8.

The Period between Lives

With regard to the period between lives, or the intermissive period, it is a common fallacy that this time is an unconscious, comatose existence for everyone. As we've already seen in previous chapters, this is far from true. Certainly many do suffer from post-mortem parapsychosis or lead simple, unthinking, robotized existences. Nevertheless, a small percentage of consciousnesses pursue busy, productive, unselfish existences during the intermission that are full of opportunities for learning, for lending assistance to others and for participating in the preparation of the next physical life. And of course, as is true in the physical world, every permutation and combination of the human condition exists between these two extremes.

Of all the factors that affect our existential seriality and how it unfolds, some specifically influence the nature of the intermissive period of the individual, including the duration, which can last from a few short hours up to several centuries in some rare cases, and the extraphysical location in which a consciousness will more permanently reside during this time.

Duration

It is thought that the duration of the intermissive period of an average human consciousness who is unremarkable in either a positive or negative sense, is roughly the same as that of an average human life—approximately seventy years. There are some notable exceptions to this. Most suicides for example, are reborn shortly after the act so spend very brief periods between lives. Sometimes they are reborn into the same extended family to allow them further opportunities to redress any karmic imbalances they may have with that particular group of people. At the other end of the spectrum, when a person has planned work he is supposed to carry out in a physical life, the investment required in the intermissive period sometimes becomes greater depending on the specific nature of the task planned, and the period between lives can become longer. For example, a life of advanced human leadership at times demands intensive, lengthy preparation over several intermissive periods.

Extraphysical Hometown

The key factor in determining the characteristics of an individual's intermissive period however is whether or not he gains extraphysical lucidity, i.e. awareness of his nonphysical condition after death and thus discards the dense energies of the energy body (second death). The majority of people don't achieve the second death, while some only manage to partially discard the energy body. In these cases, the extraphysical body remains laden with varying proportions of the energy body, and a filter effect comes into play, restricting these consciousness from accessing certain layers of the extraphysical dimension where the energies are considerably more subtle and refined.

Within the range of extraphysical layers that a consciousness can access between lives lies a kind of extraphysical hometown to which he will usually return at the end of each of his physical lives.

When we are between lives in the extraphysical dimension, we form cohesive groups with other nonphysical consciousnesses with whom we have natural rapport in terms of our level of lucidity, our thoughts, ideas, interests, behaviors, intentions, habits, ideologies and belief systems. Like always attracts like. These shared affinities have linked us to these individuals in previous lives; therefore, we also share a history and have karmic links with this group. So we can be sure of a warm welcome from the members of our group when the time comes for us to return to our extraphysical origins.

I encourage you to verify this information for yourself. One of the techniques for producing lucid out-of-body experiences described in chapter 16 is the mental target technique. You could choose your extraphysical hometown as your target, and try to pay a visit out of the body and reacquaint yourself with the members of your group who are currently between lives.

While a natural gravitation towards like-minded people is also an observable reality of physical life, the segregation between groups is much less stark than what is seen in the extraphysical dimension. To give an example, individuals who are completely unaware of their nonphysical condition between lives do not coexist with consciousnesses who are lucidly preparing for their next physical life. In the physical dimension by contrast, individuals of widely varying capacities coexist side by side on a daily basis. It is entirely possible that a serial pedophile be seated on a train between a teenage punk and a conservative elderly woman. Consciousnesses don't intermingle in this way in the extraphysical dimension. This is a feature of the physical dimension and an example of the many learning opportunities uniquely available to physical life.

Holokarma

Another factor that significantly influences the nature of our intermissive periods, as well as our physical lives, is our holokarma (from the Greek *holos* meaning whole) which incorporates our egokarma, groupkarma and polykarma.

For those not familiar with the concept, karma is the Sanskrit word for "action" or "deed." Over time, the meaning of the word has evolved to incorporate the effects or consequences of one's actions.

While numerous groups of people around the world including various Shiite Moslem sects of western Asia, tribes of West Africa such as the Igbo of Nigeria, and the Tlingit of southeastern Alaska, do not link one's karma to one's morality, most Westerners who believe in reincarnation have come to adopt the more prevalent Hindu-Buddhist doctrine of karma, which is based on an appropriate punishment or retribution for a causative behavior and includes the possibility of reincarnation in the animal bodies of less evolved species. (Stevenson, 2001)

According to these religions, karma is the catalyst that drives the multiexistential cycle, meaning one's moral conduct in one life will determine the circumstances of one's future.

Extrapolating this point backwards, so to speak, suffering is attributed to negative deeds of the past.

As we understand it in conscientiology, karma is the law of cause and effect or action and reaction. However, our understanding of the concept deviates from the Hindu-Buddhist doctrine on the issue of punishment and reward in that we don't consider a person's circumstances or experience of life, for better or worse, to be a punishment or reward, but simply the harvest of seeds planted in the past. Each and every consciousness, from a simple single-celled amoeba to the most advanced extraphysical helper, is in the process of evolution and each of us is evolving upwards. This naturally precludes the possibility of being reborn in a less evolved state. You are largely responsible for creating your circumstances for yourself. I say "largely" because not all suffering, disasters, crimes and misfortune are caused by karma. I cannot put a finer point on this. There are always several possible explanations for any given situation and we should always be aware of this fact. Some situations that seem unfair may have been planned by a helper to give us an opportunity to learn a skill that we will require in a future life. Others might be unplanned accidents, the unfortunate result of being in the wrong place at the wrong time, or the consequences of carelessness.

Equally, not all karma is negative. Think of the karma you have with your helpers for example.

Bearing in mind that we are multidimensional, multiserial consciousnesses, the karmic consequences of our actions, decisions, choices, thoughts, ethics and intentions are sometimes not apparent in this life, but only reach fruition in future physical lives and intermissive periods, and determine to some degree the location and the amount of time spent in each dimension, the company we keep both physically and extraphysically, and the amount of freedom we experience, among other things.

How this actually works becomes more apparent when we understand the three types of karma that collectively make up our holokarma.

Egokarma

Egokarma is a personal karmic account in which your actions and inactions have consequences only for you. For example, if you make some efforts to improve yourself, to perform some self-analysis, to overcome your weak traits and strengthen and build upon your strong traits, you won't suffer from the same personal limitations in your next life. This would be the karmic result of your actions.

Groupkarma

Groupkarma is the karmic account we have with the people who are closest to us, with the people we know or have known more intimately in this life and previous lives, some of whom are currently extraphysical, as mentioned earlier. Groupkarma is unavoidable during our existence on earth because human beings depend on others to survive, notably up until the age of five.

For each of us, our karmic group is composed of everyone we have ever met and have had some level of relationship with (not including passing acquaintances). So your group is made up of the consciousnesses who are, or who have been in previous lives, members of your immediate and extended family, your friends, lovers, colleagues, teachers, students, team mates, neighbors and others with whom you are perhaps working on your personal development.

Because of the natural rapport, mutual affection, energetic affinities and past history we have with those in our group, the links we share become stronger and more established over many lives, creating in turn some interesting synchronicities and increasing our chances of re-meeting these people in future lives. This is known, in conscientiology, as groupkarmic inseparability. We don't re-meet everyone in our group every life however. Some you may only reencounter once a millennium.

To give you an idea of how many people are in your group, it is hypothesized that an average person has links with hundreds of thousands of consciousnesses, both physical and extraphysical. Bearing in mind Vieira's approximation that there are up to nine extraphysical consciousnesses for every physical consciousness, we can conclude that we have many more extraphysical consciousnesses closely related to us than physical. The strength of the connections we have to various individuals in our group varies. Perhaps several thousand years ago a particular person was a member of your family every life over a series of ten or more successive lives. So you were very involved with that person then, but if you haven't met him or her in three thousand years, neither during your physical lives nor intermissive periods, you would have closer ties now with the individuals with whom you have shared more lives more recently.

We also have some level of karmic connection with a much wider group that consists of millions of physical and extraphysical consciousnesses.

The Stages of Groupkarma

The type of karma that has most bearing on the twists and turns of the multiexistential cycle is groupkarma. Bearing in mind that most of us have probably already lived many hundreds of lives, and thinking back to the uncivilized condition of mankind thousands of years ago, it is logical to conclude that at some point in the past many of us would have engaged in group activities of one kind or another that we would not be so proud of today. Did we fight wars with our group, invading other countries with no provocation and oppressing the conquered people? Did we once sacrifice children to our gods or burn "witches" and sodomites at the stake? Were we once pirates or slave traders? We have all made mistakes in the past. None of us is perfect.

On this note, it is worth emphasizing again that we acquire karma through our inactions as well as our actions. To give an example, one of the gravest instances of group inaction of the last century was the failure of the governments of many first-world countries and of various international bodies to intervene in the Rwandan Genocide of 1994 in which one million Tutsi and moderate Hutu victims were murdered by extremist Hutu militia in one hundred days. This genocide was planned. Intelligence to this effect was provided to the international community before the killings began, and global news coverage reflecting the sheer scale of the atrocities was broadcast across the world as they took place. And no one intervened. So certainly there are karmic consequences for groups of people who fail to act as a group when they should. But the responsibility for speaking out against and preventing war crimes, poverty, disease and other crises cannot only rest with governments. We also have responsibilities as societies. Did you know that 30 million people belonging to the global society put their names on the LIVE 8 list which was presented to Tony Blair as chair of the G8 Summit in 2005, to campaign against poverty, and that three billion people watched the LIVE 8 concert that year? Such is the pressure that we, as societies, can exert on the politicians of our time to act.

The karma we create with our group, whether it is through our actions or inactions, is not so easily settled or cleared. Even the more moderate, benign cases demand at least seven-and-a-half centuries of physical lives and effort, on average, to progress through the various stages that culminate in the settling of the account one has with one's group (for want of a better expression) and the liberation of the consciousness from its groupkarma. This figure represents the minimum time. It would take someone responsible for mass genocide, for example, considerably longer to be free of his groupkarma. Let's take a look at how this process unfolds.

Interprison

Sometimes there are situations in which a person cannot get out of his group because if he tries to escape, he will be killed. A situation like this can even persist over several lives. Some groups involved in unethical, criminal activities such as "extermination" groups involved in ethnic cleansing, mafias, terrorists, prostitution rings, drug networks and organizations involved in human trafficking and forced labor subscribe to such codes of behavior as a means of controlling and entrapping weaker or more vulnerable individuals. In cases like these, the condition is not just one of natural groupkarmic inseparability but one of *interprison,* in which the individual is trapped because he has profited from the unethical activities of the group. In this first stage of the groupkarma, the person is very well adapted to his group. He is in his element in fact. He is 100 percent comfortable and settled with his companions and has no moral dilemma or internal conflict about the group's activities. To the contrary, he has absolute certainty about what he's doing and brooks no criticism. This radical, extremist and less mature behavior represents the very beginning of group development.

Victimization

But as per the law of karma, every action has a consequence. So when someone involved in a group like this eventually starts to question the group's *raison d'être* and the prudence of his own engagement there, and finally manages to break free (perhaps after several lives), he will become a victim in a later life of the same antisocial organization he helped to create. Several lives spent in this phase of retribution or *victimization* may be required in order to settle one's group karmic account. Put simply, if you make a mess, you have to clean it up.

Contrary to the rather simplistic popular understanding of how this aspect of karma unfolds, there are countless ways, simple and complex, direct and indirect, subtle and obvious, in which a person can be a victim of his own group.

For example, a drug trafficker responsible for peddling heroin or cocaine in one life might suffer indirectly as a result of drugs in a future life due to his karma. He may, as an innocent passer-by and through an apparent synchronicity, be the victim of a street crime or other drug-related violence and get hurt or killed. A son or daughter of his might become a drug addict in a future life. Or he might experiment with intravenous drugs once only, in a future life, and contract the HIV virus.

Or let's say a woman runs her own prostitution business. As part of her karma she may find herself poor, uneducated and lacking in skills in a future life, with five children to support and no husband. So she could find herself in a situation in which her only means of earning a living and supporting her family is to become a prostitute. Or, perhaps she resides next to a busy brothel and is tormented day and night by the extraphysical intruders of the prostitutes and their clients, oblivious to the real cause of her stress. If she is more lucid, she might work with a charity or NGO that gives support to women who want to stop prostituting themselves, but she might have a hard life working like a donkey and being persecuted by the people who run the business—not pleasant, but a more constructive type of victimization nonetheless.

So there are many different ways in which a person can rebalance his karmic account.

Reconstruction

The period of victimization will eventually end and the individual will then enter a phase in which he begins to have enough lucidity and balance to help his former victims, members of his group whose lives he destroyed who are still stuck in the interprison and victimization phases. This stage represents the *reconstruction* of the holokarmic account. For example, perhaps someone was a chronic, abusive alcoholic in one life and caused his family much pain and distress. In a later life, when the victimization phase has come to an end, he may work in a field in which he counsels and helps people to overcome their addictions, or as a benefactor of an organization that offers assistance and support to abused people.

Freedom

After spending some time reconstructing his groupkarma, maybe more than one life, a person will become liberated from his negative karmic links. The person starts to experience real *freedom* for the first time and a quality of life that is characterized by a greater level of control over his present and future circumstances. He has choices and options open to him that he didn't have before and is not suffering from so much intrusion anymore. Someone who is at liberty to choose his area of education, perhaps pursue a career in another field altogether, who has the wherewithal and resources to live in many different countries, and leads a life filled with opportunities for personal growth and contact with others, would at least be in this phase of the groupkarma. Someone who struggles on a daily basis to fulfill the basic requirements necessary for survival does not experience this level of freedom.

Polykarma

The final phase of groupkarma (and the third type of karma that makes up one's holokarma) is when a person applies himself to developing his mental body. He dedicates himself to self-knowledge, to improving and evolving as a consciousness, and to assisting large numbers of others to do the same, including people he doesn't know. This is *polykarma*. At this level, the person doesn't ask anything for himself anymore; he has a universalistic outlook on life, consciously applies his discernment, maturity and cosmoethics (see chapter 13) and is working towards becoming free of intrusion.

Leaders such as Mahatma Gandhi and Nelson Mandela acted on their polykarmic accounts with positive actions that alleviated the suffering and improved the lives of many thousands of people, dismantling and incapacitating well-established mechanisms of physical and extraphysical intrusion in the process. Terrorists such as Osama bin Laden and rogue leaders such as Saddam Hussein, Slobodan Milosevic and Adolf Hitler, added negative polykarma to their karmic accounts, each playing the role of the physical focal point of a larger multidimensional mechanism of intrusion.

Karma is always multidimensional in nature, meaning there are also extraphysical consequences or repercussions to one's actions. The multidimensional implications of polykarma are greater than those of egokarma and groupkarma, and address more complex issues such as evolution.

Every person has his egokarmic and groupkarmic accounts open from the moment he takes his first breath on earth but only a small minority of people will open their polykarmic account.

* * *

The frequency of the rebirth of the consciousness and the duration of the intermissive periods depend for many hundreds of years on its personal egokarma and the karmic debts of its group. Additional aspects related to groupkarma that can affect our existential seriality include the existential seriality of those who are or have been blood relatives, and the level of individuality of a consciousness, as usually a consciousness lacking in individuality is governed by his groupkarma. These factors can have some bearing on where and to whom we are reborn.

When we begin to understand the dynamics and mechanisms

of holokarma, we can start thinking about what practical steps we can take to improve our own and in so doing can exercise more control over our future lives and periods between our lives. For example, on the egokarmic level, look after yourself well by ensuring that all of your physical, emotional and mental needs are met without being selfish or egocentric. To improve your groupkarma, strive to have a clear conscience with regards to all of your relationships. Take steps to eliminate any misunderstandings and resentments with frankness and sincerity and avoid causing sadness or pain. Don't victimize others and don't play the victim. To activate your polykarmic account, do good works of assistance to help not only your friends and family, but strangers—people that you don't know—and as many of them as possible.

In this way, we start to take responsibility for our holokarma and to embrace it as an important influence in our lives over which we have some control rather than as an unseen force of which we are but random victims.

Chapter Six

Clues to Past Lives

Do you know who you are?
—*Dostoevsky*

Many years ago I used to go diving regularly with some very experienced divers. One instructor in particular used to put on a kind of underwater magic show that was just fabulous to experience. As we swam alongside the reefs, examining the corals, peering into rocks and caves and bringing the vivid colors to life under the light of our flashlights, he would draw on his knowledge to expose clever camouflages, transforming apparently lifeless environments into scenes that thrived with activity.

In a similar way, suggestions of past lives are all around us. It's just a matter of knowing how and where to look. Once we develop an understanding of some subjects that might be new to many of you, such as the complete or *holo*memory of the consciousness, paragenetics (genetics that we pass to ourselves from one life to the next), pathologies of the mental body, the tendency to mimic previous lives, semi-conscious recollections of past lives and energetic affinities, we can start to perceive the clues to former existences that are discretely woven into the fabric of our everyday lives.

The concept of seriality (the series of successive lives) helps throw light on some quirks of human nature that are widely accepted as being real but are poorly understood, such as "love at first sight" and various aversions and disorders that have no apparent basis. More importantly though, through meticulous scientific research, notably that of the late Ian Stevenson MD, former head of the Department of Psychiatry and founder and director of the Division of Personality Studies at the University of Virginia in the US, seriality has been shown to be a plausible determining factor in some physical and psychological conundrums that have long baffled modern medicine, such as some birthmarks, birth defects and phobias.

Given the success of Dr. Stevenson's work, the question that naturally arises is what other enigmas might benefit from a scientific perspective that acknowledges that the consciousness survives the death of the physical body and is subject to a long series of successive lives? What existing theories that preclude this viewpoint can adequately explain all the cases of the Savant syndrome, of genius, child prodigy and exceptional talent; xenoglossy (unlearned language) or gender dysphoria, for example?

In this chapter I examine some clues to past lives, some of which seem to be the result of scientific investigation and others that can be corroborated through personal experience. In the next chapter I proffer an explanation of the mechanisms that allow past-life experiences, skills and knowledge to manifest in a later physical existence.

Phobias

In the context of past-life experiences, it seems more logical to examine children's phobias as, due to their young age, there is considerably less likelihood that the phobia could be linked to a current-life experience.

In encountering children with phobias, child psychiatrists commonly attempt to treat phobias that neither they nor the children's parents can explain in that they are not the result of any known incident or trauma nor do they correspond to a similar fear in a family member. Bearing this in mind, the hypothesis that some phobias relate to past-life traumas becomes even more compelling in light of a tentative classification of children's phobias drawn from research and clinical experience that was proposed by Miller, Barret and Hampe (as cited by A. Davids, 1974).

Among the phobias proposed were many that one could reasonably understand a child developing, such as phobias of snakes and spiders, high places, air travel, deep water, being seen naked, social interactions, getting an injection, reciting in class, and being criticized. But there were also several that would seem to defy any logical explanation in the context of the present life of a young child and, moreover, could be considered to have more relevance to past societies than present. These include phobias relating to poisoned food, germs, wars and riots, members of another race, breaking a religious law, being kidnapped and going crazy. (A. Davids, 1974)[2] Of course, a conscientious study of individual cases would be required to ascertain whether or not the roots of any phobias present in children do in fact stem from past-life experiences.

This is precisely what Ian Stevenson did for four decades, thoroughly interviewing and investigating over 2600 cases of reported reincarnation, scientifically substantiating many past-life memories by methodically sifting actual real-life experiences from intuitions, claims and beliefs. His approach was to construct a case history of each individual by corroborating the life of the personality remembered with existing historical data, such as medical and civil records, and by interviewing people still living who remembered the previous personality and who were able to confirm the stories that the child claimed to have lived.

The subjects of Stevenson's work were mostly children, the majority from countries and cultures that believe in reincarnation, who professed to remember previous lives.

In one particular study of 387 such children, phobias were found to occur in 141 (36 percent). Some of these children exhibited the phobia before learning to speak and so couldn't explain the phobia in the context of the remembered life to their family. Commonly, the phobias corresponded to the cause of death of the previous personality. One subject, a Sri Lankan girl by the name of Shamlinie Prema, for example, demonstrated two phobias as an infant; one of water, the other of buses. Her parents were at a loss to explain them. Over time, as Shamalinie learned to talk, she began to describe a previous life in which she had died at the age of eleven. She said that she had gone out to buy bread one morning and the road was flooded. A passing bus splashed water all over her and when she stepped backwards to get out of the way, she fell into a paddy field and drowned. (Stevenson, 2001)

In many instances, the children's phobias related specifically to the instrument responsible for the death of the previous personality, such as guns, knives and swords, while a few of the subjects had phobias of the place where the death occurred.

In general, Stevenson's study produced results that strongly pointed to the possibility of past lives. Among 47 cases in which the previous personality had drowned, a phobia of being submerged in water occurred in 30 (64 percent). Among the 30 cases in which the previous personality died of snakebite, a phobia of snakes occurred in 43 percent. (Stevenson, 2001)

While the actual incidence of children's phobias in the general population is difficult to quantify, according to a study by King, Hamilton and Ollendik (1994), it is thought to be between only 3 and 8 percent, making it considerably more difficult to dismiss these connections as pure coincidence.

Birthmarks and Birth Defects

Similarly, there are many recorded instances of people with birthmarks or birth defects that have no known genetic or prenatal cause.

Stevenson investigated 210 such cases in which subjects exhibited birthmarks, birth defects and other abnormalities that, according to them, were related to events experienced in a previous life. Existing medical records, often post-mortem reports, verified the recollections of many of the subjects, proving in 43 of the 210 cases the distinguishing marking or feature on the current physical body to be linked to a wound, often fatal, incurred by the individual in a previous existence. (Stevenson, 2001)

One of these files tells the story of Haşim Köybaşi, a Turkish man who had died in a postelection riot in Turkey in 1963. Haşim's postmortem report showed that he had died from a bullet that had entered his head behind the left ear. The bullet almost emerged on the right side of his neck but the examining pathologist had to make a small incision to extract it. Many months later, a female relative gave birth to a son, Metin Köybaşi, who was born with birthmarks corresponding to the entry and exit wounds of the bullet that had killed Haşim. Developing a tendency that was common in other children in Stevenson's study, as he grew older, Metin became extremely vengeful towards the man who had shot Haşim. Once, intent on shooting him, he even tried to take his father's gun. (Stevenson, 1997)

Birth defects can be defined as major deformities and are usually characterized by the partial or complete absence of fingers, toes, arms, legs, ears or other organs. As cited by Stevenson (1997), the three known causes of birth defects are genetic factors such as chromosomal abnormalities; certain infectious diseases, drugs and other toxins; and conditions that occur in the uterus when the fetus is developing, such as overcrowding during multiple pregnancies. When these known causes are excluded however, large numbers of birth defects remain unexplained with some studies showing this incidence to be as high as 65–79 percent (Wilson, 1973)

In his book *Reincarnation and Biology: A Contribution to the Etiology of Birthmarks and Birth Defects Vol. 2,* Stevenson presents

25 case studies of subjects who had major birth defects of the extremities, in other words, they were missing either fingers, toes, hands or feet. All but two of the subjects claimed that the previous personality had died a violent death, with more than half of them occurring in Myanmar (formerly Burma).

Among the Burmese subjects, some remembered lives that took place under the British rule in Burma, others had memories relating to the ensuing pandemonium of the defeat of the Japanese army in 1945, and four claimed to have been Japanese soldiers who fought and died in Burma during Word War II. The subjects' memories were consistent with the facts relating to these periods in Burma's history.

All of the previous personalities of the Burmese subjects were killed with swords with the exception of one who died in a bomb explosion. Five of the subjects claimed to have been tortured before being killed, saying that their killers had chopped off some of their fingers and toes first. This form of torture was known to have been carried out by the Burmese on Japanese stragglers separated from their army. Three of the subjects said that they had lost fingers when they raised their hands in self-defence or to plead for mercy. Unlike the others, these three manifested birth defects of the hands but not of the toes.

In considering any likelihood of a birthmark or birth defect being linked to a trauma incurred by an individual in a previous life, it is worth bearing in mind that in comparison to instances of birthmarks, most birth defects are rare. (Stevenson, 1997)

Xenoglossy and Glossolalia

Another phenomenon that sometimes puzzles modern science but may make sense in the context of past lives is that of xenoglossy. Xenoglossy is the ability to speak in a language that has not been learned in the current life. In some cases, a person can also write in the unlearned language (xenography).

Religious literature, especially that of spiritualism, is proliferated with accounts of the related phenomenon of glossolalia or "speaking in tongues" which is the ability to utter words or sounds of a language unknown to the speaker, usually as an expression of religious ecstasy. The following appears in the New Testament of the Bible for example, "And they were all filled with the Holy Ghost, and began to speak with other tongues, as the Spirit gave them utterance." (Acts 2: 4). In Christianity, the supernatural ability to speak in unknown languages was interpreted as a gift bestowed by the Holy Spirit.

Authentic cases of xenoglossy, in which a person speaks a real language that is completely unknown to him in his normal state of consciousness, are very uncommon, and properly documented cases are even rarer. Most cases of apparent xenoglossy can in fact be dismissed as a person speaking nonsense, a gibberish invented by the subconscious mind, as instances of possession or telepathic communication involving mediumism, or as fraud.

There are two distinct types of xenoglossy, recitative and responsive. In recitative xenoglossy the person is unable to converse in the foreign language but can repeat some words or phrases in rote style, without necessarily understanding what they mean. In responsive xenoglossy, the person is able to communicate in the foreign language in an intelligent manner. Authentic cases of responsive xenoglossy are much rarer than those of the recitative kind. (Stevenson, 1974)

The following example of recitative xenoglossy was cited by researcher, author and founder of the magazine *Spiritism,* Frenchman Gabriel Delanne in 1924.

An Italian family by the name of Battista, from the Rome area, lost their young daughter Blanche in 1902. Three years later Signora Battista, who was pregnant, had an experience in which the deceased child appeared to her saying she was coming back to the family, so when Signora Battista gave birth to a daughter in 1906, she and her husband (who reported the case) named her Blanche also.

When the first Blanche had been alive, the family had employed a Swiss maid who only spoke French. She had taught Blanche to sing a French lullaby. As the girl had left the family's employ soon after Blanche had died, the family soon forgot about the lullaby, so they were astounded one day to hear the second Blanche singing the old French lullaby when she was about five years old. It hadn't been heard in the Battista household for nine years. When they asked Blanche who had taught her the song she replied, "No one, I just know it by myself." (Stevenson, 1974) As the child was not able to converse in the foreign language, only recite, this was an example of recitative xenoglossy.

One of the best-known cases of genuine responsive xenoglossy is that of "T. E.," a 37-year-old housewife, investigated by Stevenson, who was born and raised in Philadelphia.

T. E.'s Russian parents had emigrated to the US from Odessa, Russia. Neither of them had ever been to Scandinavia nor knew anyone well who could speak any of the Scandinavian languages. T. E. was raised in an English-speaking society and her family spoke mostly English together.

During a session of regressive hypnosis under her husband K.E., a physician in Philadelphia, it was discovered that T. E. was easily able to enter deep trances, so he began to experiment with her more systematically. Under hypnosis one day soon after the more regular sessions began, T. E. announced that she was a man by the name of Jensen Jacoby and then briefly described his life as a peasant farmer. She spoke in a deep masculine voice. This was the first session of several conducted between 1955 and 1956 at which Jensen appeared. In the sixth, seventh and eighth sessions, Jensen communicated almost exclusively in an early form of colloquial Swedish that was spoken before the industrial revolution. All sessions from the fourth onwards were recorded except the eighth at which detailed notes were taken.

After thoroughly investigating this case and examining both the recordings and transcripts of the hypnosis sessions, Stevenson was able to establish its authenticity as an example of responsive xenoglossy by discounting any possibility of fraud or cryptomnesia (in which a language is learned early in life but later forgotten). Extrasensory perception was postulated as a third possible cause as Swedish-speaking interpreters had to be present during the sessions to test T. E.'s knowledge of Swedish, but Stevenson reasoned that this hypothesis was very unlikely as Jensen's speech was smattered with a considerable number of Norwegian words while the interpreters all preferred Swedish.

Dr. Stevenson spent over eight years working directly on the Jensen case and recruited linguists and other experts and scientists who thoroughly investigated every alternative explanation. In summary, having dispensed with the three explanations mentioned above, Stevenson concluded that it was impossible to understand this case of responsive xenoglossy without assuming that a personality who had learned Swedish before 1956 had survived the death of his physical body. This personality could be a nonphysical consciousness temporarily speaking through the hypnotized T. E. or he could be an aspect of T. E.'s own personality. While Stevenson didn't believe that the data provided a stronger evidence for either of the two possibilities, nor provide absolute proof of reincarnation, he did however propose reincarnation as a plausible hypothesis, especially as Jensen was evoked only by suggestions of regression. (Stevenson, 1974)

In more recent times, Professor Adrian Finkelstein, an established author and psychiatrist in Los Angeles, recounted the true story in *Your Past Lives and the Healing Process* of a boy, Robin Hull, who remembered his past life as a Tibetan monk. Robin often spoke in a language his mother couldn't understand. When a friend of Robin's mother who believed in reincarnation heard the strange language she invited another friend who was a professor of Asian languages to Robin's house. Eventually, the professor was able to identify the language as a dialect spoken in the northern regions of Tibet. When he asked the boy where he had learned the language, the boy replied "at school." When his mother reminded him that he hadn't started school yet, Robin said that he went to school a long time ago and then explained that he didn't like to talk about his past life because the only time he had attempted to, his mother had ignored him. With the professor's encouragement, Robin described very precisely his past life as a Tibetan monk, so precisely in fact that the professor decided to go in search of the place. He eventually found the monastery of which Robin spoke in the Kuen Lun Mountains. (Finkelstein, 1996)

If some instances of phobias, birthmarks, birth defects and xenoglossy can be shown through scientific research to be plausible manifestations of reincarnation, then it stands to reason that there may be other clues to past lives, some more commonplace, also worthy of investigation. Here are some examples that seem suggestive, to varying degrees, of a prior existence of the personality.

Prodigies, Exceptional Talents and Early Achievers

A prodigy is defined as a person who manifests exceptional talents or powers at an early age, displaying expert proficiency in a field that is usually the exclusive domain of adults. A prodigious talent, although always remarkable, is even more so when evident in a child who has had neither the time nor opportunity to acquire such highly developed skills in the current life, nor inherited a genetic predisposition towards the skill from his family.

Some of the reasons given for exceptional talent in children include a particularly strong, positive parental interest and attention in the child (perhaps because the child was an only child, was sick or was born late in the father's life), or the child spending a large portion of his time in the company of adults and imitating and being influenced by exceptional parents. (Radford, 1990) The latter reason is evident in the cases Mozart and Picasso, for example, two of the world's most famous child prodigies. These three reasons however, do not account for all cases of prodigies.

According to the "nature-nurture" theory, we are all a product of our genetic inheritance and our environment. While there are no definitive answers as to what makes a prodigy break this mold, general consensus among researchers is that a prodigy is rather the product of environment (which includes factors such as nationality, culture, level of education, religion, socioeconomic status and opportunities to practice the skill in addition to the factors mentioned in the previous paragraph) and innate talent. But what exactly is innate talent? British psychologist and author, John Radford, claims that while special talents are essentially innate, the genetic mechanism behind this is not clear. He admits that "special talents and precocity are simply unusual cases of general laws which have yet to be elucidated." (Radford, 1990)

According to the science of conscientiology, innate talents are readily explained as talents that a person can inherit (along with many other things) from himself, via his holomemory (complete or integral memory) and paragenetics. These mechanisms are explained in full in the next chapter.

Certainly it is not difficult to find examples of children exhibiting skills and strong tendencies that seem to indicate something more than behavior of an exceptional level of maturity and development, suggesting in some cases a "carrying forward" of familiar, habitual behaviors from past lives. In *Child Prodigies and Exceptional Early Achievers* for example, Radford describes a photo carried in the (London) *Times* on June 29, 1988 of Prime Minister Thatcher inspecting the press credentials of a young journalist at the meeting of

European leaders in Hanover, Germany. The journalist was 12-year-old Alexander Blume reporting for his school newspaper, *The Mole*.

In other examples cited by Radford, the *Early Times* of California, dated December 27, 1988, reported the story of Tony Aliengena, aged nine, who became the youngest solo pilot in California, taking off and landing an ultralight plane. The following year he piloted a plane around the world.

And on August 24, 2001, *The Guardian* in the UK reported the story of Arran Fernandez who, at age five, had become the youngest person to pass a GCSE exam, in mathematics. A perfect example of the environment/innate talent hypothesis, Arran was an only child who had been educated by his parents at home in Surrey but who nonetheless accomplished feats that would far surpass the expectations of what such advantages might bring when he discovered some integer sequences previously unknown to research mathematicians. These were later published in an international research encyclopedia.

If the theories relating to holomemory and paragenetics as proposed by Vieira are correct, then it stands to reason that a person would be able to inherit negative behaviors and tendencies as well as positive ones. Examples of extreme negative tendencies in children that cannot be explained away by the child's environment or genetic inheritance but appear to be innate, are similarly not so difficult to find.

Genius

A study of genius also turns up numerous examples of people of extraordinary intellectual and creative powers that challenge the nature/nurture theory, hinting instead at capacities and talents that have been learned, developed, "remembered" and perfected by the consciousness over many lives.

How else can we adequately explain the case of classical composer George Handel (1685–1759) for example, who came from a family of no musical distinction and received no formal musical training apart from lessons taken with the organist at his local church as a young child? His father was strongly against his interest in music and his mother offered him no real support. (Stevenson, 2001) Against these odds, Handel nonetheless became, during his lifetime, perhaps the most internationally acclaimed of all musicians.

The Savant Syndrome

Genius is even more difficult to explain within the limited parameters of the conventional paradigm when it manifests in people who are handicapped in almost every other way, as is the case with some sufferers of the savant syndrome. Could it be that holomemory and paragenetics also play a role in this baffling paradox of superability and disability?

An *idiot savant* (from the French *idiot* meaning idiot and *savant* whose original meaning refers to a learned or knowledgeable person such as a scholar, philosopher or scientist) is an extremely rare condition in which a mentally handicapped person, usually incapable of learning, reading and writing, can accurately access highly specific and detailed knowledge in precise fields such as mathematics, music and the arts. Dustin Hoffman famously raised awareness of the Savant syndrome in the film *Rain Man*. He played an autistic *savant* who was able to memorize a staggering number of cards played at a blackjack table yet was incapable of making simple choices about what to eat or wear.

What is most perplexing about the autistic *savants* is that they do not gain their specialized knowledge through learning. They just "know" precise, explicit information. Some, for example, are calendar calculators, such as the identical twins George and Charles who were extensively studied by Darold A. Treffert, a Wisconsin psychiatrist who has been researching the savant syndrome for more than 40 years.

As cited by Treffert in *Extraordinary People*, the first comprehensive work on this condition, George and Charles can tell you what day of the week corresponds to any past or future date you name, within a span of 40,000 years. They can also tell you all the years in which your birthday fell on any given day of the week. They cannot however perform simple calculations such as addition and subtraction.

Another case studied by Treffert that received a great deal of attention from the US media, is that of the prodigious *savant* Leslie Lemke. A prodigious *savant* is defined as a handicapped person with skills that would be remarkable even in a normal person. This was certainly Leslie Lemke's case. Leslie, who had never had any formal instruction in music, heard Tchaikovsky's *Piano Concerto No. 1* for the first time one night during his teens. It was the sound track of a film he was watching with his family. Later that night, his family was awakened by Leslie playing the piano—note for note, flawlessly and without hesitation—Tchaikovsky's *Piano Concerto No. 1.*

Leslie can do this with any piece of music, no matter how long or complex. This feat in itself is remarkable. Add to this the fact that Leslie is blind, has cerebral palsy, is severely mentally handicapped and cannot even manage to use a utensil to eat, and it would seem that some kind of paranormal explanation is called for. Conventional science, at least, has no explanation for this phenomenon. (Treffert, 1989)

The *idiot savant syndrome* was being studied as far back as the late nineteenth century by French psychologist Alfred Binet who devised the Intelligence Quotient (IQ) as a measurement of intelligence. But the condition remained a curiosity for many years. Not until recently has this apparently anomalous human condition been analyzed from what is known in psychology-speak as a modular view, in which, according to philosopher, psychologist and author Jerry A. Fodor, "many different kinds of psychological mechanisms must be postulated in order to explain the facts of mental life." (Radford, 1990) I propose that facts of mental life will never fully be explained until an acknowledgment of the past lives of a consciousness is also incorporated into such a modular view.

All the clues to past lives discussed thus far are rare conditions not commonly encountered in every day life. So let's now look at some other clues with which you or someone you know are more likely to have had some direct, personal experience.

Love at First Sight

Most of us have had the experience of feeling an "intuitive" attraction for someone upon meeting him or her for the very first time. A powerful but apparently baseless sentiment such as this can point to your past. When you "recognize" someone in this way, what you are often recognizing in fact is that person's unique bioenergetic signature, the mixture and quality of energy, thoughts and emotions that is specific to him or her, a combination that you already know well from your shared past together. So this sense of instant familiarity can, in fact, be a semiconscious recollection of a past life. Most people are unaware of this possibility however and often misinterpret the "recognition" of a stranger as love at first sight. Logically, as well as experiencing this sense of familiarity with those who were indeed our former spouses or lovers, we may also experience it with others we were particularly close to in previous lives, such as those who were once our parents, children, siblings or friends.

Aversions

On the flip side of the coin, an instant dislike or repulsion for a stranger upon first meeting may equally be a semiconscious recollection of a former enemy or adversary.

Less intense than a phobia and more prevalent in everyday life, an aversion is defined as a fixed, intense dislike or repugnance; the avoidance of a thing, situation or behavior because it has been associated with an unpleasant or painful stimulus. In cases in which an aversion has no known cause, the possibility that the stimulus may be rooted in a past existence should be considered.

For example, I know a man who is perfectly normal and likeable. He had a stable, loving upbringing; is considerate; funny and unpretentious and excels in his chosen profession. Paradoxically, he has apparently never had an intimate relationship, neither heterosexual nor homosexual, despite now being in his mid-forties. Clearly, he has an aversion to intimacy yet there is no evident cause for this. Could it be that he was sexually violated in a previous life? It is possible. Or maybe he spent many consecutive past lives leading up to this one as a religious figure, perhaps a priest or monk, whose dogma was that sex was wrong. Or perhaps he is just terribly shy but hides his inhibitions well. Again, we should never make assumptions about anything without knowing all the facts. There are many plausible explanations for such situations—the point I'm making is that explanations that have their origins in a past life are also plausible.

A cursory glance at world events reveals ample potentialities for the development of future life aversions, if not full-blown phobias, for thousands of unfortunate victims of natural and man-made disasters.

We can logically hypothesize that some Hajj pilgrims trampled to death in human stampedes in Mecca might develop an aversion to crowds in future lives; that some of the victims of the 2004 Boxing Day tsunami might manifest an aversion to the water or the ocean; or that some of the eleven million Jews, Gypsies, Poles and other European ethnic groups exterminated during the Holocaust of World War II might manifest, in future lives, a specific aversion to the German race.

Gender Dysphoria

Another area in which we could hypothesize the impact of past lives on a consciousness is that of gender dysphoria, or gender identity disorder.

Some people experience varying degrees of incongruousness between the gender they feel themselves to be and the gender they actually are. While some are content to "role-play" the sex they identify with in a homosexual relationship, others will go to extreme lengths physically, emotionally, psychologically, socially and financially to live a life that outwardly matches their internal understanding of what gender they are. This may include incorporating behaviors such as cross-dressing into their lifestyle (transvestism) or taking the drastic measure of changing their sex through medical intervention (transexualism).

Research has shown that there is no scientifically proven cause of transexualism. Nor is there any known psychological cure.

An incorporation of an understanding of multiserial realities into the counselling and treatment of gender dysphoria could potentially bring much relief to many who describe themselves as having the body of one sex and the desires of another.

Consider the following, for example. People commonly live their physical lives according to a series of safe routines that don't present any risk or challenge, routines that they like and with which they are comfortable. Some people are so attached to their routines that they endlessly repeat a variety of aspects of their physical manifestation over many lives—things like their profession, nationality, geographical location, type of partner and gender. This is known in conscientiology as existential self-mimicry, a topic that will be examined in more detail in chapter 9.

Take then the case of a consciousness who has led ten consecutive lives as a man. Imagine that the helpers eventually decide that this consciousness needs to be born as a female in the next life, in order that it can have some new experiences, learn from them and progress as a consciousness, and so it experiences physical life as a woman for the first time in more than a thousand years. In this context it is not so difficult to understand its malaise with its new gender.

By the same token, depending on the individual, an understanding of this broader reality may help a person to take advantage of and embrace the experience of being born a particular gender. It is an opportunity to gain empathy for the members of that sex through firsthand experience, to learn some new skills and capacities that the experience of being that sex affords, and above all, to develop the positive attributes of flexibility and adaptability.

It is important to emphasize that what I'm proposing is just one of many possible explanations for the conditions of homosexuality, transvestism and transexuality.

Ideological Affinities

A last example of clues to a person's past lives or intermissive periods is one that I witness regularly in class as an instructor of conscientiology.

Many students come to our courses with no prior, lucid experience of OBEs or any other paranormal or energetic phenomena. They come because they are looking to make sense of their existence, to broaden their view of reality and to understand their role within it.

Throughout our core course, the Consciousness Development Program (CDP), students are exposed to all manner of subjects that would seem fantastical or just plain crazy to the average person out on the street—all the things discussed in this book—mastery of energies, helpers and intruders, past lives and intermissive periods, out-of-body flights to other dimensions and planets, etc. Yet it is blatantly obvious that for most of our students, nothing could be more logical and rational. Often this is because they are not in fact being taught anything they don't already know, for they attended training courses during their last intermissive period in preparation for this current life in which they studied many of the topics that we teach in the CDP. In this case, the classes themselves trigger semiconscious recollections of classes attended in the intermissive period, which, in turn, translate into a strong sense of rapport with the information and ideas being discussed.

The following quotes from students confirm this theory:

> When I was first introduced to the science of conscientiology, the majority of the information which was being presented felt very intuitive and logical to me. In fact, the greater challenge and the focus of my mental effort were more in comprehending the conscientiological terminology used to describe the ideas, than the ideas themselves. (Glenn Hitchman, UK)

> After my first course with the IAC I had a feeling as if I had been travelling in a foreign country for such a long time and finally I found someone whose language I actually understood! It all felt so familiar and clear to me. (Ines Rusteberg, Germany)

Other affinities with ideologies and religions, cultures, languages, customs, habits and traditions, and even likings and cravings for foods foreign to the environment into which an individual was born, may in some cases be due to connections with experiences in previous lives.

Chapter Seven

The Mechanisms by Which Past-Life Experiences Affect Our Present Lives

Today we are the living summary of our past, the result of the addition of genetic and environmental characteristics, as well as the expression of everything that we have already lived, thought, felt and done.
—*Wagner Alegretti*

Holomemory

As mentioned earlier, according to leading theories in psychology, we are all the product of our environment (upbringing) and genetic inheritance. Yet each of the categories of clues to past lives explored in the previous chapter presents examples that cannot be adequately explained by this theory.

According to conscientiology, we are all the product of our environment, our genetics and one vital additional component—our past, which includes both our past physical lives and intermissive periods. During our intermissive periods, some people receive training, education and even undergo specific procedures to alter the extraphysical body. I mention this because our tendency is usually to think only of our past physical lives when we think of our past, forgetting that we also accumulate experiences, knowledge and wisdom during the period between lives.

The mechanisms by which the memories and experiences of our past can emerge in our present are our holomemory and our paragenetics. Together, these act as the matrix or template of the personality and the physical body of the consciousness. Let me explain.

Although we temporarily forget much of what happens

throughout our lives, every experience we ever had in every physical life and intermissive period, every incident, event, occurrence, meeting and exchange, no matter how minor or insignificant, is registered in the integral or holomemory of the consciousness that is stored in the mental body. Because we are the sum of our experiences, the holomemory then, is the original source of the personality of the consciousness, largely determining the way in which we think, behave and interact with others, and allowing many habits, attitudes, attributes, pathologies, tendencies, predilections, skills, knowledge, capacities, affinities, values and principles that have formed over lifetimes of experiences to emerge in and impact on our present.

You can access your holomemory and any detail from your past by having a projection in the mental body (a technique for producing such a projection is described in chapter 16). If you succeed in producing such a projection, you will see that the memories stored by your current physical brain pertaining only to your current physical life, represent a very small percentage indeed of your complete memory.

Holomemory also offers a plausible explanation for some unsolved cases of xenoglossy, child prodigies, exceptional talents, geniuses and the savant syndrome, such as those described in the previous chapter.

A hypothetical explanation of how it works in tandem with other determining factors could be as follows: In the case of some instances of the quite rare savant syndrome, it could be that the consciousness in question has been a genius in many past consecutive lives and that the specific skill of the person is so highly developed now that the consciousness, through his holomemory, "remembers" and manifests the skill in the current life . . . but that his helpers, perhaps even with the agreement of the individual in the period between lives, decide that in order to overcome a particular limitation, the person must be born handicapped in this life. Or perhaps his handicap is planned to help him to learn new skills that he will require in future lives as part of his evolution as a consciousness. It is also possible that the limitation was caused by a karmic factor.

Paragenetics

The other means by which our past can manifest in our present is via our paragenetics. Paragenetics are a kind of genetic coding that, unlike genetics, are not passed from one physical human being to another, but are transmitted from our extraphysical and mental bodies to our new physical body when we're reborn. So we pass this coding to ourselves from one life to the next. Working together with genetics, paragenetics help to shape the physical body and can thus be responsible for some aspects of our physical appearance.

Although these two mechanisms have not been clearly elucidated before, they have been acknowledged. The Greek philosopher Plato (c.428–347 BC), for example, once stated, "Knowledge easily acquired is that which the enduring soul had in an earlier life, so that it flows back easily." Renowned twentieth century clairvoyant and healer Edgar Cayce reached the same conclusion, explaining that "You have inherited most from yourself, not from your family. The family is only a river through which the soul flows." (Kelly, 1997)

The degree to which a person is influenced by his holomemory and paragenetics varies depending on the depth of maturity and the evolutionary level of the consciousness.

An average human being who strongly identifies with physical life and has no real awareness of his broader existence tends to be more influenced and restricted by the conditionings imposed by his genetics and environment. His behavior is driven more by the instinctive processes of survival and he is more likely to repeat experiences of past lives that do not contribute in any way to his evolution as a consciousness. For example, perhaps a person's life consists of a routine of working on a production line in a manufacturing plant, spending time at the pub every night after work, going to a football game on Saturday and eating lunch with the family on Sunday after church—a repetition of a lifestyle carried over from previous existences. For such a person, the influence of his holomemory and paragenetics would be minimal, meaning he manifests less of the original source of his personality—less of who he really is.

An individual of a more advanced evolutionary level tends to manifest more traits derived from his holomemory and paragenetics. This allows him to overcome many of the limitations of his environment and genetics, as happened in the case of Handel, as well as benefit from the more positive aspects afforded by these two factors. Such a person usually manifests a greater level of awareness of multidimensional realities, is more discerning and cosmoethical and performs better in evolutionary terms due to multiexistential "baggage" of a higher quality. As the influence of his holomemory and paragenetics exceeds that of his environment and genetics, he manifests more of who he really is.

Bear in mind however, that manifesting more traits derived from one's holomemory and paragenetics is not always an optimizing factor, as in the cases of phobias, birthmarks and birth defects for example. So sometimes the prevalence of genetics over the paragenetics can be a good thing.

If you are motivated to be more of who you really are, more advanced levels of evolution and maturity can be achieved with effort via the lucid, conscious prioritization of self-improvement over numerous lifetimes.

Pathologies of the Mental Body

With regards to birthmarks, birth defects and phobias, much of the scientific research referred to in the last chapter suggests that profound experiences such as traumas can be imprinted on the mental and extraphysical bodies so strongly that they influence the paragenetics of the consciousness, which in turn, affect the genetics of the next physical body.

Let's take the example of one of the Burmese subjects born with deformed and missing fingers, who recalled having his fingers chopped off in his previous life, prior to being executed. We can hypothesize that the trauma of the torture was so severe that when this man died and began an existence in the extraphysical dimension, his extraphysical body (the emotional body) was also in a kind of shock. The impact was so great in fact that the extraphysical body manifested without the fingers that had been severed during the man's torture. In other words, the image this consciousness had of itself, even in the extraphysical body, was of missing several fingers.

In this particular instance, this image was so strong that eventually, during this person's intermissive period, the mental body began to accept that this was the real condition of the consciousness and formed a fixed idea about it, a pathology, which caused the deformity to manifest more strongly in the extraphysical body and in turn, to reappear in the next physical body. So a pathology of the mental body is another mechanism that allows some aspects of our past to emerge in our current life.

It has to be said that such extremes are rare. A pathology of the mental body caused by a past-life trauma is more likely to manifest as a birthmark, phobia, aversion, or not at all, than as an actual physical deformity. Many types of phobias and aversions persist throughout the multiexistential cycle of a consciousness through this process, which is why it is important that we make an effort to overcome our limitations.

Another way in which a pathology of the mental body can manifest in a person's current existence is through odd synchronicities. For example, let's say a farmer is tilling a hilly field in his tractor, it rolls, he is trapped underneath it and his leg is severed in the accident. He dies a traumatic death from the loss of blood. This experience is so devastating emotionally that after death the extraphysical body manifests without the leg and in time the mental body imprints an image of its physical incarnation as being without a leg. In a future life, the farmer will have a new body with two legs and he will reestablish an image of himself as a person with two legs. But because the mental body still carries this pathology and the image of not having a leg is still strong, synchronicities can start to happen. Perhaps he will break the same leg several times throughout his life for example. Such apparent coincidences aren't always what they seem.

A Case in Point

To conclude this chapter I would like to share the details of a particularly remarkable case investigated by Stevenson in which the subject's past life produced not one but several of the consequences and repercussions discussed in the last chapter in her current life.

Ma Win Tar, a Burmese girl who remembered her previous life as a Japanese soldier, was born with major defects of both hands, with fingers missing on both, and with unusual grooves on her fingers and left wrist.

Although the details that Ma Win Tar gave of her last life were not verified, they were historically plausible. She recalled that her previous personality had been captured, tied to a tree and burned alive at the hands of a group of Burmese men during World War II. The soldier had pleaded for mercy and his life, to no avail.

Stevenson suggested that Ma Win Tar's deformities matched the loss of fingers the soldier would have incurred had he held up his hands to protect himself from a blow from a sword or to plead for mercy, although it is also possible that like other soldiers, he had been tortured and his fingers had been chopped off prior to the execution. The pattern of grooves on Ma Win

Tar's fingers and left wrist were presumed to be related to the rope marks from being tied to the tree.

At the age of three, Ma Win Tar was accidentally scalded with boiling water. Perhaps this was a synchronicity of the variety just discussed or maybe it was merely a coincidence. Either way, she subsequently developed a phobia of hot objects and fire.

When Ma Win Tar was learning to speak, her parents would point to an object and give the name in Burmese, encouraging her to repeat it. Instead, she often spoke a foreign word that her parents couldn't understand. Later, as a young child, she sang songs in a strange tongue unknown to her family. The music was also unfamiliar to them. It is not known if Ma Win Tar was speaking and singing Japanese.

With regards to other behaviors, Ma Win Tar manifested traits that were masculine in that she preferred to dress as a boy, wore her hair short, and was an aggressive and violent playmate when she was young. Notably, she had a tendency to slap other children across the face, a behavior characteristic of Japanese soldiers but quite rare amongst the Burmese.

Before she became conditioned to the Burmese way of life, Ma Win Tar also exhibited a number of other inherently Japanese traits, expressing a preference for raw foods, for sitting on the ground in the traditional Japanese posture and an aptitude for hard work, for example. She rejected out of hand many of the Burmese customs, refusing to perform the gesture of obeisance upon meeting a Buddhist monk or to adopt the Buddhist teaching of avoiding taking the lives of animals and insects.

Finally, her mother reported that Ma Win Tar had a liking for firearms that was considered to be unconventional, to say the least, in Burmese girls. Once, when her brother showed her part of a firearm he had brought back to the house, she immediately understood how its mechanism worked. Twice she expressed an interest in becoming a soldier. (Ian Stevenson, 1997)

If we continue to confine a search for the solutions to the

riddles of human life to the conventional, accepted, materialistic paradigm for existence, we shall probably continue to fail to find them. Increasingly, we need to start looking to the broader, multidimensional, multiserial context of existence, wherein the keys to understanding the more elaborate complexities of our existence lie. This fact is demonstrated amply in the case of Ma Win Tar.

Chapter Eight

Retrocognitions

> In conscientiology, just as in archeology, we do not excavate the past with pickaxes or explosives, but with tweezers, a brush, and patience.
> —*Wagner Alegretti*

Mahatma Gandhi once said, "It is nature's kindness that we do not remember past births. Life would be a burden if we carried such a tremendous load of memories." In many ways, I concur with this statement. Think of the feuds, grudges, quarrels, disputes and rivalries that would reignite every time you reencountered an enemy from your past. Think of the regrets, guilt, shame, obsessions and passions that would plague you. Much of the karma we have with those closest to us would never be resolved if we all carried baggage that we'd brought from past lives with us. The fact that we recommence each physical life with the memory slate wiped clean, so to speak, provides us with opportunities to reestablish old relationships from a fresh perspective and to settle some karmic issues.

Nonetheless, there is much of value to be learned from remembering our past lives and anyone with the interest, multi-dimensional self-awareness and willingness to devote the time and effort required to recover memories of their past, stands to greatly benefit from this fascinating phenomenon.

This chapter summarizes the research on retrocognitions of conscientiologist and author Wagner Alegretti, who has been researching the projective experience and its associated phenomena and implications since 1980. After meeting Vieira in 1982, Alegretti became a founding member of the International

Institute of Projectiology and Conscientiology (IIPC) in 1988. Several years later, all IIPC offices outside of Brazil formed the International Academy of Consciousness (IAC) of which Alegretti was named, and is at the time of writing, president.

Past-life recall, popularly known as regression, is technically known as retrocognition, from the Latin *retro* meaning back and *cognition* meaning knowledge or to know. A retrocognition therefore, is the process in which the memory of any event from one's past lives, including those spent in the extraphysical dimension between lives, is transferred from the mental body of the consciousness to the physical brain, coming into the area of direct awareness of the individual.

What Defines a True Retrocognition?

As retrocognitions are often experienced during an altered state of consciousness in which there is likely to be some level of discoincidence between the extraphysical body and the physical body, one of the most challenging aspects of the phenomenon is knowing how to be sure that you've had a retrocognition; in other words, knowing how to distinguish the real thing from a dream, a fantasy, or a flashback of a moment in your present life that you had forgotten (e.g. a flashback of a film set in an historical period that you saw when you were a young child).

According to Alegretti, to be sure that a retrocognition is genuine, you should have at least ten coherent retrocognitions about the same experience. So if you have a recollection that you think might be a retrocognition, make note of it in writing and file it in the "to be confirmed" folder to await further verification.

Second, a true retrocognition is remarkable for the quality of the experience in that the minute details of the past event are amplified to the point where you relive it. You are there. You see all the elements that make up the setting—the era, the culture, the location, the weather; you feel the emotions; you understand your relationship with the people around you and perceive the effect they have on you; you hear the sounds and music, the voices and words. A real retrocognition that brings all these factors into play will not be a mediocre experience but will have impact. It will move you in some way. It is this exceptional intensity of the retrocognitive phenomenon that separates it from a common dream or fantasy.

It is also important to note the appreciable differences between retrocognitions and flashbacks. In flashbacks, you are an observer of a scene in which you are involved, whereas in a retrocognition you are an active participant. People also sometimes confuse retrocognitions with what they believe to be time-travel. When you are involved in a scene in which you experience the same sensations as being alive in the physical body but you cannot change or affect your thoughts or actions, you are having a retrocognition.

Robert Monroe recounts several episodes in his first book, *Journeys Out of the Body,* in which he "took over" the life of and "temporarily displaced" the individuality of another man in a sort of double life led while out of the body in an extraphysical dimension. In this other life, he had an ongoing relationship with a woman and her children, a job and a home, etc. and although he was actively involved in the events that took place there he was unable to influence or change what happened in any way. Because of this, it seems probable that Monroe had a series of retrocognitions relating to the same period of his past rather than a double life.

Third, retrocognitions often have some connection to our present life, revealing why we have a specific limitation or skill. For example, a man who likes to date several women concurrently might have a retrocognition that places him in a culture that permits polygamy. A woman who is bossy, conceited and accustomed to being the center of attention might recall a privileged life as a noble woman or royal.

Retrocognitions are also usually of deeply emotional moments. These are the occasions we are most likely to remember from our past as well as our present lives. But don't expect the memories to come prettily ordered in sequence with the most recent life first. They will be random and may relate to an intermissive period as well as a physical existence.

The Benefits of Retrocognitions

Beyond satisfying our natural curiosity, retrocognitions can provide us with important insights into why we are the way we are—why we suffer from certain limitations, blockages, fears and phobias; why we have a particular Achilles heel and other weak traits; why we have remarkable strong traits that have clearly not been inherited from our family and why we are sometimes driven by powerful intuitions that are difficult to rationalize.

In accessing our own personal historical files and finding out where we have lived, who we have been and what we have accomplished or failed to achieve in past lives, we are presented with invaluable opportunities to solve some of the problems and dilemmas we create for ourselves. In this way, retrocognitions can be therapeutic; curing or relieving some traumas and even physical illnesses.

For example, perhaps you have a retrocognition in which you recall being aboard a sinking ship, understanding your certain fate of drowning a terrifying death many long minutes before succumbing to the cold water or sharks. This would explain a phobia of the water or a fear of being at sea. In a similar fashion, the trauma of a former death through suffocation or smoke inhalation might manifest in this life as a respiratory illness.

In instances such as these, the retrocognitive process allows the sufferer to contextualize and isolate the trauma, and to consider it with the emotional balance that distance allows. This process can diminish the intensity of the effects of the trauma, which in turn makes it harder for extraphysical intruders (who are attracted by that variety of the energy that the subconscious memory produces), to connect to the individual.

Another tangible benefit of retrocognitions is that they shed a long light of truth on the nature of the past connections or associations we have had with various people close to us in this life, offering opportunities to "recycle" relationships that have already endured over many lives and that will continue on into the future due to the strength of the karmic links. In many cases, the retrocognition will confront us with the choice of either repeating certain behavioral patterns in our relationships or doing something new.

For example, perhaps a single mother whose possessive son never approves of her choice of partner and sabotages her attempts to find love, has a retrocognition and sees that she also tolerated his possessiveness and interference in her private life in a previous incarnation, only then their roles were reversed—he was the parent and she was the child. If she understands anything at all about karma, she can conclude that their intimate connection will probably bring them together again in a future life and that unless she makes an effort to change the status quo of their relationship and assert herself now, she will suffer his dominance over her again.

For those who have the maturity to reflect upon the nature of the relationships they've had in the past with people who are close to them today, a healthy dose of sincerity is required to take best advantage of the opportunities to grow that are presented by retrocognitions. We need to be honest about the quality of the connections we share with some people. Empathy and understanding for others, and the wisdom and grace to forgive the past will also help create the space necessary for change and for something new to grow.

Although there are a number of benefits to recalling past lives, the greatest value is in remembering the most recent period between lives. These periods are harder to recall though because they took place in the extraphysical dimension where the existence is a radically different experience to life on earth. We don't even breathe there. So even former physical lives that occurred 3,000 years in the past are easier to recall than an intermissive period that ended only a few decades ago.

A conscious recollection of our last period between lives is such a unique tool for self-knowledge and should be prioritized, because this type of retrocognition might allow us access to the details of the plan for this life that was made for us at that time. Some of us were even involved in conceiving the plan for our upcoming physical life and agreed to it, prior to being born. This life plan, task or mission (in other words, our purpose in life) is an important area of conscientiological research and will be examined in depth in chapter 10. Recalling what we planned to do in this life can have far-reaching consequences. It enables us to see how and where we waste our time, and may prompt us to reprioritize our lives if necessary, to streamline our efforts, energy and resources for the accomplishment of more worthwhile tasks related to our karmic obligations and to our growth and evolution as consciousnesses.

So we can see that the phenomenon of retrocognition can be a catalyst for personal change and growth. It can provide a variety of opportunities to overcome shortcomings, dissipate energetic blockages, heal psychosomatic scars, relieve some physical illnesses, improve our group karma and enhance our self-understanding.

Factors That Block and Inhibit Retrocognitions

Considering the obvious value of the phenomenon, it is frustrating that it is such an elusive experience, but there are many factors that block and inhibit the retrocognitive process.

The process itself works like this. The physical brain, which is only acquired by the consciousness at the commencement of its current physical life, does not hold any memory of one's past lives because it didn't exist then. It is the extraphysical and mental bodies that store the memories of the consciousness, the holomemory being stored in the mental body. So in order for us to access this information, the memories have to be "downloaded" from the more subtle bodies of manifestation to the physical brain.

Low Multidimensional Self-Awareness

One of the factors that blocks this process in the majority of people is a very low level of multidimensional self-awareness, meaning that most people have no knowledge, direct experience or interest in their own nonphysical realities and no motivation to learn. How can a woman preoccupied solely with the rigors of daily survival, who believes that after death she will cease to exist, lucidly recall her most recent intermissive period? How can a man concerned only with the accumulation of material wealth hope to discover the intricate multiserial path of his existence to date? This is not to say that either of these scenarios is impossible; they are not, but they are unlikely.

Lack of Maturity

Another factor that impedes the "download" of memories of past lives to the physical brain is lack of maturity. When we look around us it is plain to see that many people can't even cope with their current life and regularly escape the disappointment, tedium or stress of their reality through drugs, alcohol and medications. If the challenges and demands of this life are too much to deal with, how would these same people cope if they remembered the shames, injustices, sorrows, fears and hardships of previous lives?

Some Memories of Past Lives are Blocked to Spare Us Pain

In addition, the exposure of the nature of past relationships with those close to us would, in many cases, be too difficult to live with. Could you remain balanced and positive knowing, for example, that one of your relatives was your intruder for several hundred years, or that you once had a sexual relationship with an individual who is a member of your immediate family in this life? In the same way the automatic mechanism of memory repression sometimes takes over to protect us from reliving the trauma of past events in this life, the consciousness blocks memories of past lives to spare us the pain. Sometimes the helpers also intervene to protect us from the impact of disturbing memories that would have negative repercussions and they actively prevent the recall of certain lives or periods of our past. They generally allow the recall of milder moments and bring memories in a manageable ascending order of impact.

Energetic Blockages

Energetic blockages, particularly in the frontal chakra, which is located between the eyes, and the crown chakra, which is located at the top of the head, also hinder the flow of information between the nonphysical brain of the extraphysical body and the human brain. The chakras are also responsible for the exchange of energy between the extraphysical body and the physical body so in order for the information to flow freely, the chakras must be open. A good technique for improving the performance of these two chakras is called the cranial circuit of energies. It involves exteriorizing energy out through the crown chakra and then absorbing energy through the frontal chakra, exteriorizing again through the crown chakra and so on until you perceive the energy flowing in a circuit. Practice this for 10–15 minutes and then reverse the direction of the flow for another 10–15 minutes. Regular practice and mastery of the vibrational state will also greatly help to reduce energetic blockages in the frontal and crown chakras and facilitate the flow of information from the parabrain to the brain.

Poor Physical Memory

Poor physical memory can also inhibit lucid retrocognitions. If you can't even remember what you had for dinner last night, how can you hope to remember lucid projections that you experienced in previous lives? Factors such as stress, a lack of nutrition in the diet and lack of sleep, as well as the regular use of drugs like alcohol, tobacco and marijuana similarly do not favor conscious retrocognitions.

The Shock of Rebirth

A major factor responsible for our inability to recall our past is the shock of rebirth, which contrary to popular belief is usually more traumatic than the shock of death. When the physical body dies, the consciousness is freed from the limitations of the more restrictive dense energies of the physical dimension and enters a phase of its existence where it is more expanded, in which it manifests a greater percentage of its true self.

When we are preparing to be reborn again, gestating in our mother's womb, the consciousness attaches itself to a body that is nothing more than a collection of cells. When the consciousness is born, there are automatic processes in place for crying, suckling milk and dirtying the diapers, but little else. There is not even a scrap of self-awareness. The consciousness has to learn everything—how to talk, walk, think, be self-aware, etc. from scratch. Through the process of entering a physical body whose brain is empty and needs to learn everything, the consciousness suffers a massive restriction of lucidity. This abrupt interruption in the continuity of lucidity is very traumatic and profoundly affects the consciousness and generally blocks memories of other existences.

These are the main reasons why we don't remember our past lives.

Precautions

Before we look at some tips and techniques for overcoming these blocking factors and producing retrocognitions, it is important to mention the following precautions to insure you are well-prepared for the experience and to avoid any negative effects:

- In dredging up memories of the past you will probably evoke some extraphysical consciousnesses associated with the events recalled, so it's important to have a good level of energetic self-defense. This can be achieved by working with the vibrational state.
- Avoid any self-intrusions that may be caused by indulging feelings of shame or guilt, and avoid obsessing over past existences.
- Be mature and discerning about what you tell others about your retrocognitions and who you share your recollections with. Not everyone will be equipped to handle information about their past so be circumspect about what you tell to whom. And don't use retrocognitions as a means of seduction.

Although it is possible for several people who know one another to each have separate, individual retrocognitions of a previous life shared together, participating in group regressions in which everyone is physically together is not advisable, as it is possible to experience a retrocognition of another person in these situations. While on the subject, whether in a group or alone, in general it is not advisable to be regressed by someone else, as hypnosis can in some cases be an invasive mechanism. It should, therefore, be used as a last resort to alleviate or cure a serious problem such as a phobia, for instance, and then, only by an experienced, balanced and cosmoethical hypnotherapist. To explore our past in search of self-knowledge, we need to have the tools in our own hands and not be dependent on anyone else. The ideal is that we learn to willfully self-induce a retrocognition through the practice of a technique, or to acquire enough lucidity of our seriality so that retrocognitions can spontaneously occur while the consciousness is manifesting in either the physical, extraphysical or mental body.

As a final precaution, don't waste any information gained via successful retrocognitions by repeating the mistakes of your past.

Tips for Recalling Past Lives

There are several practical things you can do to gain insights into your previous personalities and to optimize your chances of successfully recalling your past existences, such as the following:

- Study the clues to past lives mentioned in the previous chapter. Identify your tendencies and preferences and all of the things with which you have an affinity. Take note of how you feel in certain cities and countries. Do you feel more at home in a country other than the one in which you were born? List the languages you speak; your hobbies and favorite pastimes; as well as any major illnesses, accidents, patterns of energetic blockages, birthmarks or birth defects, phobias, aversions or traumas you have.
- Identify your physical and emotional Achilles heel. These are your mega-weak traits. Make a list of your other weak and strong traits. The most sincere way of doing this is to ask others to draw up these lists for you. And don't ask only the people who like you, but also the people who you don't get along with so well. These people will likely be more forthcoming with their criticisms. To achieve the best results, reassure everyone that there will be no repercussions for their brutal honesty. Compare the lists and

identify where the consensus lies. Any incorrect perceptions you have about yourself will be brought to your attention, so this exercise will help you see yourself for who you really are. And who you really are is the result of your past. For example, are you consumed with your own self-importance, is your ego out of control, can you not accept someone else's authority, do you have a taste for the high life? Chances are you were a leader or held a position of some privilege and power in a previous life.

- Study closely your immediate and extended family and wider circle of friends, particularly those with whom you spend the most time. These are the members of your groupkarma—people with whom you have already lived many lives. Make note of the type of people you like to have around you. What characteristics distinguish the group? Are they artists, tradesmen, businessmen, intellectuals or criminals? Are they altruistic, hedonistic, materialistic or religious? Are they open-minded or governed by societal norms? Studying your group and the things you do together you will provide some clues to the things you did together in the past.
- Keep a diary in which you record your projections, episodes of intrusion, and any psychic perceptions such as clairvoyance, telepathy or intuition you may have. All these may hold clues to past lives.
- Train your physical memory so it doesn't degenerate. Give it a regular workout. Ask your doctor if there are supplements that could improve its performance.
- Nurture the attributes of curiosity and neophilia. In other words, open yourself to new experiences and ideas by traveling to new places, talking to new people and participating in new activities. When you are interested in your life, you observe more, remember more and provide the mental body with plenty of stimulation.

- Strive to achieve and maintain a good level of emotional stability. The ideal condition for achieving lucid retrocognitions is one in which we are open and curious and our rationality is more dominant than our emotionality. A good technique for improving emotional balance is to aim to achieve ten consecutive days without having an emotional outburst such as throwing a temper tantrum, crying out of self pity, drinking too much or getting horribly depressed. And then try to beat that record and last eleven days and so on. If eventually you manage to stay emotionally calm for 100 days, or even more, you will see that you are a different person.
- Exteriorize energies in your bedroom to cleanse and improve the quality of the energetic field and to create the protective shield that was explained in chapter 4. This will facilitate quality sleep, which is important, as a lack of it can block our memory.

Techniques for Producing Retrocognitions

Beyond these practical tips for optimizing our chances of recalling past lives, there are several techniques for producing lucid retrocognitions that are known to work. Although success cannot be guaranteed, anyone with the motivation, determination and will to succeed can achieve positive results.

- Try to increase the quantity and lucidity of your out-of-body experiences. As the memories of our past lives are stored in the mental body and the parabrain of the extraphysical body, we can more readily access this information when the consciousness manifests directly in these vehicles of manifestation, as happens during an OBE or during other altered states of consciousness in which the extraphysical body is partially separated from the physical body, such as the hypnagogic and hypnopompic states (the period between wakefulness and sleep and vice versa, respectively).

- Choose meeting one of your helpers outside of the body as a target for a conscious projection. Ask him something specific about one of your previous lives. But be responsible with your motivation for wanting to know.
- Another target could be to meet with the mentor of the helpers in your karmic group, the advanced extraphysical consciousness with whom you agreed what your purpose in this life would be during your last intermissive period. Ask him to remind you what you agreed if you don't already know.
- Or try to project to your extraphysical hometown. There you can meet the extraphysical members of your groupkarma and be reminded of the relationships you have shared in the past.
- Study some personalities, both contemporary and historical, that interest you and whom you admire. Draw up a list of names and then study each of them to see if you resemble any of them. If you find someone whose traits are uncannily similar to yours, it is possible that either you were that person or that he or she was a member of your karmic group. Again, file the information in the "to-be-confirmed" folder, pending further verification.
- Perform a retrocognitive self-hypnosis. This is how it works. First, prepare to have a projection. Imagine you're on the edge of an expanse of lawn. In the middle of the lawn there are a series of steps that lead down into a corridor. Picture yourself slowly and calmly going down the stairs, counting in reverse order as you go, 30, 29, 28, etc., and know that what awaits you at the end of the corridor is your past. Say things to yourself between taking the steps and counting the numbers such as "I am

getting closer to a previous life." "My helpers will help me." "I am not afraid." "I have no anxiety or fear." "I will not be surprised." "I will remember everything when I return." You can pre-record the prompts and play them back for a more effective self-hypnosis. When you reach the end of the corridor you will see many doors on both sides. Use your intuition to select one. Don't panic if you open the door and are confronted with a scene from your past. This technique is known to work but it might take some practice to achieve results so be prepared to persist.

- Experiment in a retrocognitarium such as can be found at the Center for Higher Studies of Conscientiology (CHSC) where Vieira is based at the Iguassu Falls in Brazil. This is a laboratory for self-research that has been especially designed for producing retrocognitions. Architectural, psychological and energetic conditions, among other physical and nonphysical elements, have been arranged in such a way as to diminish external interference from the environment and to enhance opportunities for recalling past lives. Everyone is welcome. Another retrocognitarium is planned for the research campus of the International Academy of Consciousness (IAC) in Évoramonte, Portugal. Or, if you are sufficiently motivated, you can build your own.

If you devote the time and invest the effort into putting these tips and techniques into practice, and if you persist with your efforts, you will predispose yourself to having retrocognitions.

I would like to conclude this chapter by quoting from an essay written by Alegretti whose book, *Retrocognitions: An Investigation into the Memory of Past Lives and the Period between Lives,* I highly recommend to anyone interested in furthering their knowledge of this subject.

The most efficient approach to retrocognitions is: have as many retrocognitions as you can of your past lives to know what you should not be doing again (negative repetition), and have retrocognitions of your last period between lives to know exactly what you should be doing. In this way you will have a much better chance of taking advantage of the opportunities presented to you by life for learning and helping the evolution of others. (Wagner Alegretti)

PART THREE

The Evolution of the Consciousness

The great history of out-of-body exploration is just beginning to be written, and at its core this history is truly about the evolution of the consciousness beyond the façade of matter.
—*William Buhlman*

Chapter Nine

The Evolutionary Process

> Apply yourself both now and in the next life. Without effort, you cannot be prosperous. Though the land be good, you cannot have an abundant crop without cultivation.
> —*Plato*

A third fundamental principle of conscientiology is that the consciousness evolves.

All life-forms share the common objective of evolving. Even the simplest single-celled organisms have a basic instinct to improve and become more complex.

If we take into account the broader, more detailed picture of what it means to be a consciousness as has been described in the previous chapters, it is clear that physical life, rather than being meaningless or arbitrary, provides us with a sophisticated, challenging environment that is rich in opportunities to better ourselves and to mature—in other words, to evolve.

Once we begin to recognize this and to purposefully engage in our evolution, life starts to take on more meaning, for the real currency of life is what lasts, what we take away with us when we die. Our status in the extraphysical dimension is not determined by how much wealth we accumulated in the previous life but by our level of evolution. So if we return to the extraphysical dimension when we die in a better condition than when we last left it to be reborn, and if we helped others to do the same during our lifetime, then we can leave this life with the deep satisfaction of knowing that we made it count.

The process of our evolution has already been taking place for many thousands of years and it takes place wherever we are along the multiexistential cycle, bearing in mind that we are multidimensional beings—sometimes our focus is physical, sometimes it is extraphysical. During all of our past lives and intermissive periods we have had many experiences, we've made mistakes and hopefully learned something from them, we've acquired new intelligences and skills, we've increased our knowledge of a range of subjects, we've developed new capacities and attributes, we've experienced a variety of relationships with others, and as a result of all this we have become wiser and have evolved into more complex beings.

You will remember from the previous chapter that during the process of rebirth the consciousness suffers a massive restriction of lucidity during which the memories of previous existences are blocked. So in order to evolve, to build upon the extensive knowledge, experience and wisdom that we've already accumulated during our past lives, first we have to recover our awareness of what we already know. Fortunately, the process of gradually manifesting more of the personality that we really are is to some degree quite a natural one. This is how it works.

Recovery of Awareness

When a consciousness is reborn, on the first day of life in the new physical body, it has almost no awareness of itself or anything else. But from that day on, each day it breathes in the new physical body, it recovers its awareness through the regular everyday experiences of life. As we grow, we experience emotions; we go to school to study our language, history, science and maths; we play games and sports; we make connections with others and we start to develop our own personality. We recover many things that we knew before and we start to be more of who we really are. In other words our awareness starts to return.

The "Basement" of the Consciousness

The phase that lasts from the age of two until the end of puberty, however, is when our level of awareness is at its poorest. This phase is known in conscientiology as the "basement" of the consciousness, or the *consciential basement*. What is in your actual basement? If it's anything like mine, it's probably home to a chaotic pile of trunks, boxes and moldy old suitcases filled with things you don't use or need any more, and other rubbish that should have been thrown out long ago. In a similar fashion, the consciential basement is a period during which we exhibit behavior that will be of no use to us once we become adults and that we need to get rid of at some point. For example, children love to play tricks like ringing old people's doorbells then running away, just to disturb them. This shows a lack of respect for others. Most of us probably did plenty of things like this when we were young, but if we wouldn't do them now that we are adults, they do not represent who we really are. Take another example. Let's say a child likes to torture insects for fun by picking off their limbs and wings. Perhaps this is just his consciential basement. But if he's still amusing himself by torturing insects when he grows up, if he hasn't overcome this tendency from his consciential basement, then it would seem that this behavior represents who he really is—the person doesn't respect life in general.

So the consciential basement is the phase during which the individual knows more but is manifesting less; it is when the consciousness manifests as a poor resemblance of itself.

The consciential basement includes traits such as aggression and egocentricity, an inability to concentrate, lack of organization, lack of maturity and respect and attitudes that are not ethical. Many fears and insecurities also reside at this low level of awareness. So the consciential basement is like the sewerage of the personality, for want of a better expression.

The lower chakras predominate during the consciential

basement, i.e. the spleen chakra, umbilico-chakra and sex chakra. These chakras are related to the primitive needs of physical survival, things like territorialism, food, water, shelter, sex and other forms of gratification but not to things like studying or self-improvement. During the conscientia basement a person is a slave to the energies of these lower chakras rather than the master of them. This prevents the individual from recovering full awareness of who he really is and inhibits his evolution. An example of this is when a person becomes obsessed with sex. He (or she) spends so much time thinking about it that he finds it difficult to concentrate on anything else, and the need for gratification becomes the focus of his life. In situations like this a person's decision-making abilities are often negatively affected as his rationality is completed dominated by his physical urges.

So the starting point for investing in our evolution as consciousnesses is to overcome our conscientia basement, i.e. our infantile tendencies and our "animal" drives and instincts. In order to become the maximum of who we really are, this should ideally be achieved between the ages of 18 and 26, the age at which we reach biological maturity.

Factors That Keep Us Stuck in the Conscientia Basement and Tips for Overcoming Them

Genetics

Examples of traits inherited via our genetics that can keep us stuck in the conscientia basement include laziness, self-indulgence, low self-discipline or self-motivation, mean-spiritedness, aggression, arrogance, isolation from others, and manipulation and control of others, to name a few.

A good technique for overcoming these and other traits that paralyze our evolution is the strong and weak traits formula. In the previous chapter, I described how you can correct any false perceptions you may have of yourself by asking others to draw up a list of your strong and weak traits. You can use the resulting list for this exercise, or, if you're not ready to involve others, you can make this a personal exercise that you do alone. Success in this case, of course, depends on your willingness to face yourself with sincerity. Once you have the list, put the two columns, strong traits and weak traits, side by side. Our strong traits dynamize our efforts to evolve, so the aim of this exercise is to maximize the evolutionary profit you can derive from them by seeing how you can use them to overcome your weak traits.

For example, perhaps you are the type of person who hates conflict of any kind and because of it you fail to stand up for yourself properly. That is a weak trait that may be undermining your efforts to achieve what you want at work or in your personal life. But perhaps you identify that one of your strong traits is your inherent self-respect. So your aim is to start behaving in a way that is coherent with that and to stop people from walking all over you even if the price to pay means having to deal with conflict.

Another example, perhaps even knowing it's not ethical, you love to gossip and involve yourself in other people's business. This is one of your weak traits. But maybe on your list of strong traits you identify that you have a strong will. So the idea is that you use your will to force yourself to walk away from any situation in which others are gossiping. Every time. No exceptions.

Paragenetics and Holomemory

Other factors that can keep us stuck in our consciential basement are our paragenetics and holomemory. As they transport scars accumulated from past life traumas to the current life via the extraphysical and mental bodies, they may be the cause of unhealthy pathologies and neuroses such as addictions, aversions and phobias that range from the mild to the obsessive.

For example, perhaps you have a phobia of enclosed spaces that is crippling your self-confidence, preventing you from realizing your true potential and hindering your evolution. Or perhaps you have suffered an ordeal such as a rape, a violent attack, or a car accident in which others died, and the resulting trauma has had so much impact that you feel unable to work or function as a normal member of society.

The solution to these types of hindrances is to be prepared to let go of attachments to and repercussions of traumatic experiences.

If we hold on to traumatic experiences and the effects they have on us, be they physical, emotional or mental, we condemn ourselves to suffering from them repeatedly in our future lives. We have to face them at some point either in this life or a future one, so it might as well be today.

Environment

Environmental factors that can hinder us from overcoming our consciential basement stem from the physical environment and the culture into which we were born. For example, were you pressured to marry and have children at a young age—was your life filled with commitments and obligations to others before you even knew who you were? Did the religion in which you were raised brainwash you into not questioning its dogmas? What level of education did you have access to?

Some of these factors are difficult to deal with because we have been conditioned to accept them from a very early age. There is a solution to overcoming them, however, and it lies in being prepared to think as an individual, independently of others. This may mean you have to go against the accepted norms of society, even against the beliefs of your friends and family, and rely instead on your own analysis, judgment, personal experiences and reference points when deciding how to prioritize your life. This will undoubtedly be challenging to some extent but the alternative is to live your life a bit like a sheep, unquestioningly following the rest of the flock—behavior that favors stagnation not evolution.

Tips for Recovering More Advanced Levels of Awareness (i.e. Awareness of Who You Are beyond the Physical Body)

We have already seen how, during the period between lives, some lucid individuals are fully conscious of the fact that they are no longer alive in the physical sense; they are aware that they have died; that they have had many previous lives and that they have many lives yet to live. Some, already understanding that the consciousness evolves, plan their next physical life in such a way as to take best advantage of the opportunities to further improve and develop. More about this specific planning is explained in the next chapter.

One of the great challenges that such individuals face as they move through physical life is to recover this more advanced level of awareness; that is, to remember their multidimensional, multiserial existence, and their more advanced skills such as their psychism or their ability to master their energies. If they manage to do this, they can then live their lives in a way that is more coherent with what they planned during their last intermissive period, if they choose.

If you are still reading this book, there is every chance that you are just such a person—that you were lucid in your last period between lives. How do I know? Because these ideas make sense to you, otherwise I assume you would have stopped reading long ago. As I mentioned in chapter 6, many of these ideas are prompting semi-conscious retrocognitions, just helping to remind you of what you already know.

Study Multidimensional Realities

When we study the complexities of multidimensional realities, we trigger the download of information from our mental body, reminding ourselves of so many things we knew and understood before we were born. We start to recover awareness of who we are beyond this physical body, awareness that has been temporarily blocked by our physical existence. My point here being—study the consciousness and all its associated phenomena—read and learn with discernment not only from conscientiology but from a wide variety of sources, and see where the consensus lies. This will prompt you to recover your more advanced levels of awareness until hopefully the maximum amount of awareness corresponding to your evolutionary level has been regained.

Put Theory into Practice

Assuming that we manage to gain this awareness and have experiences that enable us to *know* that we are much more than just the physical body, then in order to evolve we must apply what we know. To know something in theory is not enough because without application nothing changes. Resisting change, however, is a well-documented human foible. In general, people far prefer to stick to the familiar habits that don't present them with any challenges or risks and with the routines that make them feel safe.

But we have two choices. We can either rely on routines and stick to what we know—for most people this means prioritizing short-term concerns that relate to the current, physical life such as survival, and beyond that, material wealth, comfort, pleasure and status. Or we can consciously make decisions based on the fact that as consciousnesses we still have hundreds of lives ahead of us along our multiexistential journey. Increasing your maturity, and thus evolving, requires that you want to live your life in a manner that is coherent with the fact that you are more than just the physical body, that you are a consciousness; and if necessary, that you undertake some personal "recycling" and start to live in a way that is consistent with this reality.

Let me give some examples of the sorts of changes you may

consider initiating if you decide you want to "recycle" your life and prioritize your evolution:

- Let go of attachments to materialism, prestige and indulgence. Of course there is no requirement for anyone to suffer in order to evolve; everyone is entitled to have a decent life, to have a roof over his head, food on the table three times a day and a reasonable level of comfort. But what do we really need beyond that? We can dedicate our lives to accumulating more and more money, properties and cars but we can't take these things with us when we die. They are of no use to us in the extraphysical dimension and they won't be waiting for us when we return to physical life next time. But what else could we achieve with all the time we spend accumulating and maintaining material possessions? What else could we do with our wealth? Who could we help?
- Be determined to be more of who you really are (according to your multidimensional, multiserial history) and be consistent with that throughout your life. Refuse, for example, to allow yourself to get stuck in a rut in which you accept less than what you deserve. If you are not happy with your boyfriend or girlfriend, don't keep complaining about it, do something about it. If you are in a poorly paid profession that you despise, retrain and find something that is more suited to you.
- Make an effort to get rid of behavioral patterns that you justify to yourself even though you know they are not positive. For example, do you fly off the handle at the slightest provocation or inconvenience, making the people in your life tiptoe on eggshells around you, and blaming your short fuse on their frustrating behavior? If so, work at overcoming your weak traits. Don't take them with you into your next life.

For sure, it is easy for me to sit here and write these things and just as easy for you to read them, right? But what about actually doing them? In some cases we're talking about unravelling deep-seated habits and attitudes that we have had for many, many lives, so where and how do we begin?

Harness the Power of Your Mental Body

The key to destroying the root of your problems and recycling your life lies in harnessing the power of your mental body. A good place to start is to apply one of its most powerful attributes, your will, to transform your thoughts, intentions and ideas, and then to align your behavior so it is consistent with them. If you remember what was explained in the chapter on bioenergy, when we alter our thoughts our energies follow suit, as the two are inextricably linked. When you change the way you think, you create a new energetic field around you that will open you up to synchronicities, intuitions, connections and relationships with others that will support what you are trying to achieve.

For an immersive experience in the processes and consequences of changing the way you think, I recommend seeing the highly motivating film *The Secret*. Although it doesn't address the mechanisms of what happens when you change your thoughts from a multidimensional perspective, interviews with high-profile philosophers, authors, healers and ordinary folk alike, provide many real-life accounts and examples of how immensely powerful our thoughts are. Remember, what you think—is. If you truly believe you can accomplish anything you set your mind to, you will. If you truly believe that you are persecuted and that everyone is against you, life will not flow in your favor.

Other attributes of the mental body that are invaluable tools in our evolutionary toolbox are our concentration and attention. If we can develop our capacity to continuously fix our attention on a predetermined objective, the sky is the limit in terms of what we can achieve. We can learn and master some new types of intelligence for example, intelligence of course being another attribute of the mental body. Once upon a time intelligence was measured by one's intelligence quotient (IQ) only, but nowadays it is recognized that intelligence is multifaceted. To take psychic intelligence as just one example of a form of intelligence; think how fantastic it would be if you could develop yours to the point of being able to accurately interpret what was going on around you extraphysically at any given moment and to respond appropriately with your energies to reduce intrusion in your life, increase interaction with your helpers and provide practical assistance to individuals in need. Such an accomplishment would have a significant impact on your level of evolution, and believe me, you *can* do it!

I offer these few suggestions to give you a flavor of the power of the mental body. Look back over chapter 1 that describes the bodies of manifestation of the consciousness—will, concentration, attention and intelligence are just some of the many positive attributes of the mental body listed there. Familiarize yourself with the others, for these are the keys to your evolution. Think about improving those that you already possess and developing those that you don't.

Existential Self-Mimicry: The Stagnation of Consciential Evolution

To conclude this chapter, I would like to expand a little upon the subject of existential self-mimicry, which I briefly referred to in an earlier chapter. It is pertinent to bring it up here because existential self-mimicry is what results when we become complacent with life and don't see any point in changing. It is what results when we don't consciously and actively manage our evolution. Self-mimicry is when we repeat, *ad nauseam*, the same human experiences, professions, partners, lifestyles, nationalities, gender, choices and priorities over many physical lives. It is when there is nothing new from one life to the next. It is a common human tendency to repeat past lives because most of us prefer to do what is easy and what we know. So if we want to better ourselves, we need to identify and eliminate any unnecessary self-mimicry from our lives.

Reading back over this chapter, I can understand you might be feeling a little overwhelmed at this point, thinking that it is beyond your capacity to bring about the changes you feel you need in your life. If so, it might help to keep in mind the following excellent advice from Confucius who wrote:

> "A journey of a thousand miles begins with a single step."

Chapter Ten

Life Plan

> Would any one of us undertake even a journey of a few hundred miles without knowing why, without having some purpose? And yet, so many of us live, undertaking not a chance task, but the great Task of life itself . . . and yet we ask not why.
>
> *—J .J. Van Der Leeuw*

Was My Life Planned?

I would like to preface this chapter by saying that much of the information presented here lies well beyond the conventional paradigm for existence and that there are few experiences you may have had in your normal everyday lives that will enable you to immediately verify some of it for yourself. I refer you back to the introduction in which I explain in detail the many sources of Vieira's research. And as always, I encourage you to use the techniques and other tips described in part 4 to have your own lucid experiences outside the body that will enable you to confirm, or otherwise, the contents of this chapter for yourself.

Some elements of the lives of all of us were decided or planned prior to our birth during our most recent period between lives.

How much planning is undertaken in preparation for a person's upcoming life is largely a function of his level of lucidity between lives. There would be little point in a helper formulating a sophisticated life plan for a consciousness who doesn't know he will have another life and is therefore unable to participate in the process. If the plan isn't stored in the individual's own holomemory, there can be no clues suggestive of a deeper purpose in life for him to retrieve and act upon once he has returned to physical life.

In circumstances like these, helpers who are specialists in evolution will at least plan where and to whom a consciousness will be born, but beyond this, little may be arranged.

Individuals who *are* lucid between lives and aware of the evolutionary process that is natural to all consciousnesses, are often motivated to take advantage of what physical life offers to advance their evolution, to resolve some karmic debts from the past and to contribute towards the evolution of others. A detailed, more complex plan can then be devised during the intermissive period for the accomplishment of these goals. While an individual can be quite involved in planning his future life, the intervention and overall vision of the helpers is nonetheless required to bring together the myriad details of one's personal history and holokarma to create the optimal strategy. (Alegretti, 2004)

The life plan relates specifically to the second half of physical life. During the first half of our lives, up until the age of around 35, we are busy maturing and building a foundation of sorts for our physical existence. We receive an education, we study or train in a profession and then establish ourselves in a long-term job or career; this provides us with some level of financial stability, which in turn enables us to put a roof over our heads. Many people also establish their life partnership during this period, fulfilling their daily needs for love, affection and sex. So during this phase of life we prepare the foundation necessary to support us in the execution of our life plan. The life plan then is devised with the intention of executing it from the age of around 35 onwards.

The life plan is intended for execution during the "executive" phase of physical life.

Of course there are always exceptions to the general rule and a small number of more lucid individuals may become aware of their life plan and start acting on it at an earlier age.

Having a life plan does not mean that it is your fate to carry it out. Don't forget, you always have the right to exercise your free will. So even if you were involved in planning the details of your forthcoming life, and you remember what you planned, you can always choose to do something different. Fate is a myth. This is evidenced by the fact that a relatively small percentage of people with a life plan actually succeed in executing it. The reasons for this are explained later in the chapter.

The purpose of having a life plan then is to optimize the opportunities for the evolution of ourselves and others.

In theory, the evolution of the consciousness is a personal individual experience, but on a practical level humans evolve much faster in groups—through interacting with others. To give an example, imagine there is a hermit who, in pursuit of "enlightenment," decides to spend his entire life meditating alone on top of a rock on a mountain peak, isolated from the whole of humanity. While he may develop his capacity to control his thoughts and his ability to master some altered states of consciousness, do you think his isolation will help him to evolve faster? No it won't, simply because there is a limit to the amount and variety of challenges he will face and therefore a limit to how much he can learn and improve himself in one lifetime. Being in a group on the other hand, requires that we develop the skills needed to deal with all the issues that arise from our relationships with others. For example, do you have the maturity to accept the authority of your superiors at work? Can you cope with having your weak traits exposed as happens when you develop an intimate connection with someone? Are you prepared to make sacrifices to help others or do you only offer assistance when it costs you nothing? And whom do you help? Is it just your family and friends or do you also help people you don't know?

A physical life that is rich in relationships and contact with others, with challenges and experiences, presents us with opportunities to evolve every day.

The life plan is always pitched at the exact level of a person's capacity, taking into account his personal strong and weak traits; meaning, everyone is capable of fulfilling his purpose in life as long as there is no self-corruption. Self-corruption is when we betray our own principles; it is when there is no coherence between what we know and what we do. In other words, if we fail to accomplish what we planned to do in life, the problem is not in the planning but in the execution.

Having said that, the life plan is not set in stone, but is mutable. It is constantly being updated and redefined to take best advantage of the opportunities that come our way, and to allow for those opportunities we miss as well as for unforeseen circumstances. So there are back-up plans in place. For example, perhaps your original life plan required that you live in a particular country where you would have opportunities to address certain karmic issues with your group. So you were born there but let's say at a very young age your country was invaded, your people became refugees and dispersed, and you were separated from your family and taken to live in a foreign country. In cases like this, the helpers will modify your life plan to take into account your new circumstances. So the life plan is flexible, but we should take care not to use this as an excuse not to do it.

Mini and Maxi Life Plans

Not everyone has a specific plan for the upcoming physical life. Consider this fact: more than half of the world's population—over three billion people—lives on less than two US dollars per day.[4] For them and many others trying to live on little more, the daily ordeals of survival consume all of their time and resources. Their experience of existence is closer to an instinctive type of life based around fulfilling biological needs.

But any individual who was lucid during the period between lives will have a life plan or a specific purpose to his existence that falls into one of the following two categories: the mini life plan or the maxi life plan.

The Mini Life Plan

The mini life plan is a smaller, simpler plan that is dedicated to addressing egokarmic and groupkarmic issues. As it is more concerned with personal issues and less concerned with evolution, it is usually not so complex. For example, a person is born into a certain family to deal with his groupkarma. He then marries and has five children and perhaps ends up supporting his aging parents or a disabled sibling as well. He is the epicenter, the pillar of his family unit, and does a wonderful job of assuming responsibility for the many people dependent on him. This is an example of a mini life plan dedicated to addressing one's groupkarma.

Although the mini life plan is not so complex, that is not to say it can't include multidimensional aspects. A shaman in Africa who acts as a bridge between humans and extraphysical consciousnesses as part of his work as a healer is also dealing with his groupkarma. It is still a mini life plan, but it has a multidimensional perspective.

The Maxi Life Plan

The maxi life plan is a more advanced strategy that is undertaken knowingly and is dedicated to addressing polykarmic issues, i.e. issues that have ramifications for the whole of humanity. Cosmoethical behavior; personal incorruptibility; a fraternal, universalistic attitude and assistance to others beyond one's immediate family and friends, chiefly through clarification (when you teach others to help themselves), are the hallmarks of a maxi life plan. A hypothetical example of a maxi plan is a life intentionally dedicated to combating the exploitation of the weak by the strong. Some of the wealthiest corporate retail manufacturers, including globally recognizable brands, earn vast profits by exploiting the local labor in impoverished nations around the world. Workers suffer 16-hour days, endure constant risks to their health and safety, live in over-crowded housing and are paid barely enough to survive on for their efforts. An individual who chooses to work with an international organization, such as the International Labor Organization (ILO), who purposely devises and implements programs aimed at educating vulnerable workers on basic employment rights and local labor laws, could be executing a maxi life plan.

Other examples of maxi life plans include dedicating one's life to: brokering peace in the Middle East; inventing an affordable cure for AIDS; campaigning against the global destruction of the planet; challenging nations to improve their human rights; and researching sustainable energy resources.

Adaptability and more constant modification are usually required at this more advanced level. You may need to develop yourself to deal with people from many different countries and cultures or you may need a special physical body, one that has an exceptionally strong immune system and doesn't easily fall ill, for example.

But not all maxi life plans have a multidimensional component. Take the example of physicist Albert Einstein. His revolutionary theories shaped our current understanding of space and time but his life plan addressed physical realities only. Another example is that of Mahatma Gandhi, who obtained independence for India, freeing one billion Indians from British rule through a nonviolent campaign of civil disobedience. There was no multidimensional element to his life plan as such. A maxi plan that did have multidimensional aspects is illustrated well by the life of the late Jose Arigo, a celebrated Brazilian psychic surgeon who healed many thousands of sick and dying people while channeling a consciousness he claimed was formerly a doctor.

The level of complexity of a person's life plan, therefore, is not determined by the presence or absence of transdimensional work. What distinguishes a maxi plan from a mini plan is whether or not a person is consciously looking for evolution for himself and others. To put it another way, a life plan completed unconsciously is a mini plan.

The thresholds that separate mini and maxi plans are didactic only. Consider the case of a primary school teacher who loves his job and is excellent at what he does. If he spends 40 years of his life teaching young children how to be the very best they can be, inspiring confidence and openness in them, and helping them to realize their every potential, then he is working with individuals beyond his own groupkarma and is executing a kind of *midi* life plan.

Success and Failure in the Endeavor to Carry Out One's Life Plan

Completion of our life plan, regardless of whether it is a mini or maxi life plan, is essential for our evolution. While some people strive to complete their task, others waste the opportunity that life presents to them and fail in this endeavor.

Generally, people who are aware of their purpose in life and dedicate themselves to fulfilling it, fall into one of two categories.

In the first category are those who are initially off track with what they planned but later correct themselves, get back on track and go on to complete their life task. To give an example, perhaps someone with lucidity in the intermissive period who had already been a doctor in previous lives, planned to become a plastic surgeon in his forthcoming life to help underprivileged people with physical deformities. Let's say that the person was then born in the US and trained to become a plastic surgeon but was seduced by the money to be made in cosmetic surgery and established a thriving business and comfortable life for himself in Los Angeles. So he dedicates himself to consumerism for several years and is off track with what he planned. At some point, however, something happens to make him question his choices in life. He undergoes an internal renovation that then brings about an external shift in the form of a new career. He joins Doctors Without Borders and spends the rest of his professional life traveling third-world countries, using his skills as a plastic surgeon to help alleviate the suffering of poor people born with deformities and victims of war and genocide.

For some people in a situation such as this, reprioritizing their life to give proper attention to their life plan can be a huge challenge. Perhaps by the time they realize they need to make changes, they already have commitments in the form of partners who have no interest in improving themselves, children who take up all of their time, or a job that is not ethical. So some of the changes they make to get back on track with what they planned, both internal and external, can be quite extreme. But at the moment a person decides to rearrange his life and prioritize his inner reform, he will attract the attention of helpers who will come to assist, so he is by no means alone in his endeavors.

In general, individuals in this category are more influenced by their environment and genetics than by their paragenetics.

In the second category are those people who are never off track with what was planned but are very clear about what they want to do from a young age. They prioritize their lives to facilitate the accomplishment of their purpose in life and start fulfilling it before the age of 35.

People like this know what they're supposed to be doing from adolescence. They already have some awareness of their intermissive period and of a "mission" in life as these realities are still "fresh" so they start looking for answers, planning their lives and giving assistance to others before reaching adulthood. They probably know what their profession should be and choose something that will both enable them to help more people and provide them with the financial security necessary to support their own development.

When such people make the major decisions about life such as choosing a partner or deciding if they want to have children, they invert the tendencies and norms that society imposes on us and end up with fewer commitments that prevent them from pursuing their life plan. For example, rather than living solely to become parents, they prefer to develop their psychism, master their energies and work with polykarma. So these individuals don't adopt society's values and this is because the influence of their paragenetics is stronger than the influence of their environment.

People who fall into the latter category have a greater chance of completing their life plan than those in the former, but what is important is not when you gain awareness of your purpose in life, but whether or not you fulfill it. In one of his books entitled *Our Evolution*, Vieira describes the successful completion of one's life task as "the greatest triumph of the human consciousness."

Ten Reasons We Fail to Complete Our Life Plan

When we are sidetracked from our evolution and the execution of our life plan was not satisfactory, we often experience a kind of indefinable discomfort or frustration with life.

Some life plans are not accomplished because the person died prematurely. But the majority of people with a life plan fail to execute it for other reasons. It is roughly estimated that only a quarter of people who have a life plan, be it mini or maxi, manage to fully complete it. This is not altogether surprising when we consider all the sources of opposition and interference, both internal and external. Let's take a look at ten of the major culprits.

Reference Points and Conditionings

Society and our external environment in general pressure us with strong ideas, assumptions and expectations. Most wealthy western societies are conditioned towards robotic, routine behavior lacking in self-awareness. Their references points for success are material wealth, professional status, marriage and children, thus the self-propagating cycle of the nine to five, the mortgages, the prestigious schools, the holidays, and so on it goes.

Perspective

A perspective of existence that focuses only on physical life and fails to include multidimensional, multiexistential realities such as energetic fields, past lives, future lives and karma.

Emotionality

Emotionality usually has the effect of clouding our rationality and diminishing the clarity and serenity of our decisions.

Relationships

Partners who are skeptical of or oppose the idea that we are more than the physical body.

Physical Intrusion

Sometimes our families or partners henpeck and pressure us to do what they want, e.g. run the family business, have children, etc. Are the members of your evolutionary group helping you or preventing you from achieving your life plan? Remember, some of our intruders are not extraphysical.

Extraphysical Intrusion

And then there are those who are. Many life plans with great potential for productivity are thwarted by extraphysical intrusion. In most cases this happens because people are both unaware of the process of intrusion and don't know how to de-intrude themselves.

Extraphysical Blind Guides

Other extraphysical interference can come in the form of blind guides who prefer us to mimic past lives—to live the same kind of life and do the same things that we did together with them in our past.

Self-Mimicry

Yet often we need no encouragement from our blind guides. We want to mimic our past because we prefer to do what's easy and what we know rather than face the unknown.

Procrastination and Postponement

These are the scourges of existential completism.

Lack of Motivation

A lack of motivation for inner reform is an internal problem, one that comes from inside of us. If we are looking for excuses not to carry out our life plan and to have a calm, comfortable life instead, they're easy to find. The bottom line is that many people make excuses because they're unwilling to pay the price of evolution—and there is a price to pay. My own experience of attempting to fulfill what I understand to be my purpose in life is that it requires effort, tenacity and sacrifice, and is full of challenges. But when the going gets tough I remind myself that my interest in fulfilling my purpose in life is not conditional on it being easy and I just keep going.

To explain this another way, take a look at the diagram opposite.

The dot in the center of the inner circle is the consciousness and the inner circle is the comfort zone. When we live life within our comfort zone we experience lower levels of stress, conflict,

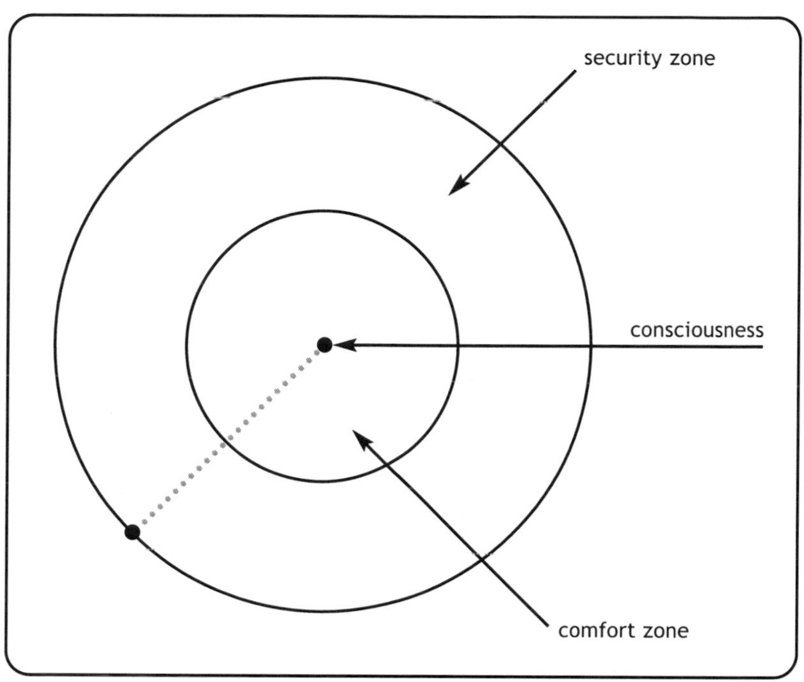

Comfort zone and security zone (Santos, 2003)

challenge and risk but there are still problems. We may feel frustration, disappointment and even angst because we are off track with our life plan. So while life is manageable in the comfort zone it is ultimately unfulfilling, because there is no growth at this level.

The next ring out is the security zone. Although life here doesn't demand anything of us that's beyond our capacity, we are faced with and have to handle complex situations. Life is more stressful and unpredictable, but we are happy because we are on track with what we planned. Realistically, we can't expect to evolve without stress, because if there's no stress we're not being challenged or stretched. We should aim to live our lives at the outermost edge of the security zone; in other words, at the very limit of our capacities, because this is where evolution takes place. So the question you need to ask yourself is, what price, if any, are you prepared to pay for your evolution?

These are ten examples of the more common sources of interference that prevent people from successfully executing their mission in life.

At a certain point in time, the helpers recognized just how difficult it was even to remember one's life plan in physical life, let alone execute it. So, in the same way that we are here, learning about other dimensions and studying the evolution of the consciousness, the helpers developed a course in which lucid *extraphysical* consciousnesses study the physical dimension and evolution during the period between lives, with the objective of successfully executing their life mission in the forthcoming physical life. This course is known as the intermissive study course.

The Intermissive Study Course

As I mentioned in chapter 3, the helpers have different areas of specialty or expertise. The helpers who oversee the intermissive course, known as evolutionary orientors, are experts in evolution, are more advanced in terms of evolution than most other helpers and are the mentors of the helpers of our evolutionary group.

During the intermissive course, evolutionary orientors and helpers give a series of theoretical and practical classes on subjects such as multidimensional self-awareness, seriality, life plan, hindrances to evolution in the physical dimension, free will, the practice of lucid projection, bioenergy, polykarma, retrocognitions and cosmoethics. It is quite obvious then why those of you who have attended an intermissive course will feel a sense of affinity with the ideas discussed in this book.

While intermissive study courses are accessible to all consciousnesses who are motivated to attend, there are some commonsense prerequisites for joining. To be eligible you must have

- passed through the second death and recovered extraphysical lucidity, i.e. realized you are no longer alive in the physical sense, or in the event that you died as a child, you must have recovered the condition of extraphysical adulthood;
- acquired some multidimensional experience, e.g. accept existential seriality as a reality;
- and already achieved a reasonable evolutionary level.

How Our Life Plan Is Decided

Optimizing Opportunities for Evolution

As mentioned at the start of this chapter, assuming we are lucid during the period between lives, we can participate in the analysis and planning of our forthcoming physical life. We do this in conjunction with a team of extraphysical helpers who map out its key themes. The evolutionary orientor of our karmic group will make some final suggestions on the plan that we will most likely accept.

Of course the key consideration that is taken into account when putting together the life plan relates to the conditions that will optimize our evolution. Who will be the most suitable parents for us, can they provide us with a decent education, which potential life partners can support and assist us in our goals, what nationalities and cultures can provide conditions that are appropriate and optimal for us?

Often the evolutionary orientor gives us two or three options of where and to whom we could be born (he may even get involved in creating some synchronicities that allow our future parents to meet if they haven't already), and then we can choose the option that we want. But while you might choose, say, option A as it will provide you with an opportunity to address certain aspects of your development that you think should be prioritized, the evolutionary orientor may bring other points to your attention that you didn't think were so important and would be best addressed by option B. So while he doesn't impose anything on you—the decisions are primarily yours—he is there to help you to see the bigger picture.

Matching Skills with Needs

Another strategy he uses to help formulate our life plan is an analysis of our strong and weak traits, as he aims to match up our skills with our own individual needs, with the needs of our group and with those of humankind. For example, some instructors and volunteers involved in conscientiology around the world, rather than waiting for their next intermissive period to start planning their next life, are already anticipating future lives in China. There are some parallels between the Chinese culture and conscientiology, particularly with respect to the understanding of bioenergy. These individuals would be able to assist in China by providing a more updated, scientific context for some of their cultural aspects, and in so doing, help China to bridge to the West at a time when it will arguably be the dominant power on the planet.

Evolutionary Partners

Something of great interest to many people actively pursuing a life plan is to identify the person that they planned to spend their life with (if they are not already with that person). But just like the life plan itself, the evolutionary partnership we planned is not *destined* to be, as such. In most instances, several sets of potential partnerships will have been identified. Partner A (for want of a better expression) is usually the person who will most optimize the opportunities for your evolution and is also the person with whom you would share the highest level of spontaneous love, intimacy and connection. If unexpected events or circumstances prevent you from meeting your partner A (e.g. he or she dies in a car accident while still a teenager) or you don't connect with this person as planned, the helpers will try to arrange for you to meet your partner B, C or D, etc. As you can imagine, this can require a lot of work on their behalf.

To explain how our evolutionary partner is selected, the partnership itself is one that lives in coherence with the fact that we are more than just the physical body; it focuses on and prioritizes the accomplishment of the life task of each partner, and it achieves results in terms of the evolution of both partners.

So our partner in evolution is an individual who helps us to

- fulfill our purpose in life,
- analyze our strong and weak traits,
- become more mature and cosmoethical,
- become more willing and able to help others,
- master our energies,
- develop our psychism,
- and become more aware of the multidimensional and multiserial aspects of existence.

And you do the same for them. In time, you share substantial areas of each other's life plans and you support each other in their execution.

It is important to understand however that the evolutionary partnership is not a type of utopia in which all relationship problems are resolved. Challenges will always be faced when one is consciously trying to evolve.

Finding Your Evolutionary Partner

Perhaps you are already with your evolutionary partner, or perhaps you recognize that the person you are with is not supportive of your efforts to grow and evolve, or even prevents you from accomplishing what you planned. Or maybe you are single. If you are looking for your evolutionary partner, the important thing to remember is that common underlying feelings and ideas will always draw likeminded people together. Living your life in coherence with the ideas associated with the evolutionary partnership will cause you to shine energetically and create synchronicities that facilitate you meeting others who share similar broad goals.

Moratoriums

When a person was supposed to die (e.g. jumps out of a plane and his parachute fails to open at 8000 ft.) and receives an extension of life (e.g. lands in a haystack thick enough to cushion his fall), sometimes this is referred to as a moratorium, meaning the person was granted a kind of reprieve from death. Sometimes a person is granted what is known in conscientiology as an existential moratorium, which is an extension of physical longevity granted for the specific purpose of allowing more time to accomplish part of or to complete a life plan. Again, it is the evolutionary orientor who is responsible for such an intercession. A near-death experience (NDE) in which a person meets his orientor and obtains information that prompts an evolutionary crisis that results in significant changes to his life is an example of an existential moratorium. This can happen when a person is sidetracked from his life plan.

There are two types of existential moratoriums.

Minor Existential Moratorium

A minor existential moratorium is when a person was going to die but is given more time to complete his life plan regardless of whether it's a mini or a maxi. Nominated for a Nobel Peace Prize in 1998 and highly regarded as a man of forgiveness, tolerance, peace and compassion, it seems likely that the late King Hussein of Jordan received several minor moratoriums to allow him further opportunities to complete a maxi life plan—to broker peace in the Middle East. To quote a book about his life written by his fourth wife, Queen Noor, "Attempts on King Hussein were the stuff of legend." At the age of 16, he survived the first attempt on his life (the first of more than ten, and the same one in which his grandfather King Abdullah was assassinated) when the bullet aimed at his chest hit a medal that his grandfather had insisted he wear that morning. He went on to survive an air ambush by Syrian MiG jets, road ambushes, attempts to poison his food and nose drops, wars with various Arab neighbors and invasions by the PLO. He fought off coup attempts and overcame renal cancer in 1992 before finally succumbing to non-Hodgkin's lymphoma in 1999. (Queen Noor, 2005)

Major Existential Moratorium

A major existential moratorium is when a person has successfully accomplished a maxi life plan and was going to die but merits and is given new tasks by the evolutionary orientor and additional time to execute them. In such cases, the helpers may sponsor "renovations" to the person's physical body to support the moratorium.

Melancholy and Euphoria Related to Failure or Success in One's Life Plan

When people are off track with their life plan they sometimes become melancholic, without knowing why. An imprecise malaise that they can't quite put their finger on settles in their gut and life feels empty and unfulfilling. Failure to complete the life plan sometimes manifests therefore as depression or even as a mid-life crisis—for what is a mid-life crisis but an intangible sense of having failed?

Do you know any cantankerous old people who are "glass half empty" pessimistic? This, too, can be a common manifestation of melancholy associated with the realization that one has led a superficial existence and done little of value—and in the case of the aged, one that is further exacerbated by the knowledge that it's too late to start over.

What about you? If you died right now would you feel satisfied with what you have accomplished so far?

Melancholy related to the unsuccessful execution of one's life plan can also be experienced after death, particularly by those who are more lucid. This is known as extraphysical melancholy.

If you have a life plan, your evolutionary orientor may sponsor a panoramic review of your life after your death so you can analyze, evaluate and learn from your performance with his guidance, and also understand that your every thought, action and inaction had consequences for others.

How do you think you would you feel if, during your life review, you saw that you had all the opportunities, resources and contacts to successfully execute your life plan but you got off-track and failed? This is what causes extraphysical melancholy. This is a particularly distressing condition to be in, as we know that not only through making inappropriate choices did we miss opportunities to evolve, but that those opportunities can never be recovered.

On the other hand, when you know you are on track with your life plan you can feel euphoric. You are aware of your plan, you know you can accomplish it, you are filled with the strength and energy to do so and you are motivated to advance further in the next life. It is normal that you will also encounter problems and challenges because this is the nature of evolution, but they don't get you down.

You can also experience euphoria after death—extraphysical euphoria. You look back on your life with the evolutionary orientor, and seeing that you managed to accomplish your life plan as intended, you feel a deep and abiding sense of satisfaction and fulfillment.

Chapter Eleven

Identifying Your Purpose in Life

> If you go to work on your goals, your goals will go to work on you. If you go to work on your plan, your plan will go to work on you. Whatever good things we build end up building us.
>
> —*Jim Rohn*

Even though appearances can suggest that all is well in our world and that our life is on track, e.g. we have a fulfilling career, financial independence and family and friends around us, sometimes we feel empty inside. We have a strong intuition that something is missing from our lives—that there is something else we are supposed to be doing only we don't what that is. These sensations can indicate a life plan we haven't yet fulfilled.

If you feel this way, start asking yourself the question, "What am I here to do in this physical life?"

It's a big question, obviously, and setting about finding the answers can seem daunting. Fortunately there are several tools and resources at hand to help you to recall or identify your life plan. Take a look at the following:

Personal Strong and Weak Traits Formula

You have already learned in previous chapters how to identify your strong and weak traits. I would recommend for this purpose that you tap into the knowledge and experiences that your friends, family, colleagues and even foes have of you, to enrich and bring more objectivity to the lists of your personal traits. Remember, your strong traits include all of your qualities, attributes, aptitudes, capabilities, skills, intelligences and talents while your weak traits include your vices, defects, limitations, inabilities, bad habits and immaturities.

The resulting lists, two columns side by side, hold clues not only to your past, but also to your present. How so?

First, our life is planned in such a way that the accomplishment of the goals we set ourselves requires that we draw on our unique combination of positive traits. It makes sense to draw on as many of our strengths as possible if we are striving to achieve something significant, doesn't it? So for the purpose of this exercise, rather than analyzing each of your strong traits in isolation, try to see what is unique about the *combination* of your strengths. Let's go back to the example of the plastic surgeon in the previous chapter who was making his fortune performing breast enhancements in LA and was off-track with his life plan. If he had applied the strong and weak traits formula to arrive at the conclusion that he should leave LA and take his skills to the third world, we could hypothesize that he identified a combination of strong traits along the following lines:

- an education in medicine
- surgical skills and the "stomach" for the profession
- a second language as he was raised in a bilingual environment
- an ability to easily learn other foreign languages
- a strong will and determination to achieve set objectives
- compassion for the suffering of others
- adaptability
- humility

You can see that for the doctor to take his highly specialized skills to the world's poorest countries, where the supply of such skills is low but the need for them is high, is in keeping with how life plans are formulated. The doctor both wanted and was able to do his aid work effectively because of his medical training and compassionate nature, his language skills, and his ability to adapt to foreign cultures and less comfortable living conditions.

So then, what about you? You don't have to be a surgeon or a politician or a rock star with a conscience to have something worthwhile to offer or something meaningful to do with your life, so don't underestimate yourself. Remember, no two people are exactly the same, even identical twins. Try to identify what is special and unique about your set of positive traits. And then see how you can use them to help yourself and others. This will provide you with some clues as to your purpose in life.

Second, our life is also planned to provide us with opportunities to face and overcome our weak traits. Let's consider again the hypothetical case of the doctor. Perhaps he had a fear of flying that he had to overcome in order to execute his life plan. Perhaps he was inherently a shy person but the nature of his work turned him into a minor celebrity in his field of work so he had to learn to cope with the attention.

Again, what about you? If you are hiding in the safety and predictability of your comfort zone, embrace the opportunities to confront your weaknesses and fears. If you do this of your own accord, you avoid the crises and traumas that result when circumstances beyond your control force you to. This is assuming control of your life. This is evolution.

Personal Reciprocation Formula

Another formula that can help us to identify and understand our life plan is the personal reciprocation formula which, in a nutshell, is this. Is there a balance between what you have received from life and what you have given back? What did you receive from life? Did you have a good education? Do you have a rewarding job or career, a loving partner and family? Was your upbringing devoid of any hardship? Sometimes during the preparation phase of our lives, the helpers further invest in us by providing us with additional opportunities that will help us to execute our life plan later in life. So try to think if you received anything unusual or uncommon when you were growing up. For example, did you have a mentor who took a special interest in you, did you inherit money or a property, did you grow up bilingual or trilingual, did you have access to the best universities or professions through family connections, did you have many lucid OBEs or other psychic episodes as a child, did you meet a partner who was very supportive of your personal development, etc?

What if you have had all these means to evolve, the helpers have invested in you and everything has been in place to support your evolution since you were born but you don't evolve? Then these things you have been given are luxuries and privileges that you take for granted. After the age of 35, we have to think about reciprocating, about giving something back to life. And we can do this by assisting others. When thinking about how our assistance can have the greatest net effect on others, there are two things to bear in mind. First, strive to engage in actions that have the greatest collective impact—it is better to help 1000 people than just one person. And second, assistance generally falls into one of two categories—it is either consolation or clarification. I will define these in greater detail in chapter 12 but briefly, as I've mentioned before, when we clarify others we teach them how to help themselves, and this is the very best kind of assistance we can give.

So for the purpose of this exercise, I suggest you make a list of all the things that you have received from life so far and then list everything that you have given back. Is there a balance? If not, and you are already into the second half of your life, start thinking about how you can reciprocate today. Once you begin to pay back, according to the suggestions given, your life plan will begin to unfold.

Lucid Out-of-Body Experiences

The most effective means of identifying our purpose in life is to learn how to produce lucid projections at will, because there are several ways in which we can discover our life plan outside of the body. For example:

- When we have lucid OBEs it is possible to access our holomemory, in which the details of what we planned for this life prior to being born are stored.
- You could choose to meet with one of the helpers who was responsible for developing your life plan. He might say, "Look you have forgotten what we agreed and you are off track. Remember, we planned that you would do x, y and z, etc." But take note, if you recall experiences like this out of the body you have to be sure that (a) they were lucid experiences and (b) you were communicating with a helper, not an intruder or blind guide.
- Or you could try to meet with your evolutionary orientor while out of the body.
- Another target for a lucid projection could be your extraphysical hometown. This is where you attended the intermissive course and did your training and preparation for your current physical life, so it will be easier for you to recall your life plan if you reach this target. There, you can also meet the extraphysical members of your groupkarma, some of whom may be able to confirm your recollections.

What will determine the level of success you have with all your projective objectives is the strength of your will, so don't consider any of these targets to be beyond your capability. Be determined. Don't give up.

Retrocognitions

Producing a retrocognition of your most recent intermissive

period is another technique for recalling your life plan. You can try the retrocognitive self-hypnosis technique as described in chapter 8, or you could book a session in a retrocognitarium, a laboratory especially designed to facilitate the recollection of past lives and intermissive periods, more details of which were also provided in chapter 8.

One-Year-More Technique

Once we have either obtained some clues to or have identified our purpose in life, there are a couple of useful techniques we can employ to dynamize its execution, should we be in need of some extra impetus.

The one-year-more technique is a technique that can help us when our motivation starts to flag, and is very simple in its strategy—live every year as if it were your last.

Imagine you went to visit your doctor today and he told you, "Sorry, but you have a terminal illness and you will die in exactly 365 days from today." Meaning, you have only one year left in which to fulfill your life purpose. What would you do with the remaining time? What would you *not* do? Imagine this is actually your situation. Adopting this posture can inspire and motivate us to reprioritize our lives and to realize several years' worth of obligations that make up our life plan, in just twelve months. In this context, here are some useful steps to consider taking for the next 365 days.

- Identify the projects and goals that you have fostered for a long time but haven't yet managed to fulfill and draw up a schedule that is geared towards accomplishing these priorities in one year.
- Eliminate all activities that are unnecessary for the achievement of your priorities.
- Be disciplined, sleep a little less and give yourself some extra time.

- Identify your most powerful strong trait and increase what you can produce from it.
- Produce as much as you can from your time and energy and from the opportunities that come your way, without compromising your health.
- Improve your karma by nurturing positive relationships with your family, friends, colleagues, adversaries, and even your pets; and express your affection and fraternity to all people.

50-Times Technique

Another technique for dynamizing your life plan is the 50-times technique, which works like this—whatever you need to do properly and with quality, do it 50 times. For example, do the vibrational state 50 times a day; learn every technique for leaving the body properly by attempting each one 50 times; dedicate 50 times longer to every worthwhile task undertaken; have 50 times more motivation and 50 times more attention.

In other words, develop the positive attributes of perseverance and tenacity and see the evolutionary results for yourself.

Books and Courses

Other resources I can recommend that are useful in both the identification and galvanization of one's life plan include a book by Waldo Vieira entitled *Existential Program Manual. Existential program* is the term coined by Vieira that refers to the "specific programming of each human personality for their new life in this physical dimension." (*Vieira,* 1997)

The International Academy of Consciousness, which has educational centers around the world, and the Brazil-based International Institute of Projectiology and Conscientiology both offer courses that are specifically designed to assist interested individuals to identify their life plan. Please refer to the appendix for contact details of these organizations. They will be glad to provide you with additional information.

Precautions

A final word or two about the realities of attempting to discover your true direction in life.

First, you should prepare yourself for the possibility that you won't learn all of the details of your life plan in advance. So if you have an idea, a clue, a hint as to what you should be doing with your life, don't stand still, move in that direction. Put one foot in front of the other. From your new position, more ideas will be revealed and things will gradually become clearer as you keep moving forward.

Second, as is the case with all endeavors, bear in mind that life is rarely perfect. So while it would be ideal if all our needs could be taken care of and life was calm and stress-free before we started thinking about executing our real purpose in life, this may never happen. As I said in the previous chapter, if you want to find excuses not to fulfill your life plan you will always find them. "I don't have enough money, I don't have a girlfriend, I don't own a house yet, my mother is sick, etc." I am not advocating being reckless or failing to assume your responsibilities—not at all. I'm just cautioning against procrastination.

If you have any clue as to your life plan, don't wait; act on it in some measure today.

Chapter Twelve

Holomaturity

> Consciential evolution is the journey of the consciousness from immaturity to maturity.
> —*Waldo Vieira*

Types of Maturity

At its core, the process of evolution is a function of increasing one's level of maturity. If we are striving to become lucid multi-dimensional beings, then it is just as important that we know how to behave with maturity outside the body as inside the body. Cosmoethics are morals that help us to do this, as they are applicable everywhere we go, both physically and extraphysically. We will discuss cosmoethics at length in the next chapter. But for now, let's consider what it means to be mature.

Maturity can be defined as the state or quality of being fully grown or developed. It is when something has reached a level of readiness or perfection, such as when a fruit is ripe or a plan is ready to be implemented. As human consciousnesses, we have three different types of maturity:

Physiological Maturity

Physiological or biological maturity is when the body is fully grown; this is usually reached at around the age of 26. It may appear that the body has stopped growing earlier but our long bones are still producing new cells up until the age of 26. The exact age at which we reach physiological maturity varies from person to person and there are also some differences between men and women, as girls tend to mature biologically more quickly than boys. It is also commonly believed that women age more quickly than men but as yet there is no evidence to support this. At any rate, we can say that by the age of 26, the body has reached its full potential.

Psychological Maturity

On average, we reach psychological maturity at the age of 35. Up until this time we are acquiring psychological maturity through learning about ourselves and how to deal with all the different types of people we come into contact with in society. It is when we are adept at managing the various relationships in our lives, those we have with our family, relatives, partners, bosses, colleagues, friends, neighbors, teachers, students and pets, that we have psychological maturity. We know how to stand up for ourselves and deal with confrontation calmly; we are flexible and able to make concessions within reason; we have learned how to properly consider the needs of others; we're not too demanding and selfish; we are able to take responsibility for others, etc.

Psychological maturity can be recognized in people who are stable, and balanced in their opinions and emotions. We see that teenagers haven't yet acquired this type of maturity because they are impulsive and highly charged emotionally. They tend to create mountains out of mole hills, dramatizing little problems into big issues.

While it is possible to acquire psychological maturity by the age of 35, obviously it's more difficult to measure than physiological maturity. The nature of some cultures can also either facilitate or hinder its development. There are indigenous people living in remote rain forests in Brazil, for example, who don't really experience adolescence. As soon as the boys reach sexual maturity they are considered to be adults, meaning their carefree days of childhood are over by the age of 13 or 14 and they have to assume all the discipline and responsibilities of manhood. In circumstances like these, individuals can reach psychological maturity very early.

Intellectual Maturity

Several criteria need to be met in order to acquire intellectual maturity, which is generally reached around the age of 50. They include the following:

- We need some life experience to be able to accomplish something intellectually. Very rarely do we see children or teenagers proposing new laws in physics, or writing new theories in psychology, economics or mathematics, for example. Renowned intellectuals such Einstein and Jung were not young when they wrote their masters' theses. One of the most intellectually challenging roles in the world is to be the democratically elected leader of a country so, in principle, a high level of intelligence would be a prerequisite for the task. Accordingly, the majority of the presidents of the United States were between 50- and 59- years old when elected to office.
- Another criterion for intellectual maturity is the ability to analyze and criticize knowledge, an ability that not everyone has. Some people believe everything that they read about dieting, for example, even ideas or principles that contradict one another. I have also met many people who have extensively studied one particular subject related to multidimensionality, such as past lives, and believe everything they've ever read on the subject, to the point of defending opposing theories. This shows that they lack the ability to discern that one line of thought is better than another because of x, y and z. So intellectual maturity is also about knowing how to differentiate things that appear to be close to one another.
- The opposite of this strong trait is what is known as Manichaeism. Manichaeism is when we see things as black or white, right or wrong. To give an example, according to the religion in which I was raised, abortion is

always wrong. But real life is not quite so simplistic. What if a female patient in a coma is raped by a staff member while she's in the hospital and becomes pregnant? What if a 12-year-old girl is raped and becomes pregnant by her father? What if a woman has multiple fetuses growing in her womb, but due to overcrowding the lives of all of them are at risk? Would abortion be wrong in these cases? So intellectual maturity also requires that our discernment be well developed; that we have the ability to see the bigger picture, which includes the many shades of grey between the black and white. The more shades we can see, the better.

- Someone with intellectual maturity can also associate ideas, meaning they can combine their logic, rationality and intelligence to make new connections or associations between (apparently) unrelated disciplines. Quantum physics, which connects traditional physics to philosophy, is a good example of an association of ideas. This ability shows that a person's thinking is rich and has depth. But, again, we can't expect it from people who are too young.
- The intellect of a person with intellectual maturity is multifaceted, meaning he has acquired different types of intelligence; e.g. linguistic, musical, spatial, psychic, evolutionary, mathematical, etc.
- We can all be consumers of intellectuality such as we are when we pursue an academic course or read a book. But when a person can produce something intellectual, such as a research scientist, inventor, composer or writer (and in certain cases, an artist) does, this is an indication (rather than a criteria) of achievement of intellectual maturity.

Holomaturity

In each life that we've had we will have acquired some level of physiological and psychological maturity. Some people, in some lives, will also have acquired varying levels of intellectual and energetic maturity. Now think of the cumulative value of these maturities over many lives, for this accumulation builds up inside the consciousness. In addition to this, we also gain experience and wisdom, and therefore maturity, in between lives. Maybe some of us dedicated our intermissive periods to helping others, visiting other planets and learning about extraterrestrial extraphysical communities, or to taking advanced intermissive study courses, etc. It is this accumulation of the overall maturity of the consciousness that is known as holomaturity.

Holomaturity is best defined as the maturity of the consciousness based on the consciential paradigm, which acknowledges that the true nature of the consciousness extends far beyond the boundaries of the physical realm.

Recognizing Mature Consiousnesses

If we are projected outside the body or in between lives, how will we recognize the extraphysical consciousnesses who are more mature? As we can change the way we look in the extraphysical dimension, the appearance of an extraphysical consciousness is a very poor indicator of his level of maturity. A mature consciousness can look like a baby. An immature consciousness can look like an old man. So appearance tells us nothing.

A lot of information about a person is carried in his energies and, of course, we can feel the energies of others outside the body. So when you perceive that a person is detached, wiser, more serene and lucid, settled within himself and has a good level of cosmoethics, you will easily recognize that this is a mature, evolved consciousness.

An extraphysical consciousness who is not mature has none of these traits and this will also be apparent in his energies. In the case of the post-mortem parapsychotics for example, you will sense that they have a very low level of maturity and self-awareness, that they are lost, confused and distressed.

Even in the physical dimension, appearances aren't a reliable indication of the maturity of a consciousness. It's not uncommon to encounter a woman in her forties with the emotional maturity of a teenager, or a fully grown man with the egocentric perspective of a child. On the other hand, sometimes we see young people and children who show excellent wisdom and balance, giving advice, counselling, perhaps even comforting their parents. So this is a mature consciousness inside a physically immature body.

Examples of Maturities and Immaturities of the Consciousness

Now that we understand in broad terms what holomaturity is, let's get down to the actual detail of what it means to behave with a level of holomaturity in daily life. The most important thing to understand is that the standard or usual behavior of a mature consciousness will always be cosmoethical. Here are several examples of such behaviors, each one listed with the corresponding immaturity that manifests when the maturity is not present.

Rationality / Emotionality

Rationality

When we have rationality, our thinking is driven by our mental body so we think with clarity and make decisions based on pondering all the variables in a situation. We also have control of, or less dependency on, emotions. The more mature we are the less interested we are in emotions and emotionality. But this is not repression. Nor is it to say that we are without feelings. We have feelings, but we're not unbalanced by them.

Emotionality

By contrast, when we are emotional we make decisions based on impulse and volatility, and our thinking is not sophisticated or complex. This is immaturity.

Science / Mysticism

Science

Adopting a scientific approach to life means you analyze everything according to the evidence and the facts. You accept nothing less.

Mysticism

A mystical approach to life, on the other hand, means that you accept things that are a mystery. According to the dictionary, a mystery is anything that remains unexplained or unknown or is not fully understood. To accept anything that has no verifiable basis is immature.

Assistance to Others / Egocentrism

Assistance to Others

Assistance is part of a normal, mature life. We help others when we give them our energy, our time; when we share our knowledge, experience and ideas; when we clarify them, listen to them and support them. Sometimes the best way to help is to give money if money is what's needed. Other times, the smallest gesture will have the greatest effect.

The person with a propensity for assisting others is someone who came to physical life to serve others and is conscious of doing so in his everyday life. This person has discovered what it is to be useful.

Egocentrism

Egocentrism is a complex concept, as it starts with something that's not exactly negative. As children grow up they believe themselves to be the center of the universe. This is a normal part of human development and in normal circumstances it leads to the development of healthy self-esteem and other positive traits. Later on however, during adolescence, we discover that the world doesn't revolve around us. When people don't adjust to this realization and continue to be egocentric into adulthood, egocentrism becomes negative, for this is just selfishness. Selfish people don't want to help others, don't make a proper contribution in life and allow others to shoulder the burden of their responsibilities.

In truth, many people are selfish to some extent. Even those who know they should assist others and make an effort to do so, do it in a self-serving way, helping only the people who are close to them, usually their first and second families.

Universalism / Sectarianism

Universalism

Universalism is all about inclusion—it is when you consider all people and identify and integrate yourself within the community, the state, the nation, the continent, the planet and the universe. Universalism therefore is the practice of not segregating anybody. Some good examples of universalism are: the defense of human rights; the principles of pacifism and nonviolence; disarmament; the preservation of nature; the global minimization of pollution; and international campaigns to prevent the spread of infectious diseases, to fight child labor and to eradicate poverty. A universalistic viewpoint will lead us to become less private, less selfish or egotistical, and better able to coexist with others.

A good friend of mine lived in six countries across Europe, the Middle East and Africa when he was growing up and told me how surprised he was when he came to London to start his secondary schooling at the age of 12, to meet boys his own age who had never been outside the UK and so held that there was only one way of doing things—that being the British way. So a lack of exposure to different points of view is not ideal for developing this trait.

Sectarianism

Sectarianism or bigotry, the corresponding immaturity, is the act of separating or discriminating against others. Some examples of sectarianism are racism, chauvinism, sexism, ageism, patriotism and classism. Classism is very much in evidence in the UK with the monarchy at the top of the hierarchy followed by the aristocracy, then the upper class, middle class and lower classes. It is also alive and well in India where people discriminate against one other on the basis of caste. Teenagers are among the worst segregators of all—separating off into little cliques and groups that exclude others, and bullying kids who don't fit the mold.

So what about us—how often does our universalism fail? In what situations do we still separate people? How do we exclude others? Give it some thought. This will help you to achieve a better level of holomaturity. If others outside of the group of people we choose to be with need us, we have to be ready to help. Outside the body we see very primitive extraphysical people, and others who are not balanced, who are ugly or deformed. Can we give assistance to these consciousnesses, clarify them or heal them with our energies?

Determination / Accommodation

Determination

Are we determined to evolve as consciousnesses and deal with the pressure of swimming against the tide? Are we ready to "unlearn" some things we know and create some new thought processes? Are we prepared to step out of our comfort zone, prioritize things that don't bring us status or respect, give up some things that we like, and make some sacrifices?

Accommodation

Or are we accommodated in our lives, living a safe, predictable existence that doesn't present any challenges or risks? Are we unwilling to do anything new? Are we just repeating our last life?

Clarification / Consolation

Clarification

If you give a person a fish, you feed him for one day. If you teach a person to fish, you feed him for the rest of his life. This is clarification. Clarification is when you help someone to help themselves, so it is a more advanced level of assistance.

It's when you give advice in order to deal with the *cause* of a problem. Sometimes the effects of clarification last forever, such as if you if teach or empower a person to recycle and heal his own life. It's from your mental body to the mental body of the other person. But be aware that clarification involves saying "no" more often. What if your sister is being abused by her husband, who is violent towards her and then apologetic by turns, and who has manipulated her into "understanding" and accepting his behavior? What does she need from you—your agreement that her husband is justified in hitting her? No. Clarification is to say "No, this is wrong; this is not acceptable behavior under any circumstances," even if it's not what your sister wants to hear. So do you provide some clarification for other people once in a while? Or do you offer only consolation? Or do you not give any assistance at all?

Consolation

To provide consolation is to sympathize, comfort, listen, provide support, and offer a shoulder to cry on. It's when you use your emotions to alleviate the emotions of another. But with consolation you treat the symptoms not the disease, so it is an emergency procedure, a short-term solution, a superficial cure only. That said, it's better to give consolation than no assistance at all.

When you become proficient at working with your energies, sometimes people will ask you to perform energetic healing. This is consolation. And when people are weak or ill, this is the right thing to do. Imagine a woman loses a child. She will be fragile and grief-stricken, so the best thing you can do it to provide consolation, including energetic healing to calm her during the crisis. It is certainly not the time to give a strong lecture. But we don't want anyone to become dependent on us, so once the crisis has passed and the person is strong again, we should clarify them. In a situation like the example given here, this might mean explaining that no one ever really dies; that the child has returned to the extraphysical hometown where his extraphysical family will provide support; and that the karmic connection between a mother and child is the strongest there is, meaning that your friend and her child will share future lives together—they will be together again.

Polykarma / Egokarma

Polykarma

We have already discussed karma but it is worth emphasizing here that polykarma—when the consequences of your actions reach large numbers of people that you don't know—is an act of a mature consciousness.

Egokarma

Egokarma is a trait of a less mature consciousness, when your actions have consequences only for you.

Main Brain / Sub-Brain

Main Brain

Our main brain, the encephalic or cerebral brain, is located in the head. This brain guides the behavior of a person who is more mature.

Sub-Brain

The sub-brain, abdominal brain or belly brain is a center of bioenergy located in our abdomen that relates to the lower three chakras; the umbilical-chakra, the spleen-chakra and the sex-chakra. Human beings have more neurons in their bellies that control digestion, release hormones and perform other functions than some animals have in their main brain. Our intestines, for example, produce 80 percent of the serotonin in our bodies. So the sub-brain plays an important role in our physiology and, as it runs on automatic pilot, we don't have to consciously manage many of the body's functions, which is wonderful.

But if a person is ruled by this brain, his behavior bypasses the logic, rationality and discernment of his mental faculties and is driven instead by his instincts, desires and physiological needs. For example, he may eat or drink too much or be controlled by his sexual impulses. Sex is a good thing but maybe we dedicate only 5 percent of our time and 10 percent of our thoughts to it, so if a person is thinking about sex 100 percent of the time there is something wrong. This sort of obsession can lead to sexual crime. Territorialism is also belly-brain behavior. A dimension of gang warfare, for example, arises from the instinctual defense of territories.

Energetic Control / Uunconscious Intrusion

Energetic Control

The capacity to install the vibrational state and to exteriorize energy at will, anywhere, anytime, in any condition, and thus be free of intrusion, is a trait of a mature consciousness. A person does not start to gain any significant amount of control over his bioenergies before passing through the first death. Once this has occurred it usually takes several lives to reach a good level of energetic control and maturity. There is also a stronger correlation between bioenergetic maturity and holomaturity than with holomaturity and the other maturities mentioned earlier in this chapter.

Unconscious Intrusion

Or do we have no energetic control at all? Are we intruded and not even aware of it?

Will / Psychological Crutches

Will

Our will is a powerful attribute of the mental body. Using our will, we can learn to defend ourselves energetically, clear ourselves of energetic blockages, develop our psychism, leave the body with lucidity, understand our purpose in life and overcome some weaknesses and limitations. When our behavior is driven by our will, we are the masters of our own reality, meaning we don't need to be led by someone else. A strong will is an attribute of a mature person and a quality often seen in leaders.

Psychological Crutches

Psychological crutches, on the other hand, are external objects that we lean on, that we use to protect ourselves or to prop ourselves up when we believe that we are not capable of standing on our own two feet.

A lot of insecure people become dependent on all sorts of psychological crutches that they use for a variety of purposes, such as to increase their psychic capacities, to improve their health, to acquire wealth and power, to feel more confident, to seduce the opposite sex and for protection. Some examples of pyschological crutches are: drugs, prescription medications, alcohol, tarot cards, ouija boards (for evocating or summoning extraphysical consciousnesses), crystal balls, charms, horse-shoes, talismans and objects of superstition such as rabbits' feet.

Having lived in several countries, I have witnessed people of a variety of cultures and religions using their God or god/gods and goddesses as a crutch. Did you get hit by a bus and lose both of your legs? Thanks to (insert name of favorite god)! If not for him you would have died! Never mind that you couldn't be bothered to walk 100 meters to the pedestrian overpass and instead tried to cross a busy six-lane highway on foot. This sort of behavior is typical of many religions whose adherents believe that it is their God or god who decides their fate and that they don't have any control over their lives. It is a way of absolving themselves of responsibility for their own reality.

It has to be said that many psychological crutches do in fact make us feel good. Usually this is because people who use them *believe* that they have certain powers, so the effect is the same as when subjects taking part in medical trials respond positively to placebos thinking they are taking actual medication. But think for a minute. If we are multidimensional, multiserial beings who can read what is going on around us physically and extraphysically through the mastery of our energies; who can effectively defend ourselves against any type of intrusion; who can heal and unblock ourselves and who can dynamize our own evolution through the application of the attributes of our mental body, then do we really believe that a rabbit's foot is more powerful than we are? Certainly it didn't help the rabbit.

Even the projective techniques that we use to leave the body are a kind of crutch. We don't want to become dependent on them; ideally we will be able to leave the body through the application of our will rather than via a bunch of technical procedures.

We don't want to be dependent on or slaves to anything or anyone. If we are leaning on psychological crutches of any sort, remember that we can't take them with us when we die. They're useless to us when we're between lives. So it's better that we dispense with them now and get used to the idea that we are the masters of our own reality.

Standard Conduct / Exception Conduct

Standard Conduct

Standard conduct is what we do most of the time. If we are striving to attain a better level of holomaturity and to evolve, all the mature traits listed in this chapter should become our standard conduct, our normal behavior.

Exception Conduct

Exception conduct is what we do exceptionally and/or when there is no other way. To give an example, if a teenager experiments with drugs at school one day as an exception, just to try, then no problem. But if the experiment leads to addiction and becomes standard conduct, then there is a problem. The exception conduct has become the standard conduct. Another example—healing people with energies should be exception conduct. The standard conduct for all the conscientiological organizations is to teach people to heal themselves.

So what about your life? What behaviors of yours are exception conduct that should become standard conduct? Do you give assistance to others as an exception only? And vice versa. What standard conduct do you have that should become exception conduct?

Lucid Personal Prioritization / Slave of Social Commitments

Lucid Personal Prioritization

Do we prioritize our evolution? Do we give up doing some things that we enjoy in order to make time for our evolution?

Slave of Social Commitments

Or do we prioritize social commitments instead, such as birthday parties, engagement parties, office parties, dinner parties, baptisms, weddings, anniversaries, family dinners, balls, nights out with friends, etc. Of course there's nothing wrong with any of these things. But we all lead full lives, so if we are serious about improving ourselves, then we need to *make* time to practise our energy techniques and projective techniques, keep a diary of our dreams and projections, develop our mental attributes, read books, identify our strong and weak traits, discover our purpose in life, etc. If we are going to invest time in our evolution, we have to give it the priority it deserves.

If you don't think you have to give anything up for your evolution, that you have time to do everything you want to do, it might be useful for you to analyze your daily utilization of time and calculate how many hours you actually have at your disposal each day to invest in your development.

Daily Utilization of Time

The chart opposite, which is used in the IAC's Consciousness Development Program, is designed to help you understand how and where you spend your time. Fill in the middle column with the number of hours you spend on average each day doing the activity listed in the left column. In the right column, add up the total number of hours to arrive at a final figure of hours accounted for each day in the bottom right hand corner. I have started the calculations with examples for the first two activities.

Is your total somewhere near 24 hours? When we do this exercise in class at the IAC we find that for most people it is. So if we want to evolve, many of us will have to rearrange our lives in order to find the time to do it. And there are several ways we can do this. We can multitask more—perhaps you can read while you are travelling to work, learn a new language by listening to a CD in the car, or catch up on your phone calls from your mobile while walking the dog. Or, you can think of ways to save yourself time. One thing that works for me is to order my grocery shopping online and have it delivered to the house. This service is now available in many big cities around the world and is usually free for a minimum order. This alone can save 2–3 hours a week. And then there's just plain old sacrifice peppered with a healthy dollop of common sense. In the grander scheme of our multidimensional, serial existence, how important is watching our favourite soap-opera every night?

Be aware, however, that if you are going to reprioritize your

Activity	Amount of time - hours	Accumulated hours
Sleeping	8	8
Commuting/travelling	2	10
Watching TV and relaxing		
Socializing, e.g. going out for dinner or to the cinema, parties, meeting friends for coffee or drinks etc.		
Preparing and eating meals		
Working (to earn a living)		
Personal hygiene, e.g. taking a shower, brushing teeth, applying make-up, shaving, styling hair, dressing etc.		
Miscellaneous: personal administration such as paying bills, posting letters, housework, talking to family and friends on the phone, visits to the doctor and dentist, car maintenance etc.		
Shopping (including grocery shopping)		
Exercise		
Other		

Personal prioritization chart

life in favor of your evolution, you should do it with maturity, balance, wisdom and without any drastic attitudes. Do you have a family to take care of, an elderly relative who is dependent on you, other karmic issues that require your attention, responsibilities in your community outside of the scope of your work, etc.,—*and* you want to evolve? Then all these commitments and priorities must be executed in parallel, cosmoethically, and with discernment. Evolution is no excuse for not fulfilling your responsibilities.

As we focus more on our evolution, we find that we do more, we are busier, we use our time more productively and efficiently, we have less time for doing nothing and little time to waste.

Chapter Thirteen

Cosmoethics

The highest virtue here may be the least in another world.
—*Kahlil Gibran*

I begin this chapter by acknowledging the additional, significant research and development of Vieira's original ideas on the subject of cosmoethics conducted by Wagner Alegretti. Alegretti offers a course on cosmoethics and many of the ideas he has contributed are explored in this chapter.

Cosmoethics are the very essence of holomaturity. It is our level of cosmoethics that defines our level of holomaturity. As the process of evolution is a function of becoming more mature, the relationship between cosmoethics and evolution is a very close one. In other words, if we are not cosmoethical we don't evolve.

If we are going to have lucid OBEs, cosmoethics will help us know how to behave appropriately everywhere we go, physically and extraphysically.

Ethics Versus Cosmoethics

In order to define cosmoethics, let me first define ethics. Ethics are standards of human behavior or conduct that are acceptable in a specific group of people. (Human morals, which are rules of conduct that set the standards of right and wrong, come under the broader umbrella of ethics). For example, in the UK it is considered wrong to kill others and wrong to walk around naked in public. Murder, we know, is wrong by anyone's standards. But is walking around naked really such a big deal? Native people living in hot climates all around the world don't wear clothes because the heat and humidity make it impractical. So while public nudity is morally acceptable in Australian aboriginal society, it is illegal in British society. This example demonstrates the subjective and relative nature of ethics and morals. They are not absolute, but vary across environments, countries, cultures, religions and politics.

Let's consider some examples of religious morals.

In the Hindu religion if a woman is widowed, she has to wear a white sari for the rest of her life, while widows of the Greek Orthodox faith are expected to wear black for up to two years after the death of the spouse.

Polygamy is a normal, accepted part of life in some religions, with various caveats being that limits are imposed on the number of wives a man can take and that if he wishes to have more than one he must be able to afford to treat them all equally. This same practice is known as bigamy by other religions and is outlawed in many countries, making marriage to more than one person at a time a criminal offense.

Another example: in Judaism the laws regarding the preparation of kosher foods prohibit the cooking of meat and dairy foods together; they can't be served at the same meal, and the utensils and dishes on which they are served must be separated. These rules made a lot of sense when they were created; at that time the Jewish people were living in the desert without refrigeration, and some dairy foods such as milk contain certain bacteria that, when mixed with meat and ingested, can cause food poisoning. So the kosher tradition is understandable in this context. But today, thanks to refrigeration, there is no problem in storing, preparing, cooking or serving milk and meat together, so the reason for this tradition is now outdated.

There are many such customs that are no longer meaningful, relevant or appropriate in modern society, if indeed they ever were. For example, female circumcision is still widely practiced in many African, Middle Eastern and Asian countries despite the severe risks it poses to the physical and emotional well-being of the women who endure it; some societies still condone the so-called crimes of honor; and others still forbid the use of contraception even though the earth cannot sustain its population.

Cosmoethics, on the other hand, are a more absolute, universal code of conduct that transcend the subjectivity of religions, politics, cultures, countries, continents, planets and dimensions, and are therefore applicable and appropriate in all circumstances, everywhere we go, both inside and outside of the body. They are a set of overarching ethical ideas that reflect the real dynamics of multidimensional existence as opposed to the relative, often dogmatic and limiting, morals of human society.

There are no Ten Commandments for cosmoethics. Instead they are a kind of moral philosophy—a way of thinking that helps us to avoid experiencing and causing unnecessary suffering. Unlike ethics, cosmoethics are not imposed on us via a formal system of rules or laws so they are less intrusive and allow us more freedom, but demand, on the other hand, a higher level of personal responsibility.

Let's now examine the bases that shape the way of thinking behind this cosmic code of conduct. The following are guidelines for cosmoethical behavior:

Self-Incorruptibility

An important part of cosmoethics is to live without self-corruption. What is self-corruption? The verb "to corrupt" means to destroy the integrity of; to cause to be dishonest or disloyal (especially by bribery); to lower morally; to mar or spoil; to infect, taint or make impure. *Self-corruption* then, is when we lower our *own* integrity or morals, or betray our *own* principles and knowledge. We are self-corrupt, in other words, when there is no coherency between what we know and what we do.

For example, when my mother was growing up in Australia,

people would go to the beach, slather baby oil all over themselves and stay out in the sun all day to get a fabulous tan, unaware of the risks involved. But nowadays everyone knows this is dangerous and can cause melanoma, a type of skin cancer. So if we avoid the hottest part of the day by going to the beach early in the morning and later in the afternoon, and wear sun block and a hat, then fine. But if we stay there all day without any protection, then this is self-corruption.

Imagine that you have a very important task in life that you planned to fulfill prior to being born, a plan that involved you helping a lot of other people. You need to live until the age of 80 to complete your task but you die from skin cancer at 40 and all the people you were supposed to assist missed out on your help. If this were to happen to you, when you die and pass to the extraphysical dimension, your helpers will tell you that you failed in your life mission because of a suicide of sorts. The same rationale applies to smoking. Smoking is a little bit of suicide every day.

Some other examples of self-corruptions are: participating in extreme high-risk sports; taking drugs as standard conduct; abusing one's authority; not helping others; blaming others for one's own mistakes; gossiping about others; the "tall poppy" syndrome (i.e. criticizing people who do well instead of admiring them); tolerating abuse of any kind; manipulating and controlling those who are weaker; benefit fraud; failing to pay adequate child support to an ex-spouse; and making donations to charities for tax purposes.

We also find examples of self-corruptions in professions; e.g. priests who abuse children, stockbrokers who engage in insider trading, doctors who smoke, dieticians who are obese, psychologists who encourage their patients to become dependent on them, AIDS-infected prostitutes who have unprotected sex, fashion designers and magazine editors who glamorize anorexic models. All these people are incoherent in their behavior.

Equally, we can be self-corrupted in the things that we omit to do; e.g. we don't get out of bed in the mornings to help our children get ready for school because we are lazy, we neglect our pets because we are lazy, we don't exercise because we are lazy! Laziness is the major stumbling block of many people who fail to complete their life task. A lot of people just want an easy life.

So ask yourself what types of self-corruptions you are prone to. Some are neatly woven and concealed into the very fabric of our daily lives, others occur only occasionally. This is a complex task that requires complete sincerity.

The helpers clearly see our self-corruptions. They don't expect us to be perfect, they are aware that we are fallible and make mistakes; but they do have a problem when they see us behaving in a way that is not coherent with what *we know* to be correct. One of the reasons that they don't make the mistakes we do is because they are not self-corrupt. (Alegretti and Trivellato, 2004)

An essential principle of cosmoethics, therefore, is that we have to apply what we know in our daily lives. To know something in theory only is not enough. If we want to evolve, we have to put the theory into practice. Make this a priority in your life.

Conscientiality

One of the ways in which we regularly fail to apply what we know in our daily lives is when we forget that we are a consciousness and live our lives as if we are the physical body.

If you have read through this book chapter by chapter, by now you will know that you are much more than just the physical body. You are a consciousness, a multidimensional, multiexistential being whose capacity to "be" transcends time and space. You have already experienced lives in different cultures, countries and maybe even planets; your future extends into eternity and the cosmos is your playground. Conscientiality is to live in a way that is coherent with these facts.

A lot of people are aware of this reality one way or another, but in theory only. They still behave like everyone else—materialistically. And materialism is the main cause of lack of human ethics. Nothing tempts people to compromise their ethics more than the promise of a fat check. Having a lucid out-of-body experience or near-death experience can have a huge impact on our ethics, because we learn that we continue after death and come to understand that we cannot escape the consequences of our actions. So OBEs often help people to start living their lives more cosmoethically.

So what is your level of conscientiality? How often are you aware of the fact that you are a consciousness? How many hours a day do you spend behaving like a human being?

The Law of the "Lesser Evil"

The law of the "lesser evil" exemplifies another principle of cosmoethics—the importance of applying flexibility to your thinking and your judgments; the importance of not being rigid in your morality or ethical standards.

For example, many people would agree that it's wrong to hunt animals since we no longer need to kill animals ourselves in order to have meat to eat. This issue is very topical in England right now with the recent ban on the traditional sport of fox hunting having met with powerful resistance. But suppose you go to Africa on vacation, your plane crashes in the jungle and while waiting to be rescued you have to hunt in order to survive. This is better than starving to death, right? It is the lesser of the two evils and therefore, acceptable in this context.

Other examples of the law of the lesser evil are:

- controlled euthanasia is better than dying a slow, painful, inevitable death
- amputation is better than death

- in certain circumstance an abortion may be better than allowing the pregnancy to proceed
- the confinement of anyone is never ideal, but incarcerating dangerous mentally ill patients, murderers, terrorists and rapists is less bad than putting the public at risk

To decide the "lesser" evil in any given situation, we have to use the attributes of our mental body—our discernment, detachment, rationality and logic. Sometimes our physical instincts, desires and needs are so strong that they overwhelm our mental body and our discernment deserts us. A desperate need for love or sex, for example, can cloud our judgment and cause us to lower our standards to get what we want. We also have to consider the consequences of our decisions in respect of time. The effects of some mistakes can last for lives. And lastly, when deciding the lesser evil, we need to be able to see all the mitigating and aggravating circumstances between the right and the wrong. The more lucid you are, the more shades of grey you will be able to see between the black and white.

Fraternity

One of the defining characteristics of the helpers is their high level of fraternity, meaning, to them, everyone matters, even intruders. So a cosmoethical attitude is one in which you want the best for, feel affection for and are ready to assist everyone, even your enemies, competitors and detractors.

Pure fraternity requires the capacity to feel the suffering of others. Not to feel empathy or compassion is a type of energetic blockage. At the other end of the scale, feeling too much can be counterproductive. I knew a man several years ago who was a kind, generous person with good intentions but I came to understand that he was so energetically sensitive that when his friends were in difficulty he would assimilate all of their emotions, become overwhelmed, and then feel compelled to distance himself from them. In terms of providing assistance to others, he was impotent. The challenge therefore is to be open to others and to feel their suffering, but to remain detached, balanced and serene in order to be able to provide effective help when you are needed.

Above all, fraternity necessitates action. It requires that you *do* things, not just think about doing things. And don't underestimate what you can do—think big! How many people can you affect with one action, one activity, or one project—one, ten, one hundred, five hundred? How much more could you accomplish if you worked with a team? The more the better. This is polykarma.

Be aware also that omitting to give assistance when you have the opportunity is not without karmic consequences. Doing nothing does not necessarily equate with being neutral. Failing to help when you can is anticosmoethical. So when considering your own level of fraternity, you need first to ask yourself, what do I *do* for others?

Thoughts and Intentions

Cosmoethics don't only apply to our actions but also to our thoughts and intentions.

In the extraphysical dimension, the action of thought is more direct than it is in the intraphysical dimension. In the intraphysical dimension we can easily mask what we really think. We can have thoughts or ideas but not express them. When projected however, our thoughts are immediately transmitted to others. We might as well be yelling our thoughts extraphysically. As a result, our helpers and intruders will always know what we're really thinking, so we should always be honest with ourselves and be aware of the *real* intention behind everything that we do. Ask yourself, "What is my real intention here? What do I really want? What outcome am I hoping to procure?"

It's good to create healthy thinking habits, to practice what we call "mental hygiene" both intraphysically and extraphysically.

So what about our thoughts? Are they cosmoethical? For example, what about sexual fantasies? Are they right or wrong? What if a person is between relationships for a period of time or his partner is away and he indulges in a sexual fantasy as an exception conduct? Even in these mitigating circumstances, a sexual fantasy about a real person is not just a thought, it's also an action. When we fantasize about someone, we send energy to that person and we end up connecting a type of energetic duct to them from which we also get something back. So unless the object of our desire is our partner, we are behaving like intruders. When we engage in sexual fantasies, we also call the attention of extraphysical consciousnesses who share our desires, so a lot of people feel uncomfortable afterwards because of the bad company they have attracted.

If we don't know about the energetic mechanisms behind fantasies, then we don't know the consequences for us and for the object of the fantasy, so this is not a self-corruption. But in our case, knowing what we now know, the least bad is that the object of our fantasy be someone that we create with our imagination rather than a real person. This will still attract some extraphysical consciousnesses but at least we are not intruding on anyone.

Another thing to be aware of regarding our thoughts is that some of us will have been leaders in previous lives. If this is your case you may have blind guides around you who were once your supporters and who still think of you as their leader. So be careful of wishing revenge on anyone or for anything bad to happen to others because some of your blind guides may rush to carry out your thoughts.

The key thing to remember is that when we are always cosmoethical in our thoughts, intentions and actions, the intruders have fewer means of connecting with us.

Personal Principles

As well as having the above guidelines to follow, it is also a good idea to develop your own set of personal principles, a kind of internal constitution, to help you be more cosmoethical on a day-to-day basis, in all the little things that you do. Here are some examples of what I mean:

- Think about leaving every place that you visit better off energetically. I'm not talking about public places, because as we saw in chapter 4 you should not just go around giving out energy in places where there is bound to be a lot of intrusion, as you will attract intruders to you. I'm talking here about the homes of friends or family that you may visit. Exteriorize your best energies there, infused with your best thoughts and sentiments, as an anonymous gesture to improve people's energetic environments a little bit. If you stay at someone's house overnight or longer, there are many other things you can also do to leave it better for your presence—help a child with his homework, offer to prepare a meal, energize a sick plant, make a new toy for the cat, etc.—so think about how you can help and contribute everywhere you go.
- Remember that insisting on anything too much, trying to influence others too much or convincing anyone of anything is intrusion.
- Don't allow yourself to get drawn into the same fights and arguments with the same people over and over again. This is a waste of your valuable time and energy. If someone constantly antagonizes you into participating in a fight, there is a simple solution for dealing with him. Tell him to go to hell and walk away.
- Make your own decisions. Know your mind and be self-

confident even if no one agrees with you.

- Respect the free will of others.
- Respect the evolutionary level of others. An example of this is, don't say more to people about the subjects in this book than people can handle. Those who have not attended the intermissive study course will find it hard to understand about consciousness, energies, evolution, intruders and helpers, so trying to force these ideas on such people is a kind of evolutionary rape. Whatever the person is capable of understanding, explain, but don't go further. This is cosmoethical. You will sense energetically when you have crossed the line.
- Don't tell people when they are intruded. Most people aren't strong enough to cope with that.
- Don't use your energies to try to change people. In this case, the intention may be good but the execution is not. (Alegretti, 2002)

To conclude this chapter, it's important to explain the relationship between cosmoethics, karma and evolution as an understanding of how these relationships work, enables us to see clearly how we can assume a greater level of responsibility for our evolution.

Take a look at this diagram.

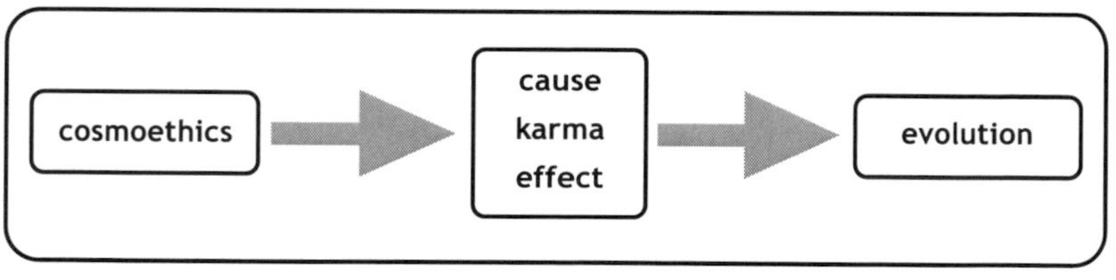

Evolutionary process

It shows that one's level of cosmoethics dictates one's karma, and karma, being the law of cause and effect, dictates one's level of evolution.

Let me give an example of how this can work. The more you help others, the better your karma will be. Think about all the different ways you can help, big and small, and don't only provide assistance when you are obliged to, but also spontaneously, because you want to. As much as you can, help in ways that clarify rather than simply console—teaching others, explaining how things work, using your experience to help others to help themselves—this is the best kind of assistance and it will give you great pleasure, too. A life full of good works of assistance to others will obviously have a positive effect on your karma. How might this good karma unfold? It might mean that you are born to a couple in your next life who completely master their energies. Imagine if as a baby your parents taught you how to move your energies in the same way that they taught you how to walk! How proficient would you be by the time you were ten? What would your level of energetic self-defense be like, how advanced would your parapsychism be, how easily would you be able to leave the body, how unblocked would your chakras be?

So can you see, the better your karma is, the better your evolution? The more we know about cosmoethics and about ourselves as consciousnesses, the faster we can evolve.

PART FOUR

The Out-of-Body Experience

> By far, the most difficult and impressive part of projection is the moment of lucid take-off from the waking state. There is no animic or psychic phenomenon that provides a greater impact. It is the one event able to provoke modification of scientific, moral and religious points of view, and has deep far reaching effects on anyone's knowledge, opinions, education, customs and beliefs. Upon experiencing the lucid takeoff . . . generations of teaching are humbled, centuries of civilizations are reduced to dust in the mind of the projector, and mountains of prejudice lose their meaning. Through personal experimentation, one dismisses all tiresome arguments. The result is peaceful certainty.
>
> —*Waldo Vieira*

The objective of this final part of the book is to provide you with information that will help you produce your own lucid out-of-body experiences in a composed, relaxed and confident manner; to recall them and to accurately distinguish them from a range of other altered states of consciousness and paranormal phenomena.

These experiences will, in turn, enable you to verify the material presented in this book for yourself.

Chapter Fourteen

Benefits of the Out-of-Body Experience

It is my hope that this book has succeeded in some measure in alleviating general ignorance of conscious projection and raising awareness of the fact that, far from being a mystical phenomenon worthy only of scepticism and ridicule, it has been researched, studied and practiced for thousands of years, and thanks to the efforts of many leading-edge thinkers throughout history, it is nowadays very well understood.

Beyond this, however, the primary objective of this book is to inform you of the many benefits of the out-of-body experience and to impress upon you that lucid projection merits a place in the modern, everyday lives of all of us.

So before proceeding with the chapters in which I will describe how to achieve your own OBEs, it is worth summarizing here the numerous benefits of being able to experience your awareness independently of your physical body.

This information will help clarify in your own mind why you are trying to leave the body and will act as a powerful incentive to do so, which in turn, will increase your chances of success.

Therapeutic Benefits

- Loss of the fear of physical death (thanatophobia)—one of the top ten phobias of humankind—through direct experience of other dimensions and other bodies of manifestation of the consciousness
- Assistance to physical and nonphysical individuals in lack and in need through the transmission of healing energies while projected

- Attainment of an exceptional "supernormal" level of health due to a reduction of personal insecurities and tension; increased self-confidence, competence, concentration and desire to live purposefully and enhanced memory and reflexes (Vieira, 2002)

Psychological Benefits

- Less significance attached to temporary material acquisitions
- Less priority given to the pursuit of self-indulgence and more priority given to assisting others
- Opportunities for extraphysical mini-breaks to physical and nonphysical destinations
- Encounters with loved ones who have passed away
- Realization that suicide is not a means of escaping one's problems

Educational Benefits

- Expansion of self-knowledge
- Substitution of ignorance, belief, faith and speculation with knowledge acquired through first-hand experience
- Acceleration of personal maturity
- Demystification of many enigmas relating to human existence

Parapsychic Benefits

- Opportunity to convert the one third of human life habitually wasted in sleep to conscious, productive activity
- Personal verification of survival after the death of the human body
- Recall of past lives—irrefutable evidence of one's own

existential seriality

- Recall of the specific purpose for this life that was planned prior to being born
- Acceleration of the development of parapsychic abilities; extrasensory perceptions; energetic sensitivity, self-control and self-defense
- Increased awareness of the energetic interactions between physical and nonphysical individuals
- Direct interaction with evolved extraphysical helpers
- Verification of the existence or absence of extraphysical intruders attached to oneself

Specific Practical Uses

- Opportunity for incarcerated and disabled people to enjoy temporary extraphysical freedom
- Opportunity for people who are lonely and have been forgotten by physical society to enjoy extraphysical social contact
- Opportunity for retirees and other available individuals to more effectively use their time (Vieira, 2002)

Chapter Fifteen

Preparation for the Out-of-Body Experience

Research has shown that a number of factors relating to how we prepare ourselves for a projection during the physical waking state prior to a projection can facilitate our level of lucidity while outside the body and enhance the recall of the experience upon returning. Having said that, all the preparations we make to project are optimizations only, meaning that a lucid projection can also occur even if we do no preparation at all.

Following is a list of variables, drawn from Vieira's research, that can influence the level of success of our projections. I recommend that you use it as a checklist in preparation for every attempt to leave the body.

External Factors

Logically, the very first thing we need to decide prior to attempting to project is where we are going to "park" the physical body. As the physical body will be asleep when we are projected, we need to leave it in a safe and comfortable location in which we have the greatest level of control over external factors such as temperature, heating, lighting, noise level and privacy. For most of us, this place will be our bedroom.

Temperature

The ideal temperature is one that will prevent the body from becoming too hot or too cold throughout the duration of the experience, and thus, from calling the extraphysical body back to the physical body. Anything at all that calls attention to the physical body will cause a projection to end, so you must be comfortable at all times. When we are too hot, we become mentally sluggish, which reduces our lucidity. Prior to applying any technique for leaving the body, you should work with energies for the purpose of making the energy body more flexible and facilitating the separation of the extraphysical body. Working with energies can make us feel colder.

Note: Be aware that if your room is air-conditioned, your body temperature will start to lower after lying still for some time so you should take this into account when setting the thermostat.

Illumination

A stable condition of semi-darkness or darkness is best, as this will diminish external stimulation and help the pineal gland to produce the hormone melatonin, which helps us to relax. A deep state of relaxation is essential to being able to leave the physical body.

Noise Level

Any noise from the physical environment will call your attention to your physical surrounds and thus prevent you from being able to focus on the extraphysical dimension so the quieter your environment, the better. Complete silence is ideal. Unfortunately, those of us who live in cities are usually subject to some degree of external noise from the traffic, aircraft flying overhead, dogs and neighbors, etc. If this is your case, an air conditioner that produces a continuous white noise can help to block out other, intermittent noises. Soft furnishing like carpets, rugs and curtains can also absorb and reduce noise.

Sensorial Stimulation

Anything or anyone touching you or making a noise while you are trying to project will disturb your attempts. This point especially relates to those of you who share a bed with a partner and/or pets. So what is your situation? If your partner snores, grinds his or her teeth, talks in his or her sleep, is restless, or pulls the duvet off you, you may need to do your projection work in another room. With regards to pets, don't have them on your bed or in your room when you are trying to project. The ideal is that you be in an environment that has no sensorial stimulation at all so try to get as close to this condition as possible.

Clothes

Nudity gives us a great sense of liberty and freedom. If you are not comfortable being naked, wear light, loose fitting clothing that doesn't restrict you in any way such as pajamas or a tracksuit.

Note however that there is not necessarily a direct connection between what we wear to bed and how we are dressed outside the body. Our appearance in the extraphysical dimension, including how we are dressed, is a reflection of how we see ourselves. So if you are 80 but the overriding image you have of yourself is as a young man, you will look like a young man when you are projected. If at the moment we "wake up" outside the body we notice that our nudity or the way that we are dressed is inappropriate for the circumstances in which we find ourselves, e.g. walking down the street in our pajamas, this can helpfully prompt us to realize that we are projected rather than dreaming and increase our level of lucidity. We can then dress ourselves any way we want.

Furnishings and Beddings

Placing pillows under your neck, knees and even arms can promote a deep sense of relaxation. So experiment with cushions and pillows until you find the set-up that allows you to be as comfortable and free of tension as possible. If you have a partner, individual blankets or duvets or a bigger bed may help reduce disturbances from him or her. Duvets and blankets shouldn't be so heavy, though, that you can feel their weight on you.

Also, try to diminish the amount of furniture and clutter in your bedroom. Have only what is necessary. If your room is cluttered with furniture, electrical equipment, art, gifts and other decorative items, from force of habit you will feel restricted in terms of where you can move when you leave the body, even though you are not.

Infrastructure

You will need a digital clock, a notepad, pencil, calendar and diary by your bed for the purpose of recording your extra-physical experiences when you wake up. The digital clock will allow you to note the time that you lie down to begin your attempt and the time you return from your projection. A calendar is useful in case you wake up not knowing what day it is and are perhaps anxious that you have to get up and go to work on a day that you don't need to. This could interfere with the recall of the projection. I will explain the purpose and benefits of recording the details of your projections and other altered states of consciousness in chapter 18.

Ideal Time

The best time to attempt to project is when the physical body is most relaxed, so there is no ideal time as this is an individual thing that varies from person to person. But we already know that darkness and silence facilitate lucid projections. So if we consider that the majority of the population goes to sleep somewhere between 11:00 p.m. and midnight we can calculate that 3:00 a.m. represents the middle of the night for most people, and is therefore the time of least noise and external interference. So this can be an ideal time to try to leave the body.

By this time the brain will also be somewhat rested from having had some sleep, which will help you to achieve a better level of lucidity, but the body will still feel tired enough to relax and be tranquil during the application of a projective technique. The pineal gland also peaks its production of melatonin in the middle of the night, which will further aid your relaxation. If you want to try projecting at 3:00 a.m., set an alarm and then take the time to wake yourself fully before your attempt, to avoid falling straight back to sleep.

Weather

No special meteorological conditions are conducive to having an OBE. If certain weather conditions affect or frighten you, delay your attempt until they have passed.

Physical and Physiological Factors

Experiment with Your Projective Posture

The position we assume when attempting a projection can help us to be more lucid outside the body and to recall the experience later. Lying on our back in the dorsal position is best as this is *not* the switch-off position for most people. Mostly when people are ready to go to sleep (i.e. black out, lose their lucidity), they turn and lie on one side or partially on their stomach. So when we assume the dorsal position we send a subtle message to ourselves that we are not switching off, we are alert and ready for anything. The idea is that you allow the physical body to go to sleep but that mentally you remain alert. This way you will be able to experience the lucid take-off of the extraphysical body. If you are not accustomed to relaxing in the dorsal position, practice! In time you will get used to it.

Avoid Food and Drink

There are two things to take into account here. First, because your heart rate increases when you are digesting a meal, you will find it more difficult to relax when you are preparing to project if you have eaten within two hours of lying down.

Second, you should avoid foods that have a high water content such as watermelon, and especially drinks that are stimulants or diuretics such as coffee and tea. So don't have anything to eat or drink within two hours of lying down to avoid being disturbed during a projection by an elevated heart rate or the need to go to the bathroom.

Note: the rate at which we produce urine often increases with energy work.

Fulfill Your Physiological Needs

Empty the bladder just prior to lying down. Constipation (blocked umbilico-chakra) can also interfere with projections, so make sure your diet is balanced.

Be Well-Rested and Relaxed

It is important to be well-rested when attempting to project to avoid immediately falling asleep. Deep relaxation is also prerequisite to being able to forget all about your physical body and environment and so as to focus your attention on the more subtle extraphysical realities.

Clean Your Nasal Passage

Clean your nasal passage well with water so as nothing interferes with your breathing.

Take a Hydromagnetic Shower

You may even like to take what's known as a hydromagnetic shower in preparation for a projection. This involves sending energies out through your crown chakra (at the top of the head) against the flow of the water when you are standing under the shower. The water will then come back and cleanse your energy body, improving the condition of your energies a little from their current condition. So if you're in bad shape energetically, this exercise will help in some measure but it won't unblock any energetic blockages, for example. Be sure to watch the water temperature. If the water's too hot you will become mentally sluggish and if it's too cold you will be too alert to relax. Also, for the first few times that you do the hydromagnetic shower, lean against the shower wall and support yourself in case working with energies makes you feel unsteady in any way.

With repetition, this exercise will help to activate your crown chakra and improve your awareness outside of the body.

Control the Monkey Within!

Remember that the physical body is just a monkey of sorts with a lot of instincts. If you are going to leave the body you have to learn to control the urge to move (scratch, swallow, blink, shift your weight, etc.) and the urge to sleep.

Psychological Factors

- Be confident that you can have a projection. With perseverance, blockages, fears and conditionings can be eliminated and everybody can achieve positive results.
- Have positive intentions that you will have an enlightening, lucid, out-of-body experience, and know that if anything worries you during the OBE, all you have to do is think of your physical body and instantly you will return to the body.
- Use your will to combat boredom, distraction and impatience for things to happen quickly. How long will you have to apply a technique before you start to leave the body? If in your case it takes around 75 minutes but you always give up on the technique after 20, you won't achieve results. So use your will to persevere in terms of time spent applying the techniques and in terms of the frequency of your attempts to leave the body.
- Be stable and calm before attempting to project. Have a

quiet frame of mind. If you try to project when you are emotional, excited, anxious, fearful or agitated, it will be more difficult for you to leave the body and your emotionality will make it harder for you to stay outside the body. So avoid fighting and arguing, watching movies that are emotionally demanding, listening to music that winds you up, playing violent computer games that leave you agitated, or doing anything else that gives you an adrenalin rush before trying to project.

- Understand clearly your objectives for leaving the body. Know where you want to go. Know what you want to do. Write it down. Want it! Be motivated by your goals and concentrate on achieving them.
- Be mentally alert.
- Remember that you are not just the physical body. You are a consciousness that is free to travel across dimensions. So forget all about your physical body and your material surrounds. Focus your awareness outwards, on the extraphysical dimension, not inwards.
- Don't have any preconceived ideas or expectations of how things should happen. For example, don't expect to float up out of the body because maybe you will sink down through the floor; don't try to force yourself out through the head because maybe your helpers are trying to pull you out through your feet. So be open. Wait to see what is happening first and then go with that.
- Above all, be ready to find yourself lucid outside the body. As Vieira wrote in Projectiology:

If you are really interested in producing lucid consciential projections or have tried to provoke such experiences, prepare yourself psychologically to accept spontaneous lucid projections because they might occur during any favorable opportunity from now on. (Vieira, 2002)

Bioenergetic Factors

Vibrational State

Installing a vibrational state prior to projecting will keep you balanced and protected while outside the body and will prevent other projected or extraphysical individuals from coupling energetically with you.

Thoughts, Sentiments and Energies

Remember from chapter 4 how our thoughts, sentiments and energies are intertwined? If we think about projecting with lucidity every day we will charge the energetic field around us with our desire to project and create connections that will facilitate and support our endeavors. So have materials related to lucid projection around your house—have books on the subject next to your bed, posters on the wall, watch DVDs about OBEs, visit quality websites regularly, listen to relevant radio interviews on the internet, etc.

Extraphysical Conditions

Don't forget to think about what is going on around you nonphysically and to cleanse the energies in your bedroom and house regularly so as the extraphysical conditions are positive and balanced, and thus conducive to your efforts to project.

Parapsychic Factors

Parapsychic Perceptions

How well-developed are your parapsychic perceptions? Are your helpers there trying to lift you out of the body but you don't perceive them so you roll over and go to sleep? Are your blind guides there trying to stop you from leaving the body but you don't perceive anything negative so you think they are your helpers? We need to invest the time to become more parapsychic—and this will develop as a natural consequence of working more proficiently with our energies (Trivellato, 2006).

General Comments About Preparation for a Projection

Research shows that all the factors described in this chapter facilitate lucid projection. At the same time, we are all individuals and all, some or none of these optimizations may prove useful to you. So you have to practice and experiment with different conditions and find out which combinations facilitate your experiences. You will also learn which variables hinder your efforts so make a mental note of these also and be sure to address them during your preparations.

You have to experiment with all of the external, physical, physiological, psychological, bioenergetic, extraphysical and parapsychic factors that can affect your projectability and invest the time to tweak and adjust the variables until you come up with a combination that yields results. Some key variables relate to your overall energetic capacity and emotional balance, while more minor variables relate to specific personal attributes that you can control with your will, such as your level of confidence or openness. In the end, the height of the pillow under your neck might be the only thing standing between success and failure. If, however, any of the variables are completely off, you're unlikely to achieve a lucid projection. (Trivellato, 2006)

Chapter Sixteen

Lucid Projection Techniques

Projecting with lucidity at will is a skill that has to be learned. In this sense, the learning process is not dissimilar to learning a new sport or language. There are no shortcuts and no substitutes for effort and determination. If you are really serious about becoming a lucid projector, the ideal is that you practice as many techniques as possible and dedicate yourself to training your physical, energy, extraphysical and mental bodies to adapt to the specific demands of each one. I mention this so as you understand that, although not impossible, it is probably unlikely that you will have a lucid projection after trying one technique just once or twice.

While there are no perfect techniques that guarantee success, the techniques devised by Vieira that I describe in this chapter are among some of the most effective, based on the results of thousands of students of the IAC and the IIPC around the world who have applied them in practical classes.

In addition to practicing all the techniques in this chapter I recommend that you do some research and put together a set of around 15–20 to work with in total. Vieira describes 37 in detail in *Projectiology* just for starters. The aim then, after practicing each one every night for a month or so, is to identify five or six that take best advantage of your strong traits and that seem to work well for you. For example, if you have a good imagination, techniques that require that you use your imagination and visualization will be easier for you; if you have good lung capacity, you will find the techniques based around breath control easier to do, and so on. You can even combine certain elements of different techniques that suit you to create your own.

Think of your every attempt to project as an opportunity to learn from all the little details and experiences that you have and don't have any anxieties or expectations about what you should achieve beyond that.

Whatever you find difficult about a certain technique will reveal a limitation or blockage that you have and this is positive, because once you've discovered what's preventing you from leaving the body you can work on overcoming it. Maybe you find that you are not able to relax sufficiently or perhaps you discover that you have an energetic blockage in one of your chakras that is holding you in the body.

Tips

Before you lie down to apply a technique, take some time to think about how you are going to occupy yourself when you are projected. If you are busy outside the body you will avoid thinking of your physical world and increase your chances of staying projected for longer.

Some activities you can include on your extraphysical to-do list are:

- try to fly
- examine your extraphysical body
- stretch your extraphysical body
- test the capacity of your vision (can you see 360 degrees?)
- change the appearance of your face
- change your clothes
- feel your silver cord
- meet your helpers
- see if you're emitting a light.

Include a target in your agenda, something or someone you are curious to meet or a place that you are really motivated to visit.

Once you have gotten yourself comfortable and are ready to

start, there are two important steps to take before applying the projective technique.

First, you should spend 15–20 minutes working with your energies; absorbing energies from the environment around you, installing the vibrational state and sending your energies out in all directions (refer back to chapter 4 for detailed instructions on how to do these exercises). This will help loosen up your energy body, which will make it easier for the extraphysical body to detach and take off.

And second, you must relax. I am shortly going to describe the Psychophysiological Self-Relaxation Technique. It is, in itself, a technique to leave the body, but it can also be used for the purpose of helping to establish a deep state of relaxation prior to applying any other projective technique. Or you can use any other effective method for relaxation that works for you.

As you are going through the steps of any technique you will probably get distracted at some point and find that your mind has wandered off. When you realize this is happening, no problem, just go back to the beginning of the technique and start again. With time and practice you will improve your ability to concentrate.

Remember, too, that your aim with all the techniques is to relax the body enough to let it sleep but to remain lucid and alert in your mind at the same time.

Projective Techniques

The Psychophysiological Self-Relaxation Technique

A deep state of relaxation is a technique for causing the extraphysical body to gently detach from the physical body and float. You will easily recognize when the separation has taken place because you will no longer be able to feel your physical body. It will feel numb. Numbness is just one of many sensations that are commonly experienced when the physical and extraphysical bodies are in a state of discoincidence and this is completely normal. I describe this and several other sensations in more detail in the next chapter.

To apply the psychophysiological self-relaxation technique: inhale deeply—fill your lungs—then contract or tense a muscle group in your face—e.g. crinkle your forehead—hold your breath for five seconds—then exhale and relax the muscles as you do so. Then, again, inhale deeply—fill your lungs—and contract another muscle group in your face for five seconds—e.g. squeeze your eyes tightly shut—hold your breath for five seconds—then exhale and relax the muscles; and so on, moving through all the muscles in your face. You can push your lips forward, clench your jaw tight, contract your neck muscles, etc.

Continue in this manner, contracting and relaxing all the muscles in your body: your neck, shoulders, chest, arms, hands and fingers, abdominals, lower back, buttocks, upper legs, shins (pull your toes toward you), calves, feet and toes. Take all the time you need. There's no need to rush.

We often carry tension in our bodies without even being aware of it. The idea of this technique is that as you relax each muscle you will release any tension you are holding and gradually establish a more profound state of relaxation. Once you feel the body becoming numb you will know that the extraphysical body is starting to float. At this point you should concentrate on the target of your projection to encourage a full projection of the consciousness.

The Projective Target Technique

Curiosity or motivation to reach a target is a very effective technique for leaving the body. Sometimes after teaching a practical class at the IAC, I tell the students to try to project to the classroom from their homes during the night to see what object I have placed on the desk or what I have written on the whiteboard. More than once students have come in the next morning with a word written down on a piece of paper that matches exactly the word written on the whiteboard. When they have described how they captured the information, it was clear that they had had a lucid OBE as opposed to an experience with remote viewing or traveling clairvoyance. The fact that the words matched allowed them to confirm their projections.

You could set up just such an experiment yourself by asking a friend to leave an object out on his kitchen table or a colleague to draw a symbol or write a word on a whiteboard at work for you to try to see out of the body.

In these examples, a place has been chosen as the target of the projection, but you could also have a person as your target, or an idea, or you may even choose a target that relates to discovering something about yourself, i.e. a self-target. Let's have a closer look at each of these categories.

Places

This category includes both physical and extraphysical places. A physical destination could be an object or objects that you have always wanted to see, such as Monet's waterlily series at the Orangerie Museum in Paris; or a place that you have always wanted to visit but haven't had the opportunity to do so yet, such as Antarctica, the Serengeti plains or Uluru (Ayers Rock) in Australia. Or perhaps you would like to travel 30 leagues under the sea to learn what strange creatures live at such depths, fly into the heart of the Krakatau volcano in Indonesia, or visit an international space station orbiting the Earth.

Extraphysically, you might like to visit your extraphysical hometown and reacquaint yourself with the extraphysical members of your karmic group, or go to an extraphysical colony of specific interest to you, e.g. a colony of pacifists, ecologists, geniuses or politicians. Remember too that every physical place has an extraphysical "backstage." So you might choose as your target the extraphysical territory and community associated with the headquarters of the United Nations, the Peace Palace in The Hague, or with your own home or place of work. What is it like there? Who is there? What is happening there?

Places That Are Off-Limits

There are some human districts and extraphysical environments that projectors should avoid and consider to be off-limits due to the existence of potential or actual risks; such as:

- Houses that are known to be haunted by poltergeists. Poltergeists are extraphysical consciousnesses that have the ability to produce effects in the physical dimension. If you project to a haunted house, a poltergeist might be hostile towards you or even follow you home and create problems for you there.
- Places where violent crimes have been committed or where humans have been assassinated in large numbers, such as the Coliseum in Rome, the Auschwitz concentration camp in Poland, the site of the former World Trade Center in New York, and the battlefields of wars past and present. Hundreds, thousands, tens of thousands, even millions of psychotic extraphysical consciousnesses who died in deeply traumatic circumstances may still be attached to places such as these.
- Current and ex-torture chambers such as Abu Ghraib prison near Baghdad in Iraq.
- Former prison dungeons (including ruins) such as the medieval Tower of London and the Conciergerie in Paris.
- Any hostile extraphysical district.
- Other peoples' bedrooms. Everyone has the right to absolute privacy in his bedroom. In some rare cases we might be taken to someone's bedroom by a helper to carry out some assistance. This is OK as long as we are very discreet about anything we might learn there.

Beings

You could also choose a physical or extraphysical individual as the target of a projection. If you want to approach someone who is physical outside the body, make sure the person is willing to participate and get his permission to do so first. Perhaps you would like to project to someone you know who is sick and who could benefit from your energetic assistance. Or you could aim to have a joint projection with a partner, family member or friend, so your target would be to meet them outside the body at a predetermined place and time.

Or you could choose an extraphysical being as your target: your helper or evolutionary orientor or maybe someone you know who has already passed away.

Beings who should not be approached

There are some physical individuals we should not approach when we are outside the body for fear of shocking and disturbing them while they are working, should they perceive us. These include surgeons performing an operation, machine operators, truck drivers, anyone riding a motorbike, barbers who are shaving someone with a razor or anyone else engaged in potentially dangerous work.

Extraphysical consciousnesses who should be avoided include anyone who has recently died and is resting and recuperating from the shock of losing the physical body. Particularly avoid anyone who has committed suicide, as they are often extremely disturbed and/or traumatized. You could also suffer too great an impact from seeing someone you know in such a condition.

Ideas

You could also have an idea as your target, such as a new hypothesis for a scientific conundrum, a cure for a disease, or a solution to a problem or issue you're trying to resolve. Perhaps you would like to understand, for example:

- how memory suppression works
- how we can better recall our projections
- the mechanisms that allow our emotions to take control over the mental body
- the differences in time that exist between the physical dimension and the extraphysical dimension

Self-Target

A self-target is one in which your aim is to discover useful information about yourself. It might be something related to your physical body such as a health problem that could be investigated through the phenomenon known as internal extraphysical autoscopy (when you are able to see inside your own physical body while projected); or it could be related to your energy body, your silver cord or your extraphysical body. Perhaps you would like to see if your extraphysical body is carrying any scars or traumas from former lives that are responsible for some of your present life conditions, for example.

As part of the projective target technique, draw up a projective agenda. Make a list of six targets selected from the categories above, name them and order them according to their degree of difficulty. Assign a realistic deadline to achieve each target (e.g. three months, nine months, one year) based on the fact that you will practice regularly, and adjust the deadlines as you go along, according to your results.

The Elongation of the Extraphysical Body Technique

Elongation or elasticity is a natural attribute of the extraphysical body and shouldn't be a cause for concern or fear. The aim of this technique is to stretch, expand and loosen the extraphysical body (particularly the para-arms and legs) until you lose the reference points for your physical body. When this happens you will feel free of the physical body as your extraphysical body will be partially disconnected, and you can allow the extraphysical body to totally detach and float up.

To apply the technique, first relax well. When you are settled and relaxed, think about your feet and start to accumulate your energies there. When you can feel the energies gathering in your feet, focus on your extraphysical body and concentrate on growing or elongating the para-feet. Try to stretch them five centimeters beyond the physical feet. When you've done it, return to normal and relax. Repeat the exercise and try to stretch the para-feet out five centimeters again. Then return to normal and relax. Do it a third time, return to normal and relax again.

In the next step, concentrate on your head and put your energies there. Try to stretch the para-head out and relax, three times, each time as before. Go slowly. Take your time.

Start the whole process again but this time stretch your para-feet out ten centimeters each time, and your para-head out ten centimeters each time.

Repeat the process, this time stretching your para-feet out twenty centimeters each time and your para-head twenty centimeters each time.

Finally, stretch your para-feet out half a meter and while maintaining this length with your feet, stretch your para-head out half a meter. Persist with this part of the exercise as long as you need until you achieve the result.

Then, while your extraphysical body is still stretched in both directions, imagine yourself expanding like a balloon through the chest and torso area. When you start to feel a ballooning sensation (another sensation commonly experienced during the take-off of the extraphysical body—see the next chapter), your extraphysical body will be starting to detach, so at this point, shift your focus from the technique to the target that you had selected for your projection to induce the full take-off of the consciousness in the extraphysical body.

Projection through the Mental Body Technique

If you would like to experience a projection in your isolated mental body (cosmoconsciousness, *nirvana, satori, samadhi*), the state of enlightenment against which all other spiritual experiences are compared, it is important to regularly work with the mental body by studying, learning and developing its attributes to keep it active and flexible. Ideally, you should also have some experience with voluntary projections in the extraphysical body before attempting a mental projection.

You will have to choose a target *idea* for this type of projection, as any other target (such as a place or a person) will engage your emotions and thus lead to a projection of the extraphysical body, the body of our emotions.

To attract the isolated mental body, your target idea should be an elevated concept or enigmatic question that can be developed or considered from new perspectives that go beyond the boundaries of your maturity and knowledge in the ordinary, physical waking state.

Targets for a projection in the mental body are notional concepts that are outside the boundaries of ordinary life. The point of them is to break out of the boundaries of what's known. The experience is epitomized by having an epiphany—suddenly you consider the concept of infinity or spirituality or oneness and you have an expansion of consciousness in which you grasp the whole idea. In a projection in the mental body you move into an arena that has more to do with understanding and awareness than form or function.

For example:

- If you are a cosmologist, you could think about the precise notion or concept of infinity in relation to the vastness of the universe.
- If you are a physicist you could think about possible means of transcending time.

- In our case, we could try to find out how the consciousness began; how we manifested before we began the multiexistential cycle and what our level of evolution was; or we could try to find out if we ever discard the mental body and if so, how we would manifest then; or we could try to discover something new about the mechanisms of group karma.

Once you have selected your target idea and established a deep state of relaxation, you will need to forget the following three things as they will restrict your mind:

- the world of forms: length, width and height (lines, curves, spheres etc.)
- the world of space: the physical dimension, the paratropospherical dimension and the extraphysical dimension
- the world of chronological time: the past, present and future (seconds, minutes, hours, days, weeks, months and years)

Concentrate now on your target and be open to original, creative ideas.

The Extraphysical Self-Awakening Technique

If we consider that nearly all of us experience some level of separation between our physical and extraphysical bodies during the natural course of nightly sleep then a useful technique for producing a lucid projection is one that prompts us to increase our lucidity and "wake up" outside the body when we are already at least partially projected.

The extraphysical self-awakening technique is an effective method for achieving this and it works like this. When you are in the normal waking state, saturate your mind with the idea and determination of extraphysically awakening yourself anytime something happens that suggests you are projected. For example:

- you find yourself suspended in an empty space
- you notice that you're not breathing
- you discover that you are emitting your own light
- you perceive that an ordinary mirror doesn't reflect you
- you are able to confirm that nobody can hear you
- you recognize that your vision is superior to physical vision

Program yourself to think about this as often as you can, every day. Wear a watch that alerts you on the hour for example, and spend a few moments concentrating on this idea every time the alarm sounds. Immerse yourself in this technique until your extraphysical lucidity automatically increases any time you realize you are no longer in the physical dimension. (Vieira, 2002)

Chapter Seventeen

Common Sensations of the Take-Off and Return

The purpose of this chapter is to describe the various unusual, sometimes exotic, sensations that are commonly experienced leading up to a projection and also at the moment of the take-off and return of the consciousness. If you have already experienced some of these the information that follows will serve to confirm that what you think happened was real and not imagined (if you are unsure), and to reassure you that what you felt was completely normal.

For those of you who have little or no projective experience, the knowledge you will gain from this chapter will help you to avoid reacting to some of the sensations with fear or apprehension, because you will understand what is going on and know that many thousands of people before you have had the same experiences. You will also be able to anticipate the sensations, and this can greatly affect your success in leaving the body, because when you start to feel things happening there will be more chance of you maintaining control than becoming startled and unbalanced.

Regardless of your level of experience, the key point to take away from this chapter is that when you feel any of the sensations that frequently precede or accompany the take-off (or return) of the consciousness from the physical body, you should feel pleased and happy because these signs confirm that your attempt to project is working and that you are on the right track. This, in turn, should further motivate you to continue with your experiments.

Signs That a Projection is Imminent

Experienced veteran projectors who have had many hundreds of lucid projections throughout their lives, sometimes have an indication or sign that an out-of-body experience is going to occur even up to two hours prior to the actual projection. They may have a powerful intuition to go home, for example, and start making the necessary preparations. Over time and with practice they are able to identify the signs that are precursors to a projection and that enable them to forecast the event.

Less experienced projectors however are more likely to have some indication or sign that a projection is imminent immediately prior to the take-off of the consciousness in the extraphysical body. Indications that are most commonly reported include:

- vivid dreams
- dreams of flying
- dreams about lucid projection
- accelerated digestion
- sensing the presence of extraphysical consciousnesses
- the elongation of a para-arm or para-leg
- a pulsation or pressure on the chakras, particularly the frontal chakra (third eye)
- a sense of alienation from the physical body
- the perception of a flow of air or light breeze in the room
- hearing a whistling or hissing noise
- the sensation that the light in the room has become brighter

Sensations During Take-Off and Return

Other sensations are specifically related to the nonalignment of the physical and extraphysical bodies and may therefore be experienced during both the take-off and the return of the consciousness. These include:

- numbness—the temporary absence of sensitivity and therefore action of the human body; a feeling similar to having had a local anesthetic; will be accompanied by a lowered heart rate
- torpidity—apathy, lethargy, sluggishness, listlessness, unresponsiveness, inaction
- auditory and olfactory hyper-acuity—a heightened ability to hear and smell things in the physical environment using your nonphysical senses; e.g. you might hear noises from the street that usually lie beyond your range of perception or detect the aroma of fresh bread from a bakery several blocks away
- weightlessness—or lightness of the extraphysical body
- heaviness—the sensation that the physical body is a dead weight
- undulation—the instability, rocking or oscillation of the extraphysical body
- ballooning—the clear sensation that the whole body or a part of the body is growing, swelling, expanding or inflating like a balloon; occurs as a result of the expansion of the energy body
- vibrational state—in most cases, a vibrational state occurring just prior to a projection will happen spontaneously
- intracranial sounds—noises that are difficult to characterize; almost always stem from inside the cranium at the exact moment of the lucid take-off and seem to be caused by a very abrupt take-off of the para-head; various projectors report hearing intracranial sounds such as ringing, jingling, buzzing, tinkling, crackles (tinnitus), squeaks, chirps or titters
- cranial pressure—a sensation that stems from an acute awareness of the weight of the physical head at the moment of the detachment of the para-head

- sleep paralysis (also known as projective catalepsy)—the sensation of being unable to move the physical body while consciously headquartered inside it; may occur prior to or following a projection
- disconnection (or reconnection) of the extraphysical body—is sometimes accompanied by a kind of 'click' of separation which sounds like Velcro being pulled apart
- falling sensation followed by jerking awake—is caused by the swift and sudden return of the extraphysical body; usually followed by rapid breathing and a pounding heart
- tunnel effect—an intrinsic component of going from one dimension to another, can therefore occur in any type of OBE but is more common in near-death experiences (NDEs); the impression, usually immediately after take-off, of entering and traveling at great speed through a long, dark, narrow tunnel towards a point of light
- double perceptions—simultaneous perceptions of the physical and extraphysical dimensions; e.g. you may hear a police siren on the street and an extraphysical conversation at the same time
- blackout during take-off—a brief lapse in lucidity that frequently occurs during the transition of our mental operations from the brain to the para-brain, as occurs during the take-off and the landing; is so common in fact that the totally lucid take-off of the consciousness is the rarest type of take-off of all; can be combated with the force of will!

Which of these sensations you experience will vary depending on the day and the projection. You may find that all of them, only some, or none of them occur. (Vieira, 2002)

Chapter Eighteen

Recall and Analysis

Why Is It Difficult to Remember an Out-of-Body Experience?

Although most people project, at least unconsciously, every night, few of us recall our projections when we wake up in the morning.

The reason for this is very clear.

When we are projected the physical brain is asleep and not involved in what is going on outside the body; it is the para-brain that is engaged when we're projected and that stores the details of our extraphysical experiences. Successful recollection of extraphysical events depends then upon the transmission or "downloading" of the details from the para-brain to the physical brain. The structure and nature of the recollection of a projection in the isolated mental body is even richer, more complex and difficult, as the transferral of the memory is performed twice: first, from the mental body to the brain of the extraphysical body (the para-brain) and then from the para-brain to the physical brain of the human body.

I wish I could tell you there is a simple method for passing such memories from one vehicle of manifestation to another but there is none known to date, simple or otherwise. We can facilitate this process however, by improving the performance of our physical brain. Be sure to get sufficient rest and avoid being tired all the time for example; exercise your memory regularly; create new connections in your brain that accurately reflect multidimensional reality and can process experiences that lie beyond the norms of ordinary, physical life; make sure there is a good circulation of blood flowing to your brain; and consider taking vitamins or supplements that research has proven to improve mental efficiency.

The Importance of Extraphysical Lucidity to the Recall of Extraphysical Events

Many other factors can also affect our recall of extraphysical events, such as the depth of the altered state of consciousness we experienced when projected, our interest in remembering and even certain aspects of our personality. These will be discussed in more detail further on.

Probably the most important factor in determining whether or not we recall our projections is our level of lucidity outside the body. If we are lucid we understand well what is happening. We are certain that we are projected and not dreaming or in the normal, waking state, and we have control over our projections. Our lucidity, in other words, determines the quality of our experiences in the extraphysical dimension and this in turn affects our ability to remember them.

To state an obvious example, if you are sleeping outside the body in an unconscious state, you won't know that you're projected at the time and, because of that, won't be able to remember that you were projected when you wake up.

Whether we are lucid or not outside the body is not an all or nothing scenario though. We can experience different levels of lucidity when we're projected just as we can when we're awake. On a good day physically we know we can analyze things quickly and accurately, be productive, multi-task, and concentrate well on what we're doing without getting distracted. On other days we are not so lucid—we go out and forget to lock the front door, we have to take a nap after lunch, we forget an appointment or meeting, we can't remember where we left our glasses—we're just not paying attention.

Our level of lucidity can also fluctuate throughout the day. Some people are very alert as soon as they get up in the morning but then hit a wall after lunch. Others are mentally sluggish before lunch and produce their best work at night.

The energies of certain places can also affect our lucidity. Sometimes we feel drowsy when we visit a hospital, for example, because everyone there is sleeping.

Our extraphysical lucidity is no different. It varies from one projection to another, can fluctuate during a single projection, and is subject to external influences.

So as a first step towards improving the recollection of our projections, we need to try to improve our level of extraphysical lucidity. And to do this we need to work on being more lucid, more consistently, in our everyday physical lives. Try to be more alert, pay more attention to detail, focus well on what you are doing, observe what's going on around you with more accuracy and avoid overindulging in substances that can lower your lucidity in the long-term as well as the short-term, such as alcohol and drugs.

Factors That Favor Recall

While a good level of extraphysical lucidity plays a key role, many other factors can aid the recall of our projections, such as:

- our level of motivation to produce conscious projections at will;
- lying in the dorsal position (on your back);
- waking immediately after a projection;
- projecting with lucidity in the second half of the night;
- having a good memory in the normal, physical, waking state;
- orally relating the experience to someone upon awakening;
- immediately writing down the details upon awakening (the longer you wait to record the experience, the more detail will be lost);

- and simple extraphysical episodes are usually easier to remember than more complicated scenarios. For example, you are more likely to remember a projection in which you woke up outside the body and found yourself suspended in a void than a projection to an extraphysical extraterrestrial space station.

Factors Unfavorable to Recall

Research has shown that the following factors may interfere with the recall of extraphysical events:

- lack of interest in projecting, scepticism regarding lucid projection and fear of projecting. (Note: you can be subject to any or all of these factors, however, and still experience and recall a lucid projection, so it can't be said that any of these factors prevent recollection.)
- lying in the prone position (on your stomach)
- surrendering to sleep
- laziness
- intoxication
- postponing the recording of the experience
- the heavy burden of your daily commitments; for example, being consumed with thoughts of the innumerable tasks you have to complete in the day from the second you wake up in the morning is not conducive to recalling the previous night's projections.

Types of Recall

The recollection of time spent outside the body occurs in one of two ways. It may be fragmented, meaning only "snapshots" of the projection are recalled. As this type of recollection is incomplete, it is subject to mistakes and is not an efficient method of recall. But if you are willing to apply some effort you can try to piece the whole projection together by concentrating hard on trying to remember what happened just before each "snapshot" and what happened just after; linking each isolated memory to another until you are able to connect all the fragments and recall the experience in its entirety, as shown in this diagram.

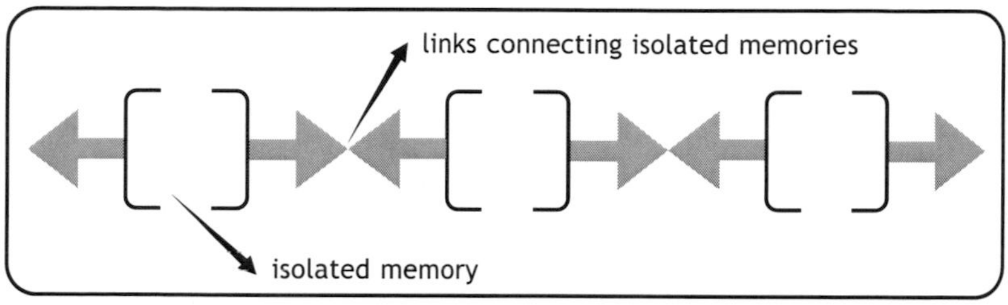

Fragmented recall

Obviously this won't work if the various snapshots recalled are related to different projections.

The most efficient method for recalling extraphysical facts is *en bloc* or continuous recall in which the projector's lucidity never lapses from the physical waking state prior to the projection, throughout the take-off of the consciousness, the time spent in the extraphysical dimension, the return of the consciousness to the physical body, and the return to the waking condition. In this sense, there is nothing to actually recall as nothing was ever forgotten. Unfortunately, this type of recall is quite rare.

Tips for Recalling Projections

There are certain measures you can take during the different stages of the projective cycle that may help you to remember the projection. Here are some tips.

Prior to the Projection

You now know that recall is closely linked to the level of extraphysical lucidity experienced during the projection. Put simply, no lucidity—no recall. So as part of your preparations to project, employ an auto-suggestion and repeat your objective ten times. "I want to be lucid outside the body and I want to recall *everything* when I wake up." In other words, program yourself to remember your experiences.

During the Night

If you wake up during the night, rather than immediately turning over and going back to sleep, wake yourself up properly and try to remember what was happening just before you woke up.

While You Are Projected

Pay close attention to what is happening when you are projected and try to memorize the events that have already occurred. And then, if you need, decide to return to your body and write down the experiences you had.

After the Projection

Resist the temptation to sleep when you wake after a projection. Instead, move your head a little to bring blood to the brain, then lie quietly for a few minutes and go over the extraphysical events twice in your mind. Immediately write down everything you remember or tell your partner if he or she is open to and can relate to your experiences. This will help bring more information and details to mind.

Upon Awakening

Sometime we wake up with no ideas or memories of anything that happened while we were asleep, so assume that we haven't had a projection. In this case, you can run a check on your physiological condition to help ascertain whether or not a projection actually occurred, as some conditions can suggest in fact that one has. For example:

- an unaltered physical position during one section of the night
- torpidity
- cracking noises in the joints
- a good physical disposition
- a full bladder
- a lowered temperature and heart rate (can be caused by a prolonged projection).

Analysis of Extraphysical Events

I have a friend who doesn't believe in out-of-body experiences, which amuses me no end because he has them all the time! I know that because he's always telling me about the wonderful "dreams" he has in which he feels as if he's awake only everything seems clearer and he perceives much more. He's usually flying in these apparent dreams and often comments on the joy of it and how much he loves to watch the landscapes change beneath him. He also tells me that when something catches his eye that he wants to inspect more closely he glides down to get a better look, and that flying so fast just feet above the ground is a huge thrill. The clarity of his thinking, his euphoria when flying, and particularly the fact that he's in control of his experiences, are all hallmarks of a lucid projection.

My friend's incorrect analysis of his experiences is very common. A lucid projection is an altered state of consciousness that people often confuse with many other altered state of consciousness such as ordinary dreams, lucid dreams, projective catalepsy, daydreams, nightmares, double awareness, hallucination, the hypnagogic and hypnopompic states (the transition states between wakefulness and sleep, and vice versa, respectively), hypnotic trances, psychedelic trips and meditation. Similarly, lucid projections can also be mistaken for a number of related parapsychic occurrences such as travelling clairvoyance, remote viewing, retrocognition, precognition, panoramic view and physical bilocation.

So I'm now going to define and examine the characteristics of some of the altered states of consciousness and parapsychic phenomena most often confused with lucid projection in case you need any help to accurately classify any experiences that lie beyond the pattern of your normal physical waking state. With knowledge and practice, and particularly if you faithfully record all of your experiences in writing, in time you will become skilled at correctly analyzing your own lucid projections.

Lucid Projection

A lucid projection is simply defined as the act of one vehicle of manifestation (either the extraphysical body or the mental body) leaving another.

Ordinary Dreams

The table opposite, based on information presented in the IAC's Consciousness Development Program, shows the characteristics that differentiate a conscious projection from an ordinary dream.

Lucid Dreams

A lucid dream (in which you know that you are dreaming and are able to enter into and participate in the dream) can be classified as a semi-lucid projection. As you gain experience of lucid projection, it is likely that your dreams will become more rational and less incoherent, permitting you to exercise your critical judgment and discover that you are dreaming. This is how a lucid dream becomes a lucid projection. The most efficient technique for inducing a lucid projection through a lucid dream, for upgrading your lucidity outside the body and gaining awareness of your projected state, is to ask yourself the following question as often as possible, in all environments and circumstances, every day for at least one month: *"Am I awake or am I asleep?"*

Conscious projection	Dream
Departure from the physical body can be detected by the projector.	No sensation of leaving the body.
An objective reality (such as when you capture information whilst outside the body that you are later able to confirm when inside the body).	Not an objective experience.
Projectors participate in and can control a projection.	Dreamers are passive, i.e. things happen to them, they do not make things happen.
Environments, scenes, images and encounters with others are real.	Images and situations are products of the imagination or nightmares; and are often lacking in rationality and coherency.
Events take place outside the physical body; projectors can even see and touch their own physical body.	Dreamers dream while inside the physical body.
It is possible to experience continuous self-awareness from the waking state prior to the projection through to the waking state following the projection, without any lapses in lucidity.	Dreams do not begin during the normal physical waking state. Dreams only occur during sleep.
Levels of awareness and mental activity can surpass what can be achieved in the normal physical waking state.	Level of mental activity can be normal, with less rationality or none at all.
Lucid projectors are aware of their normal physical lives. Can provide extra-ordinary feelings of euphoria, freedom and well-being.	Dreamers usually have little recollection of their ordinary lives. Provides regular experiences and feelings.
Sensorial stimulation causes the silver cord to retract and the consciousness to return to the physical body.	Sensorial stimulation generates further images in the dream.

Clairvoyance

Clairvoyance is the capacity to perceive the extraphysical dimension while inside the physical body. Examples of this include being able to perceive extraphysical beings and other people's auras. Clairvoyance is easily distinguished from a projection because you feel yourself to be inside the body.

Traveling Clairvoyance

Traveling clairvoyance can best be described as a set of instantaneous partial mini-projections in which the extraphysical visual capacity of the consciousness extends out and perceives nonphysical beings, images, scenes or events taking place either near to or far from the physical body. As the consciousness itself remains inside the physical body, the person is able to provide a simultaneous, live, oral report of what he perceives and again, is very aware of being inside the body.

With traveling clairvoyance, you can see things but you can't interact or interfere with anything. The maximum you can achieve is a degree of energetic presence. In a projection by contrast, you can act and participate in the experience.

The other point to clarify here is that in order for a person to communicate real-time perceptions of the extraphysical dimension through speech, the consciousness must be headquartered inside the physical brain; in other words, it is not possible to have an OBE and talk, walk, or perform any other action with the physical body simultaneously. So when people orally report "live" extraphysical events they are either channeling, imagining things, or experiencing traveling clairvoyance, remote viewing, intuition or other phenomena.

Remote Viewing

Remote viewing is basically a synonym of traveling clairvoyance. Vieira describes it in *Projectiology* as "a daydream with some flashes of awareness or clairvoyance at a distance." While traveling clairvoyance allows you to perceive things in more subtle dimensions, with remote viewing you only see things in the physical dimension—not in the extraphysical dimension. Remote viewing can also be used as a technique for prompting a lucid projection. (Vieira, 2002)

Retrocognition

A retrocognition, in which a person captures or recalls information, scenes, relationships, experiences and events related to a past life, can occur while the consciousness is either inside or fully projected outside the human body. When a retrocognition occurs during a lucid projection it is known as *extraphysical retrocognition*.

Precognition

A precognition, in which a person captures information, scenes, relationships, experiences and events pertaining to the future, can also occur while the consciousness is either inside or fully projected from the human body. A precognition that occurs during a lucid projection is known as *extraphysical precognition*.

Projective Panoramic View

A projective panoramic view, in which scenes of a period of one's life or one's entire life seem to pass before the mind's eye, is usually experienced when the extraphysical body begins to separate from the human body as the result of a critical, near-death situation. A projective panoramic view then is a type of projection.

Physical Bilocation

In physical bilocation, the extraphysical body of the projector semi-materializes outside the body and is clearly perceived by others in the normal physical waking state. I mention this here because witnesses to this type of projection sometimes confuse this rare phenomenon with clairvoyance. Physical bilocation can be considered as a more advanced kind of lucid projection.

Diary of Extraphysical Experiences

You may recall that in chapter 14, the chapter on preparing for a projection, we discussed the importance of adopting a scientific approach to your attempts to leave the body and experimenting with all the variables that affect your projectability until you find a combination that produces results.

In order to be methodical in this approach, to derive the maximum advantage from your efforts, and to progress your understanding of your personal experiences, the ideal is that you make a written report of each of your attempts to project, in the form of a diary of extraphysical events. In this, you note down the variables and circumstances related to each attempt and the corresponding outcomes, i.e. the details of the projection, parapsychic occurrence or altered state of consciousness you experienced.

This record, in time, will greatly assist you in identifying the specific combination of factors that produces results.

I suggest then that you keep an exercise book next to your bed for this purpose and that you faithfully record every aspect of everything that happened, regardless or not of whether you think it is important, as soon as you wake up. Certain memories, feelings and issues that are present at that moment might be forgotten later, so aim to capture the experience in writing while the details are fresh in your mind.

Relevant details should also be noted before you lie down such as

- the time you lie down;
- the date;
- the weather;
- your physical condition (health) and emotional state;

- your attitude towards projecting;
- anything noteworthy that happened during the day; the people you met, the arguments you had, your general state of mind and certain events, can all have a bearing on what happens outside the body. For example, a colleague of mine left our office to go to McDonalds for lunch one day and passed a homeless woman on the way. He was touched by her circumstances and I suspect felt some frustration at not being able to help her in a tangible way. Later that night he found himself projected in a colony of homeless people where he was able to give some assistance in the form of energetic healing.

Important points related to your extraphysical experiences that you should note in the diary include

- the type of projection you had, e.g. was it a leisure projection, did you experience the projection with someone else, did you perform assistance outside the body, did you have any ideas related to your past lives or to your future;
- the details of your target;
- any sensations you experienced prior to the projection and during the take-off and landing (refer to chapter 16);
- your level of lucidity, e.g.
    - were you dreaming?
    - were you aware that you were dreaming?
    - did you have some other altered state of consciousness?
    - were you aware of being projected?
    - were you only semi-lucid?
    - could you apply your will with results?
    - did your level of lucidity fluctuate throughout the projection and, if so, do you know why?

    - did you experience the condition of continuous consciousness?
- the dimensions in which you were projected—the physical, crustal, extraphysical or mental dimension;
- the dimensions you perceived;
- whether or not you reached your target;
- what caused the projection to end;
- the time you woke up.

Some final suggestions on how to get the most out of a keeping a diary:

- Be neophilic, be open to new ideas. You will experience things in the extraphysical dimension for which you have no existing frame of reference. If you try and fit everything that occurs extraphysically into your current understanding of physical reality, you will find it difficult to make sense of or interpret many of your experiences. So write down anything at all that you remember regardless of whether it makes sense to you or seems relevant at the time.
- Write just for yourself; don't adjust your style in anticipation of others reading your diary.
- Be precise, objective and informal.
- If you can, regularly transfer your notes into a computer so as they all remain together and can't be lost. And don't forget to make a back-up!
- And a final reminder—write the details down as soon you wake up. Don't postpone it. The sooner you write the report the more accurate it will be. (Vieira, 2002)

You might like to transfer your notes either in writing or electronically into a table such as the one following:

Date	
Time I lay down	
Time I woke up	
Weather	
Physical condition	
Emotional state	
Attitude towards projecting	
What happened during the day	
My target	
Sensations	
Level of lucidity	
Dream, projection or other altered state of consciousness	
What happened	
If a projection occurred, what type of projection was it?	
Dimension/s in which projected	
Dimensions perceived	
Was target achieved?	
What caused projection to end?	

Diary of extraphysical experiences

Conclusion

What we have to learn to do, we learn by doing.
—*Aristotle (384–322 BC)*

Every day we all have experiences that tell us that we are so much more than just the human body. In this book I have summarized the bases of the sciences of conscientiology and projectiology that allow us to try to better understand the mechanisms behind these events. In arriving at a more comprehensive, inclusive and realistic understanding of life, we can begin the process of consciously and proactively engaging with the unseen, although very real, aspects of existence that exert such significant influence over our lives.

While this book focuses on the benefits for the individual—of living life consistent with the fact that we are a consciousness with the inherent capacity to transcend our physicality—it is worth taking a moment here to consider the implications of applying this knowledge on a collective level.

Consider this—if the life you are living as an individual is largely the result of your personal level of holomaturity and your holokarma, then the conditions and circumstances we experience globally are similarly a reflection of the level of holomaturity and the holokarma of human society as a group. In other words, we are not the victims of global warming and its associated meteorological, ecological and economic disasters; we are not the victims of abject poverty, of famine, homelessness, of depression, addiction, obesity and innumerable other health epidemics; we are not the victims of war, terrorism and violence motivated by racial hatred, religious fanaticism and other forms of segregation. These issues and many others are, rather, the harvest of seeds that as a group we have sown in the past.

So the broadest use of conscientiology and projectiology is to show us that the way forward both as individuals and collectively is to take responsibility for all of our actions and inactions and to focus on evolving by increasing our personal level of maturity and cosmoethics, a process that intrinsically requires assisting others to do the same. As Mahatma Gandhi once said, "Be the change we want to see in the world."

Appendix A

International Academy of Consciousness (IAC)

Educational Centers

Australia, Sydney
sydney@iacworld.org
Tel: +61 (0) 2 9966 4283
Unit E6.04/599 Pacific Hwy, St Leonards
Sydney, NSW 2065—Australia

Brazil, Iguassu Falls
brazil@iacworld.org
Tel: +55 (45) 8404 5923

Portugal, IAC Research Campus (Evora)*
campus@iacworld.org
Tel: +351 268 959 148
Tel: +351 918 797 924
Herdade da Marmeleira EN 18, km 236—Cx. Postal 06
Evoramonte, Estremoz, 7100-500—Portugal
* Please telephone and book before visiting

Portugal, Lisbon
lisbon@iacworld.org
Tel: +351 (21) 386 80 08
Avenida Ressano Garcia Nº 39, 5º andar Direito
Lisbon, 1070-234—Portugal

Portugal, Porto
porto@iacworld.org
Tel: +351 22606 4025

Rua Júlio Dinis, nº 880 5º Frente
Porto, 4050-322—Portugal

Spain, Barcelona
barcelona@iacworld.org
Tel: +34 (93) 232-8008
Calle Ausias Marc, 49 5º despacho 30
Barcelona, 08010—Spain

Spain, Madrid
madrid@iacworld.org
Tel: +34 (91) 591 2587
Calle Jacometrezo, nº 15 - 5º G (Metro Sto. Domingo)
Madrid, 28013—Spain

Spain, Seville
sevilla@iacworld.org
Tel: +34 (91) 591-2587

United Kingdom, London
london@iacworld.org
Tel: +44 (0) 20 7631 5083
60 Tottenham Court Road
London, W1T 2EW—United Kingdom

United States, Los Angeles
california@iacworld.org
Tel: +1 (310) 482-0000
Toll Free: +1 (877) IAC-4OBE
3961 Sepulveda Blvd. Suite 207
Culver City, CA, 90230—USA

United States, Miami
florida@iacworld.org

Tel: +1 (305) 668-4668
Toll free: 888 234-4472
7800 SW 57th Ave, Suite 207D
Miami, FL 33143—USA

United States, New York

newyork@iacworld.org
Tel: +1 (212) 867 0807
Toll Free: +1 (800) 778 3778
151 W 46th Street, Suite 1202
New York City, NY, 10036—USA

Associate Centers

Cyprus, Nicosia

cyprus@iacworld.org
You can also contact the London office:
Tel: +44 (0) 20 7631 5083

Finland, Helsinki

suomi@iacworld.org
Tel: +358 (0) 922 433 550
Tel: +358 (0) 400 761 939
You can also contact the London office:
Tel: +44 (0) 20 7631 5083

Germany, Frankfurt

germany@iacworld.org
Tel: +49 7802 706370

Italy, Bergamo

milano@iacworld.org
Tel: +39 340 7314195

Italy, Milan
milano@iacworld.org
Tel: +39 340 7314195

Mexico, Mexico City
mexico@iacworld.org
Tel: +52 (55) 2789-5473

Netherlands, Zutphen
netherlands@iacworld.org
Tel: +31 (0) 6 41 22 79 29
You can also contact the London office:
Tel: +44 (0) 20 7631 5083

New Zealand, Auckland
newzealand@iacworld.org
Tel: +64 9 528 4649

Romania, Bucharest
romania@iacworld.org
You can also contact the London office:
Tel: +44 (0) 20 7631 5083

Sweden, Stockholm
sweden@iacworld.org
You can also contact the London office:
Tel: +44 (0) 20 7631 5083

Switzerland, Geneva
geneva@iacworld.org
You can also contact the London office:
Tel: +44 (0) 20 7631 5083

USA, Austin, TX
austin@iacworld.org
You can also contact the Miami office:
Tel: +1 (305) 668-4668
Toll Free: 888 234-4472

USA, Boston, MA
boston@iacworld.org
You can also contact the New York office:
Tel: +1 (212) 867-0807
Toll Free: 800 778 3778

USA, Gainesville, FL
florida@iacworld.org
You can also contact the Miami office:
Tel: +1 305 668-4668
Toll free: 888 234-4472

USA, Houston, TX
houston@iacworld.org
You can also contact the Miami office:
Tel: +1 305 668-4668
Toll free: 888 234-4472

USA, Phoenix, AZ
arizona@iacworld.org
You can also contact the Los Angeles office:
Tel: +1 (310) 482-0000
Toll Free: +1 (877) IAC-4OBE

USA, San Francisco, CA
california@iacworld.org
You can also contact the Los Angeles office:
Tel: +1 (310) 482-0000

Toll Free: +1 (877) IAC-4OBE

International Institute of Projectiology and Conscientiology (IIPC)

Head Office
Endereço: R. Rui Barbosa, 820, sala 903, Centro
Iguassu Falls—PR. CEP: 85851-170
Brazil
Tel: +55 (45) 2102-1448
Fax: +55 (45) 2102-1443

A full list of IIPC educational centers is available at www.iipc.org

Endnotes

1. Monroe uses the word "ring" to denote an extraphysical layer of a particular density, in this case, the paratrophosphere.
2. Miller, L. C., Barret, C. L., & Hampe, E. (1974). "Phobias of Childhood in a Prescientific Era." In A. Davids (ed.), *Child Personality and Psychopathology: Current Topics,* Vol. 1 (pp. 89–134). John Wiley, New York, 1974
3. Office for National Statistics (ONS), 2006
4. www.netaid.org
5. Centers for Disease Control and Prevention (CDC)
6. Begley, Sharon; "Beyond Stones and Bones;" *Newsweek;* March 19, 2007

Glossary

Auric coupling—the interfusing of the energetic fields of one or more individuals.

Bioenergy—the basis of the individual energetic field that emanates from and encompasses every living being.

Blind guide—an inexperienced, immature, nonphysical individual who wants to help another but does so in an anticosmoethical, subjective and self-serving manner, which may be detrimental to the recipient.

Chakra—one of several vortexes of energy that collectively compose the energy body of living beings.

Clairvoyance—the capacity to perceive the nonphysical dimension while inside the physical body.

Consciential basement—the phase of physical life from the age of two through to the end of adolescence, characterized by behavior that is infantile and driven by animal-like instincts.

Consciential paradigm—a paradigm for existence proposed by Dr. Waldo Vieira that recognizes the multidimensional nature of existence.

Conscientiology—Conscientiology is the science that studies the consciousness, investigating all of its properties, attributes, capacities, phenomena, vehicles of manifestation and lives, based on the consciential paradigm.

Consciousness, the—in conscientiology the word consciousness is used as a synonym for the mind, the ego, self, human essence or intelligent principle. More popular synonyms are the soul or spirit.

Cosmoconsciousness—an intangible, somewhat indescribable, state of expanded awareness, of all-knowingness, that allows a global view in which the entirety of all things is perceived, understood and appreciated as a single whole.

Cosmoethics—a universal code of conduct that transcends the subjectivity of religions, politics, cultures, countries, continents, planets and dimensions, and is therefore applicable and appropriate in all circumstances, both inside and outside of the body.

Déjà vu—the sense of having previously experienced something actually being encountered for the first time in physical life, from the French meaning "already seen".

Diuresis—increased production and discharge of urine.

Dream—an involuntary succession of images and situations that pass through the mind during sleep that may be imaginary or nightmarish, and therefore distorted and nonsensical.

Ectoplasm—a dense, physical form of bioenergy that emanates from the orifices of humans able to produce it; sometimes used by poltergeists to bring about actions in the physical environment.

Egokarma—the karmic account one has with oneself; the consequences for oneself of one's own actions, in accordance with the law of cause and effect.

Energy body—the vehicle of manifestation of the consciousness that acts as an interface between the physical and extraphysical bodies; the part of the energy body that extends beyond the physical body is known as the human aura.

Evolutionary orientor—a nonphysical consciousness who specializes in the evolution of one or more individuals belonging to his karmic group; who oversees and coordinates the planning of their forthcoming lives prior to their rebirth in the physical dimension.

Existential robotization—a life lacking in prioritization, purpose and assistance to others.

Existential self-mimicry—the repetition, *ad nauseam*, of the same human experiences over many physical lives.

Existential seriality—the series of successive physical lives; synonymous with the more popular term "reincarnation".

Exteriorization of energies—the conscious donation or transmission of energies.

Extraphysical—nonphysical; referring to that which lies outside of or beyond the physical state.

Extraphysical body—the vehicle used by the consciousness to manifest in the multilayered extraphysical dimension; known in conscientiology as the psychosoma, but also as the astral body, emotional body, astral double, human double, spiritual body and subtle body, among many other terms.

Extraphysical consciousness—an individual who is no longer alive in the physical sense, who no longer has a physical body.

Extraphysical euphoria—the euphoric condition experienced after death due to the satisfactory completion of one's life task.

Extraphysical melancholy—the melancholic condition experienced after death due to not completing one's life task.

Gender dysphoria—gender identity disorder.

Glossolalia—the ability to utter words or sounds of a language unknown to the speaker, usually as an expression of religious ecstasy.

Golden cord—the supposed energetic connection that secures the mental body to the parabrain of the extraphysical body.

Groupkarma—the karmic account of an individual with those who are closest to him, i.e. the people he knows or has known more intimately in this life and previous lives, some of whom are currently extraphysical.

Helper—a nonmystical, nonreligious term used to describe a nonphysical consciousness who acts as a benefactor to one or more physical individuals; more popularly known as spirit guide, guardian angel, guide and mentor.

Holochakra—the term in conscientiology used to describe the energy body.

Holokarma—the total karma that is active in the evolution of the consciousness, comprising one's egokarma, groupkarma and polykarma.

Holothosene—*holos* from the Greek meaning whole and *thosene* from combining the *tho* from thought, the *sen* from sentiment (or emotion) and the *e* from energy; refers to the information carried in the bioenergetic field produced by an individual or a group of people or inherent to a specific place.

Holomaturity—the overall maturity—physiological, psychological and intellectual—achieved by the consciousness during his multidimensional, multiexistential existence.

Holomemory—the complete, integral memory of the consciousness that retains all the facts related to his multidimensional, multiexistential existence.

Hypnagogic state—an altered state of consciousness, experienced during the period between wakefulness and sleep.

Hypnopompic state—an altered state of consciousness, experienced during the period between sleep and wakefulness.

Intermissive course—a theoretical and practical course delivered during the period between lives to extraphysical individuals who have achieved a certain evolutionary level, with the objective of preparing them to accomplish their life plan (purpose in life) in their forthcoming physical life.

Intermissive period or intermission—the period between lives.

Internal autoscopy—the phenomenon of being able to see inside your own physical body (either with the consciousness apparently headquartered inside the physical brain or projected outside the physical body).

Intruder—a term which applies to both physical and extraphysical individuals, used to describe someone who, intentionally or otherwise, negatively influences another through the transference of a combination of his thoughts, emotions and energy.

Manichaeism—a dualistic philosophy that divides the world between good and evil principles.

Mental body—the most subtle vehicle of manifestation of the consciousness; known in conscientiology as the mentalsoma.

Multiexistential cycle—the alternation of physical and extraphysical existences.

Nadis—the links and channels that connect the chakras to their counterparts in the extraphysical body; known in acupuncture as meridians.

Near-death experience (NDE)—a type of forced out-of-body experience that can occur when an individual meets the clinical criteria of death but is later revived.

Neophilia—the positive trait of being open to new ideas or novelty.

Neophobia—the negative trait of being closed to new ideas or novelty.

Out-of-body experience (OBE)—the act of one vehicle of manifestation (either the extraphysical body or the mental body) leaving another.

Para-brain—the brain of the extraphysical body.

Paragenetics—the subdiscipline of conscientiology that studies the genetic coding that, unlike genetics, is not transmitted from one individual to another but from one life of the consciousness to the next, imprinted on the extraphysical and mental bodies of the consciousness.

Paratroposphere—an extraphysical zone closely connected to earth that duplicates terrestrial environments and coexists and overlaps with human life; more commonly known as the crustal plane, the astral plane, the afterdeath world, and the spiritual world. A place inhabited by earth-bound extraphysical consciousnesses.

Physical bilocation—the extraphysical body of the projector semi-materializes outside the body and is clearly perceived by others in the normal physical waking state.

Poltergeist—a nonphysical being capable of producing direct effects in the physical dimension such as causing objects to move and creating noises.

Polykarma—the karmic account of an individual in relation to all other physical and extraphysical consciousnesses.

Postmortem parapsychosis—the condition of a nonphysical individual who is unaware that he is no longer alive in the physical sense; characterized by complete lack of self-awareness, automatic behavior, and often an unbalanced state of confusion caused by an inability to make any sense of his experiences.

Precognition—an experience in which an individual captures information, scenes, relationships, experiences and events pertaining to the future.

Projectiology—the subdiscipline of conscientiology dedicated to the study of the projection of the consciousness outside of the physical body (out-of-body experience, OBE).

Projection—the act of one vehicle of manifestation of the consciousness leaving another.

Projective catalepsy—the sensation of being unable to move the physical body while consciously headquartered inside it.

Projective panoramic view—an experience in which scenes of a period of one's life or one's entire life seem to pass before the mind's eye.

Psychic surgery—a procedure in which a practitioner's hands penetrate the patient's body without the use of surgical equipment and without causing pain to the patient. The practitioner then removes organic matter or foreign objects from the patient's body and cleans the area. The procedure is completed with the patient showing no wounds or scars on his skin. Some practitioners also use nonsurgical blades to perform operations.

Psychosoma—the term used in conscientiology to refer to the extraphysical body of manifestation of the consciousness; more popularly known as the astral body, emotional body, astral double, human double, spiritual body and subtle body.

Remote viewing—basically a synonym of traveling clairvoyance, yet only allows for the perception of beings, images, scenes or events in the physical dimension.

Retrocognitarium—a laboratory for self-research that has been especially designed for producing retrocognitions.

Retrocognition—an experience in which an individual captures or recalls information, scenes, relationships, experiences and events related to the distant past, i.e. past lives.

Self-corruption—when we lower our own integrity or morals, or betray our own principles and knowledge.

Silver cord—the energetic connection between the physical body and the extraphysical body formed by part of the energy body.

Soma—the term used in conscientiology to refer to the physical body of manifestation of the consciousness.

Teleportation—a method of transportation in which matter is dematerialized, usually instantaneously, at one point and rematerialized at another.

Traveling clairvoyance—a set of instantaneous partial mini-projections in which the extraphysical visual capacity of the consciousness extends out and perceives nonphysical beings, images, scenes or events taking place either near to or far from the physical body.

Vibrational state—the condition of maximal and simultaneous dynamization of the chakras, promoted by the conscious mobilization of one's energies up and down the body (Trivellato and Gustus, 2003); can also occur spontaneously.

Xenoglossy—the ability to speak in a language that has not been learned in the current life.

Xenography—the ability to write in a language that has not been learned in the current life.

Bibliography

Alegretti, Wagner; IAC Course "Retrocognitions"; Geneva, 2002

———; IAC Course "Cosmoethics"; Geneva, 2002

———; IAC Course "Paratechnology and Paraecology"; London, 2005

———; *Retrocognitions: An Investigation into the Memory of Past Lives and the Period between Lives*, IAC, Miami, Fl., 2004

———; "History of the Out-of-Body Experiences"; online article; www.iacworld.org

Alvino, Gloria; "The Human Energy Field in Relation to Science, Consciousness, and Health"; 1996, online article; www.thinkaboutit.com or www.twm.co.nz

Ayto, John; *Dictionary of Word Origins: The History of Over 8,000 Words Explained*, Bloomsbury Publishing, London, 1990

de Balzac, Honoré; *Louis Lambert*, Gallimard Editions, Paris, 1980

Begley, Sharon; "Beyond Stones and Bones"; *Newsweek;* March 19, 2007

Bloom, William; *Feeling Safe*, Judy Piatkus (Publishers) Ltd, London, 2002

Bowker, John (ed.); *The Oxford Dictionary of World Religions*, Oxford University Press, Oxford, 1997

———; *The Concise Oxford Dictionary of World Religions*, Oxford University Press, Oxford, 2000

Buhlman, William; *The Secret of the Soul*, HarperCollins Publishers, New York, 2001

Croxon, Paula Beyerly; *The Piatkus Dictionary of Mind, Body, Spirit*, Judy Piatkus (Publishers) Ltd., London, 2004

Delanne, Gabriel; (1924), *Documents pour Servir à l'Etude de la Réincarnation*. Editions de la B.P.S., Paris, 1924

Dennis, L.; (1924), Cited in Gabriel Delanne, *Documents pour Servir à l'Etude de la Réincarnation*. Editions de la B.P.S., Paris, 1924

Fenwick, Peter; & Fenwick, Elizabeth; *Past Lives: An Investigation into Reincarnation Memories,* Headline Book Publishing, London, 1999

Finkelstein, Adrian; *Your Past Lives and the Healing Process—A Psychiatrist Looks at Reincarnation and Spirituality,* Fifty Gates Publishing, Malibu, Calif., 1996

"Gender Identity Disorders in Children and Adolescents: Guidance for Management," Council Report CR63, January 1998, Royal College of Psychiatrists, London

Greene, Brian; *The Elegant Universe,* W. W. Norton & Company, New York, 1999

Gustus, Sandie; "Survey Research Examines the Out-of-Body Experience Phenomenon," *Psychic News* (UK), Issue Number 3694, Saturday April 19, 2003

———; "Out-of-Body Experience: A Powerful Tool for Self-Research," *Nexus* (UK, USA, Australia), Vol. 11 No. 3 April/May 2004

———; "Out-of-Body Experience: Insights into a Broader Framework for Existence;" *Kindred Spirit* (UK), Issue 71: Nov/Dec 2004

———; "A New Lease of Afterlife," *Vision* (UK), Issue 3: March 2005

———; "There's No Escape!" *Vision* (UK), Issue 6: June 2005

———; "Everyday Benefits of Mastering Your Bioenergy," *Vision* (UK), Issue 11: February 2006

———; "A Beginners Guide to Astral Projection," *Prediction* (UK), December 2007

Hagman, E. R.; "A Study of Fears of Children of Pre-School Age, *Journal of Experimental Education,* 1932

Hardo, Trutz; *Children Who Have Lived Before: Reincarnation Today,* The C. W. Daniel Company Limited, 2004 (First published in Germany in 2000 under the title *Reinkarnation Aktuell*)

Hessenbruch, Arne (ed.); *Reader's Guide to the History of Science,*

Fitzroy Dearborn Publishers, Chicago, 2000

Hollingworth, Leta S.; *Children Above 180 IQ,* World Book Co., New York, 1942, (repr. Arno Press 1975)

Jung, C. G; *Memories, Dreams, Reflections,* Pantheon Books, New York, 1963

Kelly, Joanne; *Past Lives Remembered,* Snover Publishing, Torquay, Devon, 1997

King, Neville J; Hamilton, David I; & Ollendik, Thomas H; *Children's Phobias. A Behavioral Perspective,* John Wiley & Sons, Chichester, 1994

Lewith, George; *Understanding Complementary Medicine,* Family Doctors Publication Limited in association with the British Medical Association, Poole, UK, 2002

Marks, I. M.; *Fears and Phobias,* Academic Press, New York, 1969

Miller, L. C.; Barret, C. L.; & Hampe, E.; "Phobias of Childhood in a Prescientific Era." In A. Davids (Ed.), *Child Personality and Psychopathology: Current Topics,* Vol. 1, John Wiley, New York, 1974

Moen, Bruce; *Voyage Beyond Doubt,* Hampton Roads Publishing Company, Inc., Charlottesville, Va., 1998

Monroe, Robert A.; *Journeys Out of the Body,* Doubleday, New York, 1992

———; *Far Journeys,* Doubleday, New York, 1985

Moody, Raymond; *Life After Life,* Random House, London, 2001

Noor, Queen; *Leap of Faith: Memoirs of an Unexpected Life,* Miramax Books, New York, (reprint edition), 2005

Ostwald, Peter; *Schumann: The Inner Voices of a Musical Genius,* Northeastern University Press, Boston, 1985

Radford, John; *Child Prodigies and Exceptional Early Achievers,* Harvester Wheatsheaf, Hemel Hempstead, Hertfordshire, 1990

Sheldrake, Rupert; *The Sense of Being Stared At and Other Aspects of the Extended Mind*, Random House, London, 2003

Sinason, Valerie; *Attachment, Trauma and Multiplicity: Working with Dissociative Identity Disorder*, Brunner-Routledge, Hove, East Sussex, 2002

Stevenson, Ian; *Xenoglossy: A Review and Report of a Case*, University Press of Virginia, Charlottesville, 1974 (Also published as Volume 31 of Proceedings of the American Society for Psychical Research)

———; *Unlearned Language: New Studies in Xenoglossy*, University Press of Virginia, Charlottesville, 1984

———; *Where Reincarnation and Biology Intersect*, Praeger Publishers, Westport, Conn., 1997

———; *Reincarnation and Biology: A Contribution to the Etiology of Birthmarks and Birth Defects. Volume 2 Birth Defects and Other Anomalies*, Praeger Publishers, Westport, Conn., 1997

———; *Children Who Remember Previous Lives: A Question of Reincarnation*, revised edition, McFarland & Company, Inc., Jefferson, N. C., 2001

Treffert, Darold A; *Extraordinary People*, Harper & Row, New York, 1989

Trivellato, Nanci; IAC Course "Overcoming Factors that May Hinder Conscious Projection;" London, 2006

Trivellato, Nanci; & Alegretti, Wagner; IAC Course "Dynamics of the Evolutionary Duo;" London, 2006

———; IAC Course "Goal: Permanent, Total Intrusionlessness"; London, 2003–2004

Trivellato, Nanci; & Gustus, Sandie; "Bioenergy: A Vital Component of Human Existence," *Paradigm Shift* (UK), Issue 15, August 2003

———; "Sleep Paralysis and Its Causes," *Alternative London*, Issue 2, Sept/Oct 2003

Vieira, Waldo; *Existential Program Manual*, International Institute of Projectiology and Conscientiology (IIPC), Rio de Janeiro, Brazil, 1997

———; *Projections of the Consciousness*, International Institute of Projectiology and Conscientiology (IIPC), Rio de Janeiro, Brazil, 1997, Second Edition in English

———; *Our Evolution*, International Institute of Projectiology and Conscientiology (IIPC), Rio de Janeiro, 1999

———; *Projectiology: A Panorama of Experiences of the Consciousness Outside the Human Body*, International Institute of Projectiology and Conscientiology (IIPC), Rio de Janeiro, 2002

———; *Projections of the Consciousness*, International Academy of Consciousness (IAC), New York, 2007, Third Edition in English

White, John; & Krippner, Stanley; *Future Science: Life Energies and the Physics of Paranormal Phenomena;* 1st edition, Anchor Books, New York, 1977

Zucker, Kenneth J.; & Bradley, Susan J.; *Gender Identity Disorder and Psychosexual Problems in Children and Adolescents*, The Guilford Press, New York, 1995

About the Author

Sandie Gustus B.A., Dip. Ed., MCIPR, has been a volunteer and instructor at the London Educational Center of the International Academy of Consciousness (IAC) since 2003 and has published numerous articles on the OBE and related phenomena in the UK and internationally. Born in Australia, she lives in Surrey, England, where she manages the communications function for the EMEA region for an American multinational.

Index

A

absorption of energies, 90–91
accommodations in life, 210
Achilles heel, 147, 154
actions, cosmoethics of, 226–228
Africa, 86–87, 208
African Americans, 85
after-death world. *See* extraphysical zone
afterlife
  beliefs about, 46–47
  concept of, 39
  conscientiology and, parallels between, 54
  "places" that exist in, 54
  realities in, 47
AIDS, 179, 222
alcohol, 213
Alegretti, Wagner, 26, 45, 56, 63, 67, 95–96, 136, 144, 158, 159, 219
Aliengena, Tony, 128
Allen, James, 55
ancient sciences, 38
angels. *See* helpers
Arabs, 85
Arigo, Jose, 180
Aristotle, 276
assistance to others, 207
astral. *See* extraphysical
astral body. *See* extraphysical body
astral double. *See* extraphysical body
astral energy. *See* bioenergy
astral plane. *See* extraphysical zone
attraction, "intuitive," 131
auditory hyper-acuity, 259
aura, 25, 80. *See also* energy body
  human, 23, 24, 286
auric coupling, 96
Australia, 221
aversions, 131–132
awareness. *See also* self-awareness
  of bioenergy, 87–88
  consciousness, 80
  double, 267
  elevated state of, 37, 58
  existential seriality, level of, 104
  of extraphysical condition, 47
  extraphysical double, 41
  of intermissive period or intermission, 181
  mental body, as seat of, 29
  multidimensional, 29
  of multidimensional environment, 6

during OBE, 7
beyond physical body, 168
of projected state, 268
recovery of, 163, 168

B

ballooning sensation, 253, 259
bedding for OBE, 237–238
benefit fraud, 222
benefits of OBE, 232–234
bigamy, 220
bilingual environment, 194
Binet, Alfred, 130
bioenergy, 35, 78–99. *See also* energies
awareness of, 87–88
characteristics of, 81–83
control over, 87–89
energetic sensitivity and, 87–89
fields of, 83–87
history of, 78–80
mastering, 97–99
properties of, 81–83
"Bioenergy: A Vital Component of Human Existence" (Trivellato), 81
birth defects, 120–122
birthmarks, 120–122
blackout during projection, 260
Blair, Tony, 111
blind guides, 65
behaviors of, 66–67
characteristics of, 66–67
extraphysical, 184
blood relatives, existential seriality of, 115
Bloom, William, 83
Blume, Alexander, 128
bodies (vehicles)
astral (*See* extraphysical body)
of the consciousness, manifestation of, 22–37
emotional (*See* extraphysical body)
energy, 23–25
existence of, examples confirming, 34–37
extraphysical, 26, 27–29, 34–35
mental, 29–33, 137, 139–141, 171–172
nonphysical, 7, 8
physical, 1, 23, 33–34
sleeping outside, 7
spiritual (*See* extraphysical body)
subtle (*See* extraphysical body)
Bowling for Columbine (Moore), 85
Boxing Day tsunamis of 2004, 86, 132
Brazil, 202
bribery, 221
British Medical Association, 25
Bryan, William Jennings, 102

Buddhism, 35, 38, 254
Bulhman, William, 36, 161
Burma, 122

C
capacities, exercises for
improving, 88–89
Cartesian-Newtonian model, 8
Cayce, Edgar, 138
Center for Higher Studies of
Conscientiology (CHSC), 11,
158
Center of Continuous
Consciousness (CCC), 10
Centers for Disease Control and
Prevention, 85, 86
chakras
of conscientiology, 26
crown, 26, 151, 240, 241
defined, 25–26
frontal (third eye), 26, 151,
258
heart, 26
laryngo (throat), 26, 83, 97
lower, 164–165
micro, 26
nucal (back of the neck), 26
palm, 26, 91
responsibilities of, 151
root, 26
sex, 26, 165, 212
sole, 26
spleen, 26, 165, 212
types of, 26
umbilico, 26, 83, 165, 212, 240
vibrational state of, 94
charms, 213
*Child Prodigies and Exceptional
Early Achievers* (Radford),
127–128
China, 188
Christianity, 3, 38, 123
chromosomal abnormalities,
121
chronological time, world of,
255
Churchill, Winston, 80
clairvoyance, 270. *See also*
remote viewing
clarification, 178, 210
classism, 209
clothes for OBE, 237
Coalition to Stop Gun Violence,
85
Columbine High School, 86
comfort zone, 184–185
communication mechanisms,
for helpers, 61–69
blind guides, 65, 66–67
intruders, 67–69
intrusions, 72–77
intuition, 63–65
secondary messenger, 62–63
synchronicity, 61–62
communities
extraphysical, 51–52
extraterrestrial extraphysical,
205

futuristic, 50
medical, 8
nonphysical, 50–52
paratropospheric, 42, 47–49
paratropospheric extra-physical, 43
public, 9
scientific, 8, 9
conditionings of western societies, 183
conduct
cosmic code of, 221
exception, 215
moral, 107
rules of, 219
standard, 214–215
universal code of, 221, 285
Confucianism, 38
consciential basement, 164–165
defined, 164
environment, as factor of, 167–168
factors of, for overcoming, 165–168
genetics, as factor of, 165–166
holomemory, as factor of, 166–167
lower chakras, predomination during, 164–165
overcoming, 165
paragenetics, as factor of, 166–167
traits of, 164
consciential evolution,
stagnation of, 172–173
conscientiality, levels of, 223–224
consciential paradigm, 9–10, 205
conscientiology
afterlife and, parallels between, 54
broadest use of, 276–277
chakras of, 26
defined, 9–10
fundamental principles of, 22, 56, 102, 162
projectiology, subdiscipline of, 10
science of, 56, 127, 135, 276
subdisciplines of, 10
conscious donation of energies
benefits of, 92–94
OBE, as sensations of, 91–92
process for, 91
sensations of, common, 91–92
consciousness
and the consciousness, differentiating between, 7
cosmic, 35
extraphysical, 33, 57, 68, 205–206, 213
maturities and immaturities of (*See* maturities and immaturities of consciousnesses, examples of)
consciousness, the. *See also* evolution of the

consciousness
"basement" of (*See* conscientialbasement)
bodies of, manifestation of, 22–37
consciousness and, differentiating between, 7
consciousness awareness, 80
Consciousness Beyond Life: The Science of the Near-Death Experience (van Lommel), 3, 4
Consciousness Development Program (CDP), 134, 135, 216, 268
consolation, 210–211
Constantine (film), 48
constipation, 240
control. *See also* self-control
energetic, 212
of movements, 241
over bioenergy, 87–89
conventional sciences, 8
cosmic code of conduct, 221
cosmic consciousness, 35
cosmic energy, 79
cosmoconsciousness, 36, 37, 254
cosmoethics, 219–230
of actions, 226–228
conscientiality, levels of, 223–224
ethics *vs.*, 219–221
fraternity, levels of, 225–226
of intentions, 226–228
law of "lesser evil," principle of, 224–225
personal principles, development of, 228–230
self-incorruptibility, important part of, 221–223
of thoughts, 226–228
cranial circuit of energies, 151
cranial pressure, 259
crown chakra, 26, 151, 240, 241
crustal dimensions. *See* paratroposhere
crustal plane. *See* extraphysical zone
crystal balls, 213

D

déjà vu, 6
Delanne, Gabriel, 123
dematerializations, 80
dense energies, 94
determination, to evolve consciousness, 209
dimensions. *See also* multidimensionality
crustal (*See* paratroposhere)
extraphysical, 49–50
mental, 62
nonphysical, 38–54
disconnection of the extraphysical body, 260
diuresis, 240
Doctors Without Borders, 181
dorsal position, 263
Dostoevsky, 117

double awareness, 267
double perceptions, 260
dreams, 145
  about lucid projection, 258
  of flying, 258
  lucid, 268–269
  ordinary, 268
  vivid, 258
drink during OBE, avoidance of, 239–240
drugs, 213

E

Early Times magazine (California), 128
Eastern philosophies, 38
Eastern religions, 38
ecstasy, 35
ectoplasm, 43, 80
educational benefits of OBE, 233
egocentrism, 207–208
egokarma, 109, 211
Einstein, Albert, 15, 21, 179
emotional body. *See* extra-physical body
emotionality, 183, 207
energetic blockages, 151, 225
energetic climax, 95
energetic control, 212
energetic environment, 93
energetic sensitivity
  bioenergy and, 87–89
  improving, exercises for, 88–89
energetic "shivers," 90, 92
energies. *See also* bioenergy; energy body
  absorption of, 90–91
  astral, 79
  conscious donation of, 91–94
  cosmic, 79
  cranial circuit of, 151
  dense, 94
extraphysical sphere of, 40–41
  during projections, 243
  subtle, 79
  universal life (Rei-Ki), 79
  vibrational state of, 94–97
  vital, 79
energy body, 23–25
  characteristics of, 25–26
  silver cord and, 40
environment for OBE
  bilingual, 194
  consciential basement, as factor of, 167–168
energetic, 93
external, 89, 183
extraphysical, 44
  multidimensional, awareness of, 6
  natural, 90
  nonphysical, 44
  physical, 69, 71, 167, 236, 259, 286
  terrestrial, 48
Epictetus, 78

etheric double. *See* energy body
ethics, 219. *See also* cosmoethics
euphoria, 82, 85
extraphysical, 192
  of life plan, 191–192
Europe, 208
European Spiritualism, 38
  events during OBE
  extraphysical, 262–263, 267–268, 272–275
  mystical, 37
  unexpected, 188
evolution. *See also* evolutionary process; evolution of the consciousness
  consciential, stagnation of, 172–173
  opportunities for, optimizing, 187–188
  process of, 201
evolutionary orientor, 186–187, 190–192, 197, 251
evolutionary partners, 188–190
evolutionary process, 162–173
  awareness, recovery of, 163, 168
  consciential basement, 164–165
existential self-mimicry, 172–173
  mental body, 171–172
  multidimensional realities, 168–169
  theory of, 169–171
evolution of the consciousness
  cosmoethics, 219–230
evolutionary process, 162–173
  holomaturity, 201–218
  life plan, 174–192
  purpose in life, 193–200
exaltation, 35
exception conduct, 215
existential moratoriums, 190–191
Existential Program Manual (Vieira), 199
existential robotization, 105
existential self-mimicry, 133, 184
  consciential evolution and, 172–173
existential seriality, 187, 233–234
  awareness of, level of, 104
  of blood relatives, 115
  factors affecting, 105
  groupkarma, aspect of, 115
  value of, 104
experiences. *See also* out-of-body experience (OBE)
  near-death (NDE), 1–2, 190
  of past-life, affecting present lives, 136–143
  of real freedom, 114
  subjective observation and, validity and value of, 9
exteriorization of energies. *See* conscious donation of

energies
"extermination" groups, 112
external environment, 89, 183
Extraordinary People (television series), 130
extraphysical, 22
extraphysical blind guides, 184
extraphysical body, 26
characteristics of, 27–29
disconnection of, 260
physical bodies and, relationship between, 23, 33–34
reconnection of, 260
silver cord and, 34–35
as technique, elongation of, 252–253
extraphysical communities, 51–52
extraphysical conditions, 47, 243
extraphysical consciousnesses, 213
of helper, 57
intrusions on, 69–71
of maturity, level of, 205–206
natural condition of, 33
on physical consciousness, intrusion of, 68
extraphysical dimensions, 49–50
extraphysical double awareness, 41
extraphysical environment, 44
extraphysical euphoria, 192
extraphysical events from OBE
analysis of, 267–268
diary of, 272–275
extraphysical lucidity for, importance of, 262–263
extraphysical existences, 102–104
extraphysical hometown, 106–107
extraphysical individuals, 251
extraphysical intruders, 148
extraphysical intrusion, 183–184
extraphysical lucidity, 262–263
extraphysical melancholy, 192
extraphysical precognition, 271
extraphysical realities, 48, 52, 54, 240
extraphysical retrocognitions, 271
extraphysical self-awakening technique, 255–256
extraphysical sphere of energy, 40–41
extraphysical zone, 42, 289
extrasensory perceptions, 31, 89, 234
extraterrestrial extraphysical communities, 205

F

falling sensation, followed by jerking awake, 260

fantasy, 145
Far Journeys (Monroe), 45
fear of physical death, 232
Feeling Safe (Bloom), 83
female circumcision, 220–221
Fenwick, Peter and Elizabeth, 56
Fernandez, Arran, 128
Field of Dreams (film), 55
50-times technique for, 199
Finkelstein, Adrian, 125
flashback, 145
flying, dreams of, 258
Fodor, Jerry A., 130
food during OBE, avoidance of, 239–240
forced OBE, 8, 26
forms, world of, 255
fraternity, levels of, 225–226
freedom, real experience of, 114
frontal chakra, 26, 151, 258
fully conscious OBE, 28
fully lucid OBE, 6
furnishings for OBE, 237–238
Future Science: Life Energies and the Physics of Paranormal Phenomena (Krippner), 78
futuristic communities, 50

G

Gandhi, Mahatma, 115, 144, 179, 277
gender dysphoria, 133–134
genetic factors of birth defects, 121
genetics, 165–166. *See also* paragenetics
genius, study of, 128–129
George and Charles (identical twins), 129–130
Ghost (film), 55
Gibran, Kahlil, 219
glossolalia, 122–126
God, 213–214
golden cord, 29
Greek Orthodox faith, 220
Greek philosophies, 38
groupkarma, 109–112
  aspects of, 115
  existential seriality, aspect of, 115
  stages of, 110–112
groupkarmic inseparability, 110
G8 Summit (2005), 111
guardian angels. *See* helpers
Guardian magazine (UK), 128
Gustus, Sandie, 1, 3

H

Hades, 49
Handel, George, 128–129
heart chakra, 26
heaviness of physical body, 259
helpers, 57
  behaviors of, 57–60
  characteristics of, 57–60
  communication mechanisms for, 61–69

as extraphysical consciousness, 57
interactions with, 60–61
relationships with, 55–77
transdimensional interactions of, 55–77
Hindu-Buddhist doctrine of karma, 107
Hinduism, 38, 220
history of individual. *See also* past life
bioenergy of, 78–80
multidimensional, 170
multiserial, 170
personal, 175
Hitler, Adolf, 115
Hoffman, Dustin, 129
Holocaust of World War II, 132
holochakra, 25. *See also* energy body
holokarma, 107–109
holomaturity, 201–218. *See also* maturity
holomemory, 136–138, 166–167
holothosene, 87
Holy Ghost, 123
Holy Spirit, 123
homeopathy, 80
horseshoes, 213
human aura, 23, 24, 286
human double. *See* extra-physical body
Human Energy Field (HEF), 80
human "interlopers," 71
human morals, 219
Hussein, Saddam, 115
Hussein of Jordan, 190
hydromagnetic shower, 240–241
hyper-acuity, auditory, 259
hypnagogic state, 156, 267
hypnopompic state, 156, 267

I

ideological affinities, 134–135
idiot savant, defined, 129
idiot savant syndrome, 130
Igbo of Nigeria, 107
illumination during OBE, 236
immaturities. *See* maturities and immaturities of consciousnesses, examples of
imminent projections, 258
individual needs, matching of skills with, 188
infectious diseases, 121
Inferno, 49
infinity, concept of, 254
infrastructure during OBE, 238
Institute of Noetic Science, The, 78
intellectual maturity, 203–204
intelligence quotient (IQ), 130, 172
intentions, cosmoethics of, 226–228
interactions, with helpers, 60–61

intermission. *See* intermissive period or intermission
intermissive period or intermission, 104–105, 135
awareness of, 181
characteristics of, 106
defined, 102, 104
duration of, 105
investment required in, 105
between lives, 104–105
lucidity in, 180
nature of, 105
intermissive study course on life plan, 186–187, 197
internal extraphysical autoscopy, 252
International Academy of Consciousness (IAC), 1, 14, 17, 135, 199, 245, 248, 278–283
associate centers of, 280–283
Consciousness Development Program of, 216, 268
educational centers of, 278–280
formation of, 145
London Educational Center of, 12
online OBE Survey conducted by, 26
research campus of, 158
Wagner Alegretti, president of, 45
International Institute of Projectiology and Conscientiology (IIPC), 10, 145, 199, 245, 283
International Labor Organization (ILO), 179
interprison, 112
intracranial sounds, 259
intruders, 67–69
behaviors of, 69
characteristics of, 69
extraphysical, 148
intrusions
detection of, 73–74
extraphysical, 183–184
on extraphysical consciousnesses, 68–71
mechanisms of, 75
preventing, 75–77
symptoms of, 72–73
unconscious, 213
intuition, 6, 63–65
"intuitive" attraction, 131
Inyushin, Victor, 80
Islam, 38

J

jerking awake, falling sensation followed by, 260
Jerusalem, 45
Journeys Out of the Body (Monroe), 96, 146
Judaism, 38, 220

K

Kamaloka, 49

Kardec, Allan, 2–3
karma
egokarma, 109
extraphysical hometown, 106–107
freedom, real experience of, 114
groupkarma, 109–112
Hindu-Buddhist doctrine of, 107
holokarma, 107–109
intermissive period, 104–105
interprison, 112
multiexistential cycle and, 102–116
physical and extraphysical existences, alternation of, 102–104
polykarma, 114–116
reconstruction, of holokarmic account, 113–114
victimization, 112–113
Kazakh University in Russia, 80
King Abdullah, 191
Kirlian, Semyon, 79
Köybaşi, Haşim, 121
Köybaşi, Metin, 121
Krippner, Stanley, 78
Krishna, Sri, 22

L

Laden, Osama bin, 115
Lancet, The (medical journal), 2
laryngo chakra, 26, 83, 97
law of "lesser evil," 224–225
Leadbeater, C. W., 38
Lemke, Leslie, 130
"lesser evil," law of, 224–225
Life After Life (Moody), 27
life partners, 187
life plan, 149, 174–192
completion of, 180–183
constructing, process for, 187–191
euphoria related to, 191–192
intermissive study course on, 186–187
maxi, 177, 178–180
melancholy related to, 191–192
mini, 177–178
LIVE 8 list, 111
Locale II, 48
London Blitz, 44
London Educational Center of IAC, 12
lower chakra, 164–165
lucid dreams, 268–269
lucidity in intermissive period or intermission, 180
lucid OBE, 197
lucid personal prioritization, 215
lucid projection
defined, 268
dreams about, 258
extraphysical body

technique, 252–253
for extraphysical individuals, 251
extraphysical self-awakening technique, 255–256
ideas for, 251–253
places for, 249–250
projective target technique, 248–252
psychophysiological self-relaxation technique, 247–248
self-target for, 252
techniques for, 245–256
through mental body technique, 254–255
tips for, 246–247

M

Made in Heaven (film), 55
main brain, 211
major existential moratoriums, 191
Mandela, Nelson, 115
manichaeism, 203–204
materialism, 38, 224
maturities and immaturities of consciousnesses, examples of
accommodations in life, 210
assistance to others, 207
clarification, 210
consolation, 210–211
determination, to evolve consciousness, 209
egocentrism, 207–208
egokarma, 211
emotionality, 207
energetic control, 212
exception conduct, 215
lucid personal prioritization, 215
main brain, 211
mysticism, 207
polykarma, 211
psychological crutches, 213–214
rationality, 206
recognizing, 205–206
scientific approach to life, 207
sectarianism, 209
social commitments, slave of, 215–216
standard conduct, 214–215
sub-brain, 212
time, daily utilization of, 216–218
unconscious intrusion, 213
universalism, 208–209
will, attribution of strong, 213
maturity. *See also* maturities and immaturities of consciousnesses, examples of
defined, 201
exceptional level of, 126–128
extraphysical consciousnesses of, level of, 205–206
intellectual, 203–204
lack of, 150
physiological, 201–202

psychological, 202
types of, 201
maxi life plan, 177, 178–180
McDonalds, 273
medical communities, 8
mediumship, 35
mental body, 29–30, 171–172
awareness, as seat of, 29
characteristics of, 30–31
pathologies of, 31–33, 139–141
power of, harnessing, 171–172
projection in, 137
technique of, through lucid projection techniques, 254–255
mental dimension, 53–54, 62
"mental hygiene," 76
mental projection, 29
mentors. *See* helpers
meridians, 26
microchakra, 26
Middle East, 179, 190, 208
Milosevic, Slobodan, 115
mini life plan, 177–178
minor existential moratoriums, 190–191
mission. *See* life plan
Mitchell, Edgar, 78
Moen, Bruce, 46–47
Monet, 249
Monroe, Robert, 45, 48, 56, 96, 145
Moody, Raymond, 27
Moore, Michael, 85
moral conduct, 107
moratoriums, 190–191
Morphic Fields, 87
Morphic Resonance, 87
motivation, lack of, 184–186
movements during OBE, control of, 241
Mozart, 127
multidimensional awareness, 29
multidimensional environment, 6
multidimensional history, 170
multidimensionality
bioenergy, 78–99
consciousness, manifestation of bodies of, 22–37
nonphysical beings, 55–77
nonphysical dimensions, 38–54
multidimensional realities, 14, 57, 139, 168–169
multidimensional self-awareness, 150, 186
multiexistential cycle, 102–116. *See also* karma
multiexistential realities, 183
multiserial history, 170
multiserial realities, 133
Myanmar, 122
mystical event, 37
mysticism, 207

mystics, 35

N

nadis, 26, 79, 81
nasal passage for OBE, cleaning out, 240
natural environment, 90
natural sciences, 38
"nature-nurture" theory, 127
near-death experience (NDE), 1–2, 190
negative repetition, 159
neophilia, 39, 155
neophobia, 289
new sciences, 38
New Testament of Bible, 123
night OBE, 266
nirvana, 35, 254
noise level during OBE, 236
nonphysical beings. *See* helpers
nonphysical body, 7, 8
nonphysical communities, 50–52
nonphysical dimensions, 38–54
  energy, extraphysical sphere of, 40–41
  extraphysical dimensions, 49–50
  mental dimension, 53–54, 62
  nonphysical communities, 50–52
  paratroposhere, 41–49
nonphysical environment, 44
nonphysical realities, 8, 39, 42, 150
nucal chakra, 26
numbness, 259

O

OBE. *See* out-of-body experience (OBE)
objective reality, 269
objects of superstition, 213
Oldfield, Harry, 80
olfactory hyper-acuity, 259
oneness, concept of, 254
one-year-more technique, 198–199
ordinary dreams, 268
Others, The (film), 55, 71
ouija boards, 213
Our Evolution (Vieira), 182
out-of-body experience (OBE), 1, 235–244. *See also* projections
  analysis of, 261–275
  awakening from, 266–267
  awareness during, 7
  bedding for, 237–238
  benefits of, 232–234
  clairvoyance of, 270
  clothes for, 237
  difficulty of, 261–262
  drink, avoidance of, 239–240
  external factors for, 235
  extraphysical events from, 262–263, 267–268, 272–275
  favorable factors during, 263–264

food, avoidance of, 239–240
forced, 8, 26
fully conscious, 28
fully lucid, 6
furnishings for, 237–238
hydromagnetic shower prior to, 240–241
ideal time for, 238–239
illumination during, 236
infrastructure for, 238
lucid, 197
lucid dreams during, 268–269
lucid projection during, 268
lucid projection techniques for, 245–256
movements during, control of, 241
nasal passage prior to, cleaning out, 240
at night, 266
noise level during, 236
ordinary dreams during, 268
parapsychic factors for, 243
physical bilocation during, 271–272
physiological needs during, fulfillment of, 240
precautions for, 153–154
precognition during, 271
preparation for, 235–244
projections and, 265–266
projective panoramic view during, 271
projective posture during, 239
psychological factors for, 241–242
recalling, 261–275
relaxation during, 240
remote viewing during, 270–271
rest prior to, 240
retrocognition during, 271
sensations of, during take-off and return from, 257–260
sensorial stimulation during, 236–237
temperature during, 235–236
tips for, 265
types of, 264–265
unexpected events during, 188
unfavorable factors during, 263–264
weather during, 239
zones during, 42, 184–185, 289
Oxford Dictionary of World Religions, The, 79

P

palm chakra, 26, 91
Pandora's Box, 13
para-brain, 260, 261. *See also* extraphysical body
Paradigm Shift magazine, 81
paragenetics, 166–167
parapsychic benefits of OBE,

233–234
parapsychic perceptions during OBE, 243
paratroposhere, 41–42
communities within, 42, 47–49
inhabitants of, 42–47
paratropospheric extraphysical communities, 43
partners
evolutionary, 188–190
life, 187
relationships with, 183
past life. *See also* present life, past-life experiences affecting
aversions, 131–132
birth defects, 120–122
birthmarks, 120–122
clues from, 117–135
gender dysphoria, 133–134
genius, study of, 128–129
glossolalia, 122–126
ideological affinities, 134–135
"intuitive" attraction, 131
maturity, exceptional level of, 126–128
memories blocked from, 150–151
phobias, 118–120
prodigies, 126–128
recalling, 145, 154–156
savant syndrome, 129–131
talents, exceptional, 126–128
xenoglossy, 122–126
Past Lives: An Investigation into Reincarnation Memories (Fenwick and Fenwick), 56
perceptions
double, 260
extrasensory, 31, 89, 234
parapsychic, 243
psychic, 155
real-time, 270
simultaneous, 260
personal history, 175
personal principles, development of, 228–230
personal reciprocation formula, 195–196
personal strong and weak traits formula, 193–195
perspective of existence, 183
phobias, 118–120
physical bilocation, 271–272
physical bodies, 1, 23, 33–34
awareness beyond, 168
extraphysical body and, relationship between, 23, 33–34
heaviness of, 259
physical consciousness, 68
physical death, 33–34
fear of (thanatophobia), 232
silver cord during, responsibility of, 33
physical environment, 69, 71, 167, 236, 259, 286
physical existences, 102–104

physical individual for projective target technique, 251
physical intrusion, 183
physical memory, 152
physical plane, 49
physical position, 267
physical realities, 179
physiological maturity, 201–202
physiological needs during OBE, fulfillment of, 240
Piano Concerto No. 1 (Tchaikovsky), 130
Picasso, 127
PIP (Polycontrast Interference Photography) scanner, 80
"places" that exist in afterlife, 54
Plato, 138, 162
poltergeist, 71, 80
polykarma, 114–116, 211
position during OBE
  dorsal, 263
  physical, 267
  prone, 264
  switch-off, 239
postmortem parapsychosis, 43, 44, 47, 105
postponement, 184
prana (India), 79
precautions for OBE, 153–154
precognition, 271
Prema, Shamlinie, 120
prescription medications, 213
present life, past-life experiences affecting, 136–143. *See also* past life
  case example of, 141–143
  holomemory, 136–138
  mental body, pathologies of, 139–141
paragenetics, 138–139
preventing intrusions, 75–77
procrastination, 184
prodigies, 126–128
prodigious savant, 130
projected state, awareness of, 268
projectiology
  broadest use of, 276–277
  conscientiology, subdiscipline of, 10
  field of, 60
  importance of, 10
  science of, 9, 276
Projectiology: A Panorama of Experiences Outside the Human Body (Vieira), 1, 9, 10, 38, 245, 270
projections, 244. *See also* out-of-body experience (OBE)
  bioenergetic factors for, 243
  blackout during, 260
  energies during, 243
  extraphysical conditions for, 243
  imminent, signs of, 258
  mental, 29

mental body technique for, 254–255
recalling, 265–266
sentiments during, 243
take-off to, 257–260
target ideas for, 254
thoughts during, 243
unconscious, 7
vibrational state during, 243
Projections of the Consciousness: A Diary of Out-of-Body Experiences (Vieira), 1, 10, 36, 64, 75
projective catalepsy, 35, 260, 267. *See also* sleep paralysis
projective panoramic view, 271
projective posture during OBE, 239
projective target technique, 248–252
physical or extraphysical individual for, 251
places for, 249–250
targets for, 251–252
premonition, 6
prone position, 264
psychic perceptions, 155
psychic sciences, 38
psychic surgery, 80
psychism, 213
psychological benefits of OBE, 233
psychological crutches, 213–214
psychological maturity, 202
psychophysiological self-relaxation technique, 247–248
psychosoma. *See* extraphysical body
public communities, 9
Purgatory, 49
purpose in life, identification of, 193–200
books and courses on, 199–200
50-times technique for, 199
lucid out-of-body experiences for, 197
one-year-more technique for, 198–199
personal reciprocation formula for, 195–196
personal strong and weak traits formula for, 193–195
precautions for, 200
retrocognitions for, 197–198
pyschological crutches, 213

Q

qi/chi (China), 79
Quantum physics, 204
Queen Noor, 190

R

rabbits' feet, 213
Radford, John, 127–128
Rain Man (movie), 129
rationality, 206
realities. *See also* multidimen-

sionality
afterlife, 47
extraphysical, 48, 52, 54, 240
multidimensional, 14, 57, 139, 168–169
multiexistential, 183
multiserial, 133
nonphysical, 8, 39, 42, 150
objective, 269
physical, 179
real-time perceptions, 270
rebirth, shock of, 152
recalling OBE, 261–275. *See also* out-of-body experience (OBE)
past-life, 145
projections, 265–266
reconnection of the extraphysical body, 260
reconstruction, of holokarmic account, 113–114
recovery of awareness, 163
reference points for success, 183
regression, 145
Reiki, 25
reincarnation, 101, 102
Reincarnation and Biology: A Contribution to the Etiology of Birthmarks and Birth Defects Vol. 2 (Stevenson), 121–122
relationships with partners, 183
relaxation during OBE, 240
rematerializations, 80
remote viewing, 270–271. *See also* clairvoyance
resting for OBE, 240
retribution. *See* victimization
retrocognitarium, 158, 198
retrocognitions, 144–159, 197–198, 271. *See also* past life
benefits of, 147–149
energetic blockages, 151
extraphysical, 271
factors blocking/inhibiting, 149–150
maturity, lack of, 150
multidimensional self-awareness and, 150
physical memory and, 152
producing, techniques for, 156–159
purpose in life, identification of, 197–198
rebirth, shock of, 152
seriality and, 144–159
techniques for, producing, 156–159
true, defined, 145–147
Retrocognitions: An Investigation into the Memory of Past Lives and the Period between Lives (Alegretti), 95–96, 158
Return from Tomorrow (Ritchie), 2
returning from OBE, 257–260
Rio de Janeiro, 64
Ritchie, George, 2
Rohn, Jim, 193

root chakra, 26
rules of conduct, 219
Rwandan Genocide (1994), 111

S

samadhi (yoga), 35, 254
satori (Zen), 35, 254
savant syndrome, 118, 129–131
sciences, 6, 38, 207
  of conscientiology, 56, 127, 135, 276
  conventional, 8
  natural (ancient), 38
  new (psychic), 38
  of projectiology, 9, 276
scientific approach to life, 207
scientific communities, 8, 9
secondary messenger, 62–63
Secret, The (movie), 171
Secret of the Soul, The (Bulhman), 36
sectarianism, 209
security zone, 185
self-awareness, 14, 31, 81, 144, 183
  multidimensional, 150, 186
self-control, 31, 234
self-corruption, 221, 227
  defined, 177, 221–222
  examples of, 222
  types of, 223
self-defense, 88–89
self-incorruptibility, 221–223
self-mimicry, 184
self-target, 252
sensations of OBE
  absorption of energies, 90
  ballooning, 253, 259
  conscious donation of energies, 91–92
  falling, followed by jerking awake, 260
  return, 257–260
  take-off, 257–260
  vibrational state, 95–96
sensorial stimulation
  during OBE, 236–237
  silver cord and, 269
sentiments during projections, 243
seriality, 144–159
  concept of, 117
  karma, and multiexistential cycle, 102–116
  past life, clues from, 117–135
  present life, past-life experiences affecting, 136–143
  retrocognitions, 144–159
700 Experiments of Conscientiology (Vieira), 9
sex chakra, 26, 165, 212
Sheldrake, Rupert, 87
shiatsu massage, 25
Shiite Moslem sects of western Asia, 107
silver cord
  defined, 25
  dense energies via, access to,

94
energy body and, 40
establishment of, 103
extraphysical body and, 34–35
during mental projection, 29
during physical death, responsibility of, 33
self-target and, 252
sensorial stimulation and, 269
simultaneous perceptions, 260
Sixth Sense, The (film), 55
skills, matching with individual needs, 188
sleep during OBE, urge to, 241
sleeping outside body, 7
sleep paralysis, 35, 260. *See also* projective catalepsy
social commitments, 215–216
sole chakra, 26
soma, 95
space, world of, 255
Spirit, 123
spirit guides. *See* helpers
Spiritism, 2–3, 79
Spiritism magazine, 123
spiritual body. *See* extraphysical body
spirituality, concept of, 254
spiritual world. *See* extraphysical zone
spleen chakra, 26, 165, 212
standard conduct, 214–215
Stevenson, Ian, 117–118, 119, 121, 124–125, 141
sub-brain, 212
subdisciplines of conscientiology, 10
subjective observation, validity and value of, 9
subtle body. *See* extraphysical body
subtle energy, 79
success, reference points for, 183
superstition, objects of, 213
switch-off position, 239
synchronicity, 6, 61–62
syndromes
idiot savant, 130
savant, 118, 129–131
"tall poppy," 222
Syrian MiG jets, 191

T

take-off to projections
blackout during, 260
OBE, as sensations of, 257–260
talents, exceptional, 126–128
talismans, 213
"tall poppy" syndrome, 222
Taoism, 38
Tar, Ma Win, 141–143
target ideas for projection, 254
tarot cards, 213
task. *See* life plan
Tchaikovsky, 130

techniques
  extraphysical body as, elongation of, 252–253
  50-times, 199
  for intrusions, preventing, 75–77
  lucid projection, 245–256
  mental body, 254–255
  one-year-more, 198–199
  for retrocognitions, producing, 156–159
telepathy, 6, 80
teleportation, 80
temperature during OBE, 235–236
Ten Commandments, 221
terrestrial environment, 48
territorialism, 212
thanatophobia, 232
Thatcher, Prime Minister, 127
therapeutic benefits of OBE, 232–233
third eye chakra, 26, 151, 258
thoughts
  cosmoethics of, 226–228
  during projections, 243
throat chakra, 26, 83, 97
through mental body technique, 254–255
time
  chronological , world of, 255
  daily utilization of, 216–218
  ideal, for OBE, 238–239
Times magazine (London), 127
Tlingit of southeastern Alaska, 107
torpidity, 259
Touching the Void (film), 63
transexualism, 133
transvestism, 133
traveling clairvoyance, 270
Treffert, Darold A., 129–130
Trinity College, Cambridge, 87
Trivellato, Nanci, 26, 35, 67, 81, 96
true retrocognitions, 145–147
Truly, Madly, Deeply (film), 55
tunnel effect, 260

U

umbilico chakra, 26, 83, 165, 212, 240
Umbral, 49
unconscious intrusion, 213
unconscious projection, 7
undulation, 259
unexpected events during OBE, 188
United Kingdom (UK), 208, 209, 219
universal code of conduct, 221, 285
universalism, 208–209
universal life energy (Reiki), 79
University of Virginia, 118

V

Van Der Leeuw, J. J., 174

van Lommel, Pim, 4
vehicles. *See* bodies (vehicles)
vibrational state, 94, 243, 259
  benefits of, 96–97
  of chakra, 94
  OBE, as sensations of, 95–96
  process for, 94–95
  during projections, 243
victimization, 112–113
Vieira, Waldo, 1–3, 9, 10–11, 14, 18, 36, 38, 50, 56, 64, 75, 110, 128, 144, 158, 182, 199, 201, 219, 231, 245, 270
vital energy, 79
vital fluid, 79
vivid dreams, 258
Voyage Beyond Doubt (Moen), 46

W

Wang, Solon, 38
weather during OBE, 239
weightlessness during OBE, 259
Western philosophies, 38
Western religions, 38
western societies, conditionings of, 183
What Dreams May Come (film), 48, 55
White, John, 78
will, attribution of strong, 213
world
  after-death, 42
  of chronological time, 255
  of forms, 255
  of space, 255
  spiritual, 42
World War II, 44, 122, 141
  Holocaust of, 132

X

xenoglossy, 122–126
xenography, 122

Y

Yoga, 38
Your Past Lives and the Healing Process (Finkelstein), 125–126

zones during OBE
  comfort, 184–185
  extraphysical, 42, 289
  security, 185
Zoroastrianism, 38

O is a symbol of the world, of oneness and unity. In different cultures it also means the "eye," symbolizing knowledge and insight. We aim to publish books that are accessible, constructive and that challenge accepted opinion, both that of academia and the "moral majority."

Our books are available in all good English language bookstores worldwide. If you don't see the book on the shelves ask the bookstore to order it for you, quoting the ISBN number and title. Alternatively you can order online (all major online retail sites carry our titles) or contact the distributor in the relevant country, listed on the copyright page.

See our website **www.o-books.net** for a full list of over 500 titles, growing by 100 a year.

And tune in to myspiritradio.com for our book review radio show, hosted by June-Elleni Laine, where you can listen to the authors discussing their books.